T0355899

THE

UNEVOLVED

AND

EVOLVED

ETHICS

Greg Humphrey

Unless otherwise noted, all definitions quoted in whole or in part
within this discussion of ethics were drawn from The Random House
College Dictionary, Revised Edition.

Print ISBN: 979-8-35096-987-0

eBook ISBN: 979-8-35096-988-7

TABLE OF CONTENTS

Dedication..7

Chapter 1: Why a Theory of Ethics and Leadership?........................9

Chapter 2: The Unevolved Ethic..21

Chapter 3: Discussion of the Unevolved Ethic................................51

Chapter 4: The Evolved Ethic..87

Chapter 5: Discussion of the Evolved Ethic...................................121

Chapter 6: Ethics, Needs, and Spiritual Well-Being.......................163

Chapter 7: Stages of Ethical Development and Related Topics....195

Chapter 8: Ethic and Relationships..247

Chapter 9: Evolved Leadership..289

Chapter 10: Conclusion...325

Appendix 1: The Virtues and Vices..331

Appendix 2: The Virtues and Derived Values................................333

Appendix 3: The Vices and Derived Values..................................335

Appendix 4: Meditation Aid...337

Endnotes...339

DEDICATION

This work is dedicated to all those whom I've known, all those I know now, and all those I will never know.

I know it's not much, but it is the best I could do.

CHAPTER 1:
WHY A THEORY OF ETHICS AND LEADERSHIP?

Many years ago, I became fascinated with a leadership quote attributed to Bennis and Nanus. They wrote, "Managers are people who do things right and leaders are people who do the right thing."[1] This quote led me to wonder how leaders do the right thing. Further, what helps a leader determine the right thing to do? For that matter, what is it that helps any of us know the right thing to do, and why do so many of us seem unable to know or do the right thing?

Over the intervening years, I've come to two important conclusions. First, I've concluded that underlying each example of a true leader, whether famous or relatively unknown, is an ethic that guides and motivates the leader's acts and behaviors. This ethic guides the leader's choices and motivates the leader's acts and behaviors. Second, I've come to the broader conclusion that each individual has an ethic that guides their choices and motivates their acts and behaviors. Each has an ethic that guides and motivates every act and behavior in the individual's personal, professional, and social lives.

I believe this ethic begins developing at birth and continues through stages as the individual passes through childhood, adolescence, and adulthood. This developing or developed ethic determines whether or not the individual can or will consistently demonstrate right, correct, and appropriate acts or behaviors. Further, this ethic impacts every relationship with friends, neighbors, employers, co-workers, loved ones, and spouses. It impacts every relationship with clubs, civic groups, churches, and any other organization the individual joins throughout their life. It even impacts which relationships the individual will enter and why. Finally, this ethic impacts the individual's physical, psychological, and spiritual health and well-being.

At the same time, I've also concluded that individuals do not have multiple ethics. For instance, there is not a public ethic and a private ethic. There is not a personal ethic and a professional or work ethic. Each individual has one ethic that develops as the individual matures from infancy to adulthood. This ethic and the acts and behaviors it guides is more restrained or constrained in some situations or circumstances and less constrained or restrained in others, but each individual has only one ethic. For example, in a work or professional environment, there may be guidelines, policies, standards or laws that restrain or constrain the ethic and the acts and behaviors of individuals working in that environment.

Since each individual has only one ethic, an individual who knows the right thing to do in their personal life and can consistently do the right thing will also know the right thing to do in their professional or work life. Conversely, an individual who does not know or cannot identify the right thing to do in their personal life, or who cannot consistently do the right thing in their personal life, will often fare no better in their professional or work life. Society requires guidelines, standards, codes, policies, and laws for this second group, those who do not know the right thing to do or cannot consistently do the right thing. These guidelines, standards, codes, policies and laws delineate what is right, correct, and appropriate and what is wrong, incorrect, and inappropriate.

Society also needs these guidelines, policies, codes, and laws to limit or minimize harm that often results from the acts and behaviors of those who do not know the right thing to do. Society can prosecute and even incarcerate those who fail to follow the laws intended to limit or minimize harm to Others and the collective whole. Indeed, it is for those who do not know the right thing to do or cannot consistently do the right thing that many professions need ethics training to increase the possibility that everyone will follow the rules.

Unfortunately, for this country and the world, I believe the most dominant ethic today is an ethic I term the Unevolved Ethic. I term this ethic "Unevolved" because it leads society in general, and business, entertainment (to include sports), and politics in particular, into a destructive pattern of self-interest, self-indulgence, power, greed, and avarice.

When I use the terms business, entertainment, sports, and politics, I recognize each term represents a large collection of individuals engaged in a similar or closely related activity or profession, with each member of the general collection having an ethic. For example, when I speak of business, I recognize that business is comprised of many, many individuals; each of whom has an ethic that guides and motivates their acts and behaviors. The same is true for entertainment, sports, politics, and virtually every other human endeavor. Each is a collection of individuals and each individual within the collection has an ethic that guides and motivates their acts and behaviors.

The Unevolved Ethic motivates acts and behaviors that always primarily serve the interest, welfare, and good of Self and that demonstrate little or no regard or consideration for anyone beyond Self. This ethic drives acts and behaviors that fail to consider impact or consequences except as those acts and behaviors serve the interest, welfare, or good of Self. Further, this ethic motivates acts and behaviors that are, to some degree or extent, wrong, incorrect, inappropriate, unethical, and immoral. This ethic is powered by a morality that is constantly ready to justify, rationalize, explain, and excuse wrong, incorrect, and inappropriate acts and behaviors so long as Self benefits. This Unevolved Ethic is often evidenced in power, fear, coercion, manipulation, predation, and the pursuit of wealth and material gain. However, it is also evidenced in the widespread lack of consideration and regard for other people and even the lack of regard for the planet on which we live. Unfortunately, I believe this ethic is growing stronger and spreading every day.

The Unevolved Ethic spreads in multiple ways. For instance, it spreads from one generation to the next. It also spreads through modern communications technology. It spreads through radio waves and fiber optic cables. It spreads through satellite relays and through the internet. It now reaches into virtually every region and country around the globe. It reaches into every city, town, village, and most if not all homes. It also spreads through music, movies, and television programming. It spreads through a preoccupation with the latest excesses of favorite celebrities, be they from the world of business, sports, entertainment, or politics. It spreads through marketing campaigns and advertising. Its reach is boundless. However, there is a second ethic also present in the world. This second ethic is the Evolved Ethic.

The Evolved Ethic points the way to the right thing to do. The Evolved Ethic guides and motivates right, correct, and appropriate acts and behaviors and consistently motivates acting on those choices. The Evolved Ethic guides and motivates the acts and behaviors of those who consistently manifest right, correct, and appropriate acts and behaviors. This ethic is powered by a morality that encourages the transcendence of Self and the interest, welfare, and good of Self in favor of the good of Others and the collective whole. Further, this morality powers the ability and willingness to minimalize or ignore harm that results for Self when acting in the interest, welfare, and good of Others and the collective whole. Finally, the Evolved Ethic offers the possibility for a better future, a better tomorrow for humankind and the planet as a whole.

I chose "Evolved" to describe this ethic for two reasons. First, I believe the willingness and ability to place the interest, welfare, and good of Others and the collective whole above that of Self is an evolutionary step in ethical development for any individual. The willingness and ability to place regard and consideration for Others and the collective whole above regard and consideration of Self is an evolutionary step. Second, I believe the continued evolutionary fortune of humankind and the survival of the planet on which humankind lives depends on our willingness and ability to reverse the spread of the Unevolved Ethic and to encourage the spread of the Evolved Ethic.

For clarity, I do need to take a moment here to explain a term I've used several times already. This is the term "collective whole." "Collective whole" refers to levels, with each level above Self and each level broader than the previous level. The collective whole always resides one level above the level of singular or individual Self, but includes Self. Similarly, the collective whole at each level is broader than the previous level. Finally, the collective whole can take various forms. For instance, the collective whole might be a family that includes individual Self. The collective whole might also refer to a sports team or work team that includes individual Self. As one more example, the collective whole might refer to a neighborhood or community that includes individual Self. Each of these examples refers to a collective whole that includes Self and takes a different form. At any given moment, Self is included in many, many different levels and forms of collective whole. However, and consistent with this explanation of collective whole, the term Self may refer to one individual Self, but Self may also refer to a collective form of Self. Allow me to explain.

At each successive level above individual Self, the broader collective whole that includes Self becomes a collective form of Self when considered at the next higher level of collective whole. The term "collective Self" or "collective form of Self" infers that Self exists at multiple levels. This is exactly the case. Both collective Self and the collective whole exist at multiple levels. However, the collective whole always resides one level higher than the level of referenced Self, whether Self refers to one individual or a collective form of Self. In addition, the collective whole at each higher level is broader than the previous level. In each instance of collective Self and collective whole, there is some point of commonality, some point of reference common among the individual Selves that make up each level of collective Self or collective whole.

Here's an example to illustrate collective Self and collective whole. A family is a collective form of Self and a neighborhood or community is the next higher, broader collective whole made up of multiple families. Applying this to other situations, a sports team becomes a collective form of Self and a league, with multiple teams, becomes the next higher, broader collective whole. At a much higher level, the United States of America is a collective whole comprised of 50 forms of collective Self called states. Each state is then a collective whole comprised of some number of collective forms of Self called counties or parishes. Each county or parish is a collective whole comprised of collective forms of Self called cities, towns, villages, and townships. Each town, city, or village is a collective whole comprised of collective forms of Self called neighborhoods and so on until we reach the lowest level of individual Self. Even the United States is part of a larger, broader collective whole. That collective whole includes all nation-states. Even the planet Earth is a collective Self that is part of a larger, broader collective whole. That larger, broader collective whole is the solar system, and the solar system is a collective Self that is part of an even greater collective whole called the Milky Way galaxy. Figure 1-1 illustrates levels of collective Self and collective whole.

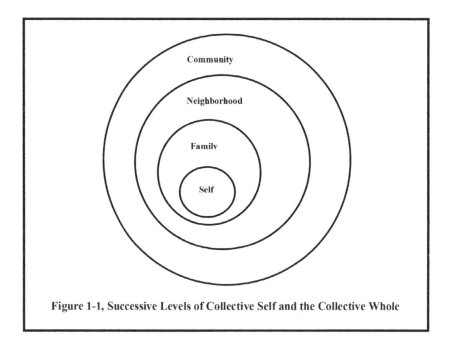

Figure 1-1, Successive Levels of Collective Self and the Collective Whole

In this diagram, the individual Self is part of the collective whole that is the family. However, the individual Self is also part of the collective whole that is the neighborhood and the collective whole that is the community. At the same time, the family is a collective form of Self that is part of the collective whole that is the neighborhood and the collective whole that is the community. Still, at the same time, the neighborhood is a collective form of Self that is part of the higher collective whole that is the community. We could continue with these examples through succeeding levels of collective whole. Each higher level of collective whole will include the lower levels of collective Self and, ultimately, each individual Self that comprises those levels of collective Self. Each successive level of collective whole transcends but includes each previous level of Self.

So, the term "collective whole" simply recognizes that Self is always part of a larger whole. Indeed, at any given moment, individual Self is part of many collective wholes that exist at many levels. This is the case regardless of whether or not Self chooses to recognize their inclusion in these many examples of collective whole. At the same time, Self is also part of many forms of collective Self and many levels of collective Self. Again, this is the case regardless of whether or not individual Self chooses to recognize their inclusion in these many forms of collective Self. Now, with the terms collective whole and collective Self explained, I also need to explain another phrase that will often appear in this discussion of ethics. This phrase is "the interest, welfare, and good of the collective whole."

When I reference the best interest, welfare, and good of the collective whole, I am referring to that which benefits or serves the collective whole, as a whole. I am not suggesting every individual Self or collective form of Self will directly benefit from that which benefits the whole. Similarly, when I reference harm to the best interest, welfare, and good of the collective whole, I am referring to that which is contrary to the good of the collective whole. That which harms the collective whole. I am not suggesting that every individual Self or collective form of Self will suffer harm from that which harms the whole. Nor am I suggesting that every individual Self or collective form of Self will even agree on what benefits or harms the collective whole. That will likely not be the case. There will be disagreement. This disagreement should not come as a surprise. More often than not, individual Self and collective forms of Self prefer to view that which is good for the whole only in terms of that which is good for Self. However, this will become clearer as the discussion of the two ethics unfolds.

I should also point out that the theory of ethics addressed in this discussion is just that, a theory. The word "ethics" is defined in part as "the branch of philosophy dealing with values relating to human conduct with respect to the rightness and wrongness of certain actions and to the goodness or badness of the motives and ends of such actions." Although the word ethics is usually construed as singular, this theory states there are two ethics: the Unevolved Ethic and the Evolved Ethic. Using two ethics in this theory offers insight into the root cause of goodness and badness, ethical and unethical, moral and immoral. It facilitates a clearer examination of the rightness and wrongness of actions or behaviors and the goodness and badness of motives and ends. It facilitates a clearer examination of right, correct, and appropriate acts and behaviors, as well as wrong, incorrect, and inappropriate acts and behaviors and the motivation behind them. For each of the two ethics, it is possible to define the ethic and the values and principles that develop from that ethic.

At their most extreme, these two ethics are best depicted at opposite ends of a continuum, along which the ethic of every individual Self resides. Along this continuum, there is a point I call the Point of Transcendence (PoT). This point is the point that separates the two ethics. It is the point at which the ethic is no longer the Unevolved Ethic. It is now the Evolved Ethic or vice-versa. The PoT is the point at which Self is consistently willing and able to transcend the interest, welfare, and good of Self in favor of the interest, welfare, and good of Others and the collective whole. It is the point at which manifest acts and behaviors consistently favor the interest, welfare, and good of Others and the collective whole. Figure 1-2 illustrates this continuum.

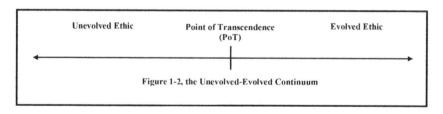

Figure 1-2, the Unevolved-Evolved Continuum

As the location of the ethic approaches the PoT, manifest acts and behaviors guided and motivated by each of the two ethics become less distinguishable. Manifest acts and behaviors guided and motivated by each ethic are more clearly evident as individual ethic moves further away from the PoT, as it moves toward the opposites. It can be said the two most extreme ends of the continuum are absolute bad and absolute good or absolute badness and absolute goodness. However, the ethic of very few individuals actually resides at the extremes. Rather, the ethic of the vast majority of individuals resides at points between the two extremes. However, knowing the exact location on the continuum of every living person's ethic would be next to impossible. To even pinpoint an acceptable sample of the total world population would be unlikely for four reasons.

First, it is impossible to extract and physically study the ethic of any individual Self. It cannot be measured or weighed. It cannot be dissected. It cannot be examined for lines of imprinted digital code. Instead, we can only look for behavioral evidence suggesting an individual's ethic. We can look for examples of observable acts and behaviors that suggest the ethic of an individual. Observable acts and behaviors become the evidence that support any conclusion concerning the ethic of an individual. Estimating an individual's ethic and where it lies on the Unevolved-Evolved Continuum through observable acts and behaviors may be possible. However, accuracy will always be suspect because direct observation of an individual's acts and behaviors is subject to compromise and interpretation. Compromise and interpretation are the second reason I believe it is next to impossible to pinpoint the exact location of ethic on the Unevolved-Evolved Continuum.

A person, aware they are being watched or observed, will likely demonstrate acts and behaviors they believe are right, correct, or appropriate in a given situation or under a given set of circumstances. They may not display the act or behavior they would demonstrate under similar but unobserved circumstances. This change in the act or behavior compromises the observed act or behavior. This compromise lessens or negates the value of the observation. Finally, even a significant number of observations under controlled circumstances would still be subject to interpretation by the observer. As the number of situations and circumstances increases, the impact of observer interpretation would also increase. This leads to the third reason I believe it is nearly impossible to pinpoint the exact location of an individual ethic along the continuum.

I believe it would take a significant number of observations, under many possible situations and circumstances, to even conjecture or generalize the location of one person's ethic along the Unevolved-Evolved Continuum. It would take observation of acts and behaviors in both public and private settings. It would take observations in social and work settings. Any estimation that did not include a wide variety of situations and circumstances would be suspect.

Finally, I believe it would be impossible to pinpoint the ethic because it is not necessarily static. An ethic can move along the Unevolved-Evolved Continuum. This movement results from perceptions, experiences, and learning as a person moves through life. This movement can be positive in the direction of the Evolved Ethic or negative in the direction of the Unevolved Ethic. The ethic can become more Unevolved, or it can become more Evolved. Finally, the ethic can evolve from the Unevolved to the Evolved ethic or devolve from the Evolved to the Unevolved Ethic. This potential for movement of the ethic along the continuum is covered in a future chapter.

As I proceed with this discussion of the two ethics, I will describe each as a composite. Both ethics are composed of three parts or components that make up the whole. I must first introduce the parts to understand the whole of each ethic. My goal in introducing the parts is not to focus a great deal of attention on the components, but rather to illustrate how the components come together to form the whole. Only by addressing the two ethics as a whole is it possible to account for the full range of acts and behaviors. I do not believe the parts or components can account for the full range of acts and behaviors. Further, only by addressing the two ethics as a whole is it possible to understand that ethic drives all acts and behaviors. It provides the motivation that underlies all acts and behaviors.

Unfortunately, over the centuries, I believe philosophers and ethicists have dissected the two ethics into many pieces and written extensively about the pieces. I believe focusing too much on the parts or pieces obscures the ability to see the whole. The result is a collection of theories of ethics that describe parts but do not, by themselves, describe the whole. Much like a picture puzzle, one can see the whole picture only by pulling the pieces back together. I will begin pulling the pieces back together by first examining the Unevolved Ethic. It is a case of starting with the more familiar and moving to the less familiar or from the more well-known to the less well-known.

In describing the two ethics, I will also examine the subjects of pleasure, pain, and the privation of pleasure. Further, I will examine the subjects of Happiness, Unhappiness and the privation of Happiness. In future chapters, I will examine the stages of development of the two ethics. I will examine the connection between the two ethics and needs, as well as wants, desires, cravings, and obsessions. I will also examine the two types of relationships and the impact of ethics on these relationships. Finally, I will close the loop by discussing the connection between the two ethics and leadership.

Understanding the two ethics and how they impact every facet of life offers the possibility of improved physical, psychological, and spiritual health and well-being. It offers the possibility of improved relationships at every level, from the relationship between one or more individuals to the level of nation-states. It offers the potential for finding meaning and purpose, fulfillment. Furthermore, it offers the potential for experiencing Happiness.

CHAPTER 2:
THE UNEVOLVED ETHIC

I refer to the Unevolved Ethic as the more familiar of the two ethics because acts and behaviors guided and motivated by this ethic are commonplace. These are acts and behaviors are often termed selfish, self-centered, self-interested, or self-absorbed. They include acts and behaviors termed self-protecting, self-preserving, self-regarding, self-promoting, and self-aggrandizing. They further include acts termed egotistical, arrogant, and narcissistic. However, they also include acts and behaviors that are thoughtless, insensitive, discourteous, impolite, and inconsiderate. Many of these are just simple acts and behaviors everyone sees or experiences in one form or another. They are acts and behaviors that seem always to manifest regard or consideration for the person acting or behaving and seem to manifest a degree of disregard or lack of consideration for everyone else.

The Unevolved Ethic guides and motivates acts and behaviors that consistently serve only the interest, welfare, and good of Self. It consistently guides and motivates acts and behaviors that maximize benefit only for Self. This ethic encourages and enables the willingness and ability to minimalize or ignore the harm that results for Others and the collective whole when Self consistently acts and behaves only to maximize benefit for Self. This ethic enables and encourages the justification, rationalization, and excuse of wrong, incorrect, or inappropriate behavior so long as Self benefits. This ethic guides and motivates consideration or regard for Others or the collective whole only when that consideration serves Self. It is this ethic that encourages materialism and living only in the present without consideration of the future. Finally, it is an ethic steeped in self-deception and moral hypocrisy.

For clarity, when I speak of harm for Others and the collective whole, I speak of harm or consequence that can take many forms. Harm may take the form of physical harm or pain for Others. It may be emotional, mental, or psychological harm or pain. It can take the form of financial harm which can further result in either physical or psychological harm or pain. However, it is important to note that harm is not limited to only measurable, quantifiable harm. Limiting discussion of harm to only measurable, quantifiable harm fails to consider impacts or consequences that are not easily measured or quantified. Limiting discussion of harm to only measurable, quantifiable harm fails to consider non-tangible harms. As a result, limiting the discussion of harm to only measurable, quantifiable harm often minimalizes or ignores the total impact or consequence when Self consistently acts or behaves only to maximize benefit for Self.

The total impact or consequence often includes building distrust, suspicion, doubt, caution, and insecurity within Others and the collective whole. It includes building jealousy, envy, resentment, and bitterness within Others and the collective whole. It results in the building of skepticism, cynicism, and pessimism within Others and the collective whole. It includes the building of dissonance and disharmony within the collective whole.

Acts and behaviors that result in these harms within the collective whole are always contrary to the best interest, welfare, and good of both Others and the collective whole. They are always contrary to the good of the collective whole at every level of the collective whole. However, as the reader will see, the willingness and ability to minimalize or ignore these harms is an essential characteristic of the Unevolved Ethic. It is a characteristic encouraged and enabled by the morality component of the ethic.

The Unevolved Ethic is composed of three components. These components are the egoistic, the hedonistic utilitarian, and the rational morality components. Figure 2-1 depicts these three components.

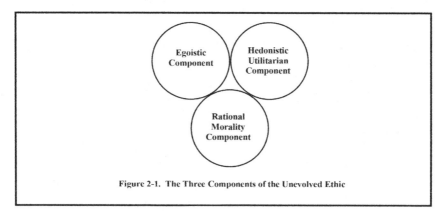

Figure 2-1. The Three Components of the Unevolved Ethic

As the discussion of this ethic progresses, I will provide examples of acts and behaviors to illustrate the parts of the ethic; however, it is important to remember that these example acts or behaviors are only indicative of the ethic if the act or behavior is part of a pattern of acts or behaviors. The overall pattern of acts and behaviors gives insight into ethic. Isolated acts and behaviors may be just that: isolated acts and behaviors. These isolated acts or behaviors may be random to the overall pattern of acts and behaviors. Isolated or random acts or behaviors are, therefore, not indicative of the motivating ethic. It is also important to remember that each act or behavior used to illustrate a component of the ethic represents the whole. Each is a manifest act or behavior guided and motivated by the Unevolved Ethic provided the act or behavior is part of an overall pattern of acts and behaviors. With this said, the first or foundational component is the egoistic component.

The Egoistic Component

By definition, the word egoistic means "selfish." "Selfish" is defined as "devoted to caring only for oneself; concerned only with one's own interest." Therefore, the term egoistic is easily associated with acts and behaviors that manifest regard for the best interest, welfare, and good of only Self. It is easily associated with acts and behaviors that manifest regard or concern for preserving, protecting, and promoting only Self. It easily associated with acts and behaviors that focus on maximizing benefit only for Self.

By contrast, egoistic is not easily associated with acts and behaviors that maximize benefit for Others or the collective whole. The term does not associate with acts or behaviors that manifest regard for the best interest, welfare, and good of Others or the collective whole, and the preservation, protection, and promotion of Others or the collective whole. Indeed, it suggests regard and consideration for Others and the collective whole only when it serves the best interest, welfare, or good of Self. It suggests regard or concern for the preservation, protection, and promotion of Others and the collective whole only when Self benefits.

While numerous theories of ethics are termed egoistic, each is generally built around the notion that individual Self should and must be concerned with Self first and foremost. These theories suggest that each Self should and must be primarily concerned with the interest, welfare, and good of Self first and foremost. These theories suggest that each individual should and must be concerned with preserving, protecting, and promoting Self first and foremost. They suggest regard or concern for Self should trump regard or concern for Others and the collective whole. They suggest that regard or concern for Others or the collective whole should be secondary to regard or concern for Self. Finally, they suggest that this focus on Self and the best interest, welfare, and good of Self is right, correct, and appropriate.

Because the focus of the egoistic component is the best interest, welfare, and good of Self, the component has its roots in what is commonly referred to as the instinct for survival. As such, the component is very useful for examining and understanding acts or behaviors that are self-protecting, self-preserving, and self-promoting. It is useful for examining and understanding acts and behaviors that minimize harm for Self. These acts and behaviors contribute to the increased survival, preservation and advancement of Self. They promote the continued welfare of Self. The continued welfare of Self serves the interest and good of Self. The continued welfare of Self maximizes benefit for Self.

However, this component is also useful for examining and understanding acts and behaviors that exceed just the survival and preservation of Self. These are acts and behaviors that also maximize benefit for Self. These acts and behaviors can even extend to those considered vain, conceited, self-righteous, self-important, self-aggrandizing and even narcissistic. However, this component is also useful for examining and understanding all acts and behaviors that focus on selfish concern for "I," "Me," "My," and "Mine."

It is useful for examining and understanding acts and behaviors that focus on "I," "Me," "My," and "Mine" since these acts and behaviors always seek to benefit Self. Self is always the primary beneficiary of acts and behaviors that manifest regard or concern for "I," "Me," "My," and "Mine." These acts and behaviors serve the best interest, welfare, and good of Self and position Self to maximize benefit for Self. Further, there is pleasure for Self in acts and behaviors that selfishly focus on "I," "Me," "My," and "Mine." As a result, acts and behaviors that always seek to maximize benefit for "I," "Me," "My," and "Mine" are always selfish and self-centered.

The egoistic component of the Unevolved Ethic will generally emphasize either minimizing harm _or_ maximizing benefit for Self. In those instances, in which the preservation and protection, perhaps even the very survival of Self is of primary concern, the emphasis of the component will be minimizing harm for Self. In those instances, in which Self's real or perceived preservation and protection of Self is not of primary concern, the egoistic component's emphasis will be maximizing benefit for Self. Regardless of whether the emphasis is minimizing harm _or_ maximizing benefit, Self is the beneficiary of acts and behaviors associated with this component. Regardless of the component's emphasis, acts and behaviors associated with this component will always be, to some extent or degree, selfish, self-centered, self-promoting, self-protecting, and self-regarding. An examination of greed illustrates the selfish, self-centered nature of this component.

Any act or behavior that manifests greed manifests either the emphasis on maximizing benefit _or_ the emphasis on minimizing harm for Self. Any act or behavior that manifests greed maximizes benefit _or_ minimizes harm to Self's interest, welfare, or good. Greed or greedy acts or behaviors are always self-protective, self-preserving, or self-promoting. "I," "Me" is at the core of all acts and behaviors manifesting greed. In all its manifestations, greed demonstrates the willingness and ability to maximize benefit _or_ minimize harm for Self, often at the expense of harm for Others and the collective whole. In each case, Self always benefits from the acts or behaviors that manifest greed. Finally, greed is always self-satisfying, self-gratifying, and self-indulgent.

Beyond greed, all self-satisfying, self-gratifying and self-indulgent acts or behaviors maximize benefit for Self. As a result, these acts or behaviors all become examples of the egoistic component of the Unevolved Ethic. Self-indulgent and self-gratifying acts and behaviors can and do lead to excess and excess always benefits Self. Both self-gratification and self-indulgence take many forms and include instant gratification and over-indulgence of Self. For instance, self-indulgence and self-gratification can take the form of gluttony. They can take the form of drug or alcohol abuse. They can also take the form of excessive consumerism or materialism. The benefit contained in each of these examples is to Self.

As a further example, the egoistic component is useful for examining and understanding the acts and behaviors of those Selves who believe there should be no limit to compensation based on knowledge, skill, talent, or ability. This component is very useful for understanding the belief that it is right, correct, and appropriate for each individual to seek and demand the highest compensation for Self's knowledge, skills, talents, and abilities. It is useful for understanding the belief that each Self is a "Free Agent" and should, therefore, act only to maximize benefit for Self, without regard for harm to Others or the collective whole. This is a very self-indulging, self-gratifying, and self-aggrandizing belief that is particularly present in business and entertainment, including sports. However, it is a very selfish, self-regarding, self-preserving and self-promoting belief traceable to the egoistic component of the Unevolved Ethic.

A related belief, also traceable to the egoistic component, concerns special privilege or special consideration for Self based on possessing unique knowledge, skills, talents, abilities, wealth or position. This belief in special privilege or special consideration is also selfish, self-centered, and egotistical. It is self-absorbed, self-important, self-regarding, and self-aggrandizing. However, there is benefit for Self that derives from special privilege or special consideration. Therefore, the belief that special privilege and special consideration is right, correct, and appropriate is also consistent with the egoistic component and the focus on maximizing benefit for Self.

Even when an act or behavior appears to benefit Others, this component dictates that Self must be the primary beneficiary of the act or behavior. This is the case even if the benefit is only a good feeling or some other intangible reward for Self. A good feeling is a reward and reward is benefit for Self. Therefore, acts or behaviors that result in a good feeling or reward for Self maximize benefit for Self. The good feeling may stem from emotion. It may stem from the reinforcement of self-image or self-concept. It may stem from the reinforcement of self-perception or how Self perceives Self. It may even stem from attention, admiration, praise, or honors for Self. It may stem from recognition, reputation, or status for Self. In each instance, the reward or good feeling maximizes benefit for Self.

Acting or behaving from emotion is one last example of the egoistic component of the Unevolved Ethic. Emotions are always tied to feelings. Feelings and emotions are unique to each individual Self. They are very subjective. Both are tied very directly to Self. They are always tied to "I," "Me" and what "I," "Me" is feeling or experiencing.

When Self acts or behaves from emotions or feelings, those acts or behaviors benefit Self in some manner. This is the case regardless of whether Self acts from a positive or negative emotion. However, it is especially true if Self acts from a powerful emotion. It is certainly the case in every instance where acting from emotions or feelings harms Others or the collective whole. However, it is also the case in those situations or circumstances where the act or behavior seems to benefit Others or the collective whole. There may be a benefit for Others in an act or behavior tied to emotions, but that benefit is secondary to the benefit for Self. The primary beneficiary of the act or behavior is still Self. In each instance the act or behavior still traces to the egoistic component of the Unevolved Ethic.

But the egoistic component is only the first or foundational component of the Unevolved Ethic. It is the foundational component on which the second component builds. This second component is the hedonistic utilitarian component.

The Hedonistic Utilitarian Component

The addition of the hedonistic utilitarian component is significant for two reasons. First, this component builds from and includes the egoistic component with its concern and regard for Self. It builds from and includes the egoistic component, focusing on Self and the best interest, welfare, and good of Self. Second, this component adds the second or complimentary emphasis to the overall ethic. If the emphasis of the egoistic component is minimizing harm for Self, the hedonistic utilitarian component adds emphasis on maximizing benefit for Self. If the egoistic component emphasizes maximizing benefit for Self, this component adds emphasis on minimizing harm for Self. Though subtle, the overall emphasis of the hedonistic utilitarian component shifts from "*or*" to "*and.*" By adding the second emphasis, the overall focus of the hedonistic utilitarian component becomes maximizing benefit *and* minimizing harm for Self.

However, even though it adds the second or complementary emphasis, the hedonistic utilitarian component will often continue to favor the emphasis of the egoistic component. By that, I mean the hedonistic utilitarian component will, to some extent or degree, favor either maximizing benefit *or* minimizing harm for Self. It will favor the emphasis that developed as the egoistic component developed. However, this does not change the overall focus of the component. The focus of this component is still Self and the best interest, welfare, and good of Self. The focus is still selfish, self-centered, self-regarding, self-protecting, self-preserving and self-promoting. Also similar to the egoistic component, this second component borrows its name from a historically well-known theory of ethics. This is the utilitarian ethic.

John Stuart Mill, the author of the essay *Utilitarianism*, referred to the utilitarian ethic as the ethic of the Greatest Happiness. Mill wrote, "The creed which accepts, as the foundation of morals, Utility, or the Greatest Happiness Principle, holds that actions are right in proportion as they tend to promote happiness, wrong as they tend to produce the reverse of happiness. By happiness is intended pleasure and the absence of pain; by unhappiness, pain and the privation of pleasure."[2]

Over the centuries, much criticism of utilitarianism has centered on the concept of pleasure. Many saw the utilitarian ethic as encouraging what Mill himself termed lower pleasure or lower values: those pleasures or values associated with more immediate bodily, sensory, or even materialistic pleasures. In his essay, *Utilitarianism*, Mill acknowledged this interpretation of Utility while at the same time explaining that pleasure also relates to higher pleasures or values.[3] These higher pleasures or values can include knowledge and wisdom, health, and friendship or relationships. Mill argued in favor of the higher pleasures as those most worth pursuing.

This recognition of higher and lower pleasures or values is important because this division still exists. As a result, the utilitarian ethic can be split into the hedonistic and pluralistic utilitarian ethic. Both the hedonistic and pluralistic utilitarian ethics focus on the utility of acts and behaviors; both are concerned with consequences, benefit and harm. However, the hedonistic utilitarian ethic is more closely associated with lower values and the pluralistic utilitarian ethic is more closely associated with higher values. In other words, the benefit of acts and behaviors associated with the hedonistic utilitarian ethic is most closely associated with more immediate bodily, sensory, and materialistic pleasure. The benefit of acts and behaviors associated with the pluralistic utilitarian ethic is most closely associated with higher values of knowledge, wisdom, health, friendships and relationships.

This division into the hedonistic and pluralistic utilitarian ethics, or in this theory, components, is critical to forming the Unevolved Ethic and, later, the formation of the Evolved Ethic. It is important since the hedonistic utilitarian component becomes the second component of the Unevolved Ethic, and the pluralistic utilitarian component becomes the second component of the Evolved Ethic. However, to really make clear why one is a component of the Unevolved Ethic and the other a component of the Evolved Ethic requires a further division or distinction.

This is a clear division or distinction between pleasure and happiness, and pain and unhappiness. This division or distinction aims to clear the confusion that results when pleasure and happiness are inferred to be the same. This division or distinction is based on how we, human beings, feel pleasure and pain but sense happiness and unhappiness. Making this division or distinction requires a short examination of pleasure and pain and happiness and unhappiness.

Pleasure is always felt by Self. Pleasure is felt by Self, and feelings are very individual. As stated, a few paragraphs ago, feelings are unique to each Self. Feelings are very subjective; therefore, pleasure is very subjective. However, it is important to note that pleasure does not refer only to physical pleasure. It may also refer to non-physical pleasure.

When I speak of pleasure, I am broadening the use of the term to include that which is pleasing to Self; that which "I," "Me" finds pleasing. I am including that which is pleasant to Self and that which feels pleasant to Self. Moreover, I am also including that which benefits "I," "Me". That which benefits Self feels good to Self. In addition, I am including that which benefits the interest, welfare, or good of Self. That which benefits the interest, welfare, or good of Self is also pleasant for Self. Finally, I am also including that which results in gain or advantage for Self. That which results in gain or advantage for Self is also pleasant to Self. Pleasure is always oriented to Self and pleasure is always felt. It is tied to the feelings of Self. Pain is similar.

Pain is likewise unique to Self and is felt. It is also very subjective. Like pleasure, pain does not refer only to physical pain. It may mean actual physical pain, but it may also refer to non-physical pain. Pain, whether physical or non-physical, is harm to Self. Here it is necessary to consider what Self finds painful. What hurts "I," "Me"? What does not feel good to "I," "Me"? Pain can include that which "I" find displeasing. That which displeases "Me" causes pain for Self. Similarly, that which causes "I," "Me" to feel displeasure is pain for Self. In addition, that which results in loss or disadvantage for Self or the interest, welfare, or good of Self also results in pain. Self feels pain when Self loses advantage or becomes disadvantaged in some manner. Loss of advantage or disadvantage does not serve the good of Self. It does not serve the good of "I," "Me". It results in pain for "I," "Me." But pleasure and pain can also refer to emotional pleasure or emotional pain.

As indicated previously, emotions are tied directly to "I," "Me." They are subjective. "I," "Me" feels emotional pleasure or pain. Anger, sorrow, grief, shame, joy, elation, and delight are all emotions felt by Self. Each emotion can and often does result in an agitated physical state. Just as actual physical pain can cause a measurable physical change in the body, each emotion is also capable of causing a measurable physical change in the body. The stronger the emotion, the greater the physical reaction caused by the emotion. For instance, blood pressure may rise or visible shaking may occur. Pulse or heart rate may increase. For some, the physical reaction may include reddening of the face or the flow of tears. All of the feelings, the emotions, and even the physical reaction to the feelings and emotions are felt by Self in the form of pleasure or pain.

Finally, pain can refer to fear. Like emotional pain, fear often results in an agitated state. This includes fear of a clear and present danger and fear of the unknown. Fear of the unknown is often less well-defined than fear of a clear and present danger, and it is often attached to that which Self does not understand. This can be a fear of the unfamiliar. The stronger a fear, the more likely the fear will result in a measurable physical change in the body. However, even less intense fear can result in a quickening of the heartbeat. It can result in the release of cortisol and adrenaline as the body prepares for fight or flight. Fear that grows stronger over time can become intense, even debilitating. It can become anxiety, paranoia, and a specific fear can become a phobia. However, in each case, the fear is felt, resulting in pain for Self.

So, whether physical or non-physical, pleasure and pain ultimately focus on Self and only Self. This point is important as Self likes to feel good. Self likes pleasure and pleasurable feelings. Conversely, Self does not like to feel bad. Self does not like to feel pain or the privation of pleasure. Generally speaking, Self will attempt to maximize pleasure and will minimize pain or the privation of pleasure for Self. Self will often judge the utility of acts or behaviors in terms of maximizing pleasure and minimizing pain or the privation of pleasure for Self. Happiness and unhappiness have some similarities to pleasure and pain, but overall, they are vastly different.

Happiness and unhappiness are similar to pleasure in that they are also individual. Each Self is capable of experiencing happiness and unhappiness. However, unlike pleasure and pain, happiness and unhappiness do not result in feelings. Rather, happiness and unhappiness result in a "sense." This sense differs from the five physical senses of smell, taste, touch, hearing, and sight. These physical senses tie more readily to physical pleasure or pain. But happiness and unhappiness result in an internal sense.

To help clarify, I associate happiness with words like contentment, satisfaction, serenity, and inner peace. In each case, these words refer to something Self senses internally. Self is internally aware of this sense of contentment, satisfaction, serenity, or inner peace. This sense of contentment or satisfaction is not associated with feelings and emotions. As indicated above, feelings and emotions result in an agitated physical state. Happiness is much the opposite. Happiness does not result in an agitated state, but rather a calm, tranquil, or peaceful state. Therefore, the term happiness, as used in this discussion of ethics, is not an emotion or emotional happiness. For this reason, throughout the remainder of this discussion of ethics, I will always capitalize the word "Happiness" to distinguish this Happiness from emotional happiness, elation, or joy. I will do likewise with the term "Unhappiness."

Like Happiness, Unhappiness does not result from feelings or emotions. Unhappiness is not perceived through the five physical senses. Instead, Self internally senses Unhappiness. In this context, Unhappiness is synonymous with terms like discontentment and dissatisfaction. Self senses discontentment and dissatisfaction. Self senses a lack of calm and inner peacefulness. Self senses an emptiness or void; an emptiness or void that wants to be filled. How Self attempts to relieve that sense of discontentment or dissatisfaction ties directly to the ethic of Self.

Through discussion of the two ethics, it will become clear that the path to relieving Unhappiness does not lie through acts or behaviors that maximize benefit and minimize harm for Self. Likewise, the path to filling the sense of void or emptiness does not lie through acts or behaviors that maximize pleasure and minimize pain for Self. The path does not lay in "I," "Me," but rather through "We," "Us." Self cannot fill this sense of discontentment, dissatisfaction, void, or emptiness for Self. Indeed, the sense of discontentment and dissatisfaction, called Unhappiness, can only be relieved through acts and behaviors that benefit Others and the collective whole.

This is the tie between Happiness and the Evolved Ethic. A clue to this tie lies within the title of the second component of the Evolved Ethic. The second component of the Evolved Ethic is the pluralistic utilitarian component. Plural means more than one. The base word plural contains an implied reference to Others or, by extension, the collective whole. However, that discussion is for later. For now, it is more appropriate to return to the discussion of the hedonistic utilitarian component of the Unevolved Ethic.

Since the hedonistic utilitarian component incorporates the foundational egoistic component, this component remains self-interested, self-regarding, and self-promoting. It continues to focus on maximizing benefit and minimizing harm for Self, first and foremost. It continues to guide and motivate acts and behaviors that serve the interest, welfare, and good of Self, first and foremost. Like the foundational egoistic component, this component also suggests that this focus on Self is right, correct, and appropriate. This component simply adds the second or complimentary emphasis to the overall ethic.

With the addition of this complimentary emphasis, the hedonistic utilitarian component guides and motivates acts and behaviors that maximize benefit and minimize harm for Self. It guides and motivates Self to pursue that which maximizes benefit and minimizes harm for Self. By benefit is intended pleasure and by harm is intended pain or the privation of pleasure. This component guides and motivates the pursuit of pleasure and the avoidance of pain for Self. The component guides and motivates Self to pursue that which feels good to Self and avoid that which feels bad to Self.

Any act or behavior consistent with the traditional meaning of hedonistic can serve as an example of this component. The focus of these acts and behaviors is always pleasure for Self. These are acts and behaviors associated with the pursuit of pleasure for Self. Indeed, hedonism is partly defined as "The doctrine that pleasure or happiness is the highest good" and "devotion to pleasure, as a way of life". These acts and behaviors might include promiscuous sex, alcohol, drug use, or any other activity focused on sensory or bodily pleasures. As another example, acts and behaviors that result in gluttony and obesity result in pleasure for Self. There is often sensory and bodily pleasure in eating and drinking Self to the point of gluttony and obesity.

However, acts or behaviors that minimize pain or the privation of pleasure for Self can also fit a description of hedonistic. For instance, failure to maintain a healthy diet and exercise minimizes pain or the privation of pleasure for Self. Failure to maintain a healthy diet and exercise does, therefore, result in pleasure for Self. The utility of hedonistic acts or behaviors is always to Self. Even the inability to practice hedonistic acts or behaviors could result in pain or the privation of pleasure for Self. Therefore, to minimize this pain or privation of pleasure, Self will selfishly defend hedonistic acts and behaviors as right, correct, and appropriate.

Another example of an act or behavior that always maximizes benefit and minimizes harm for Self is the telling of a lie. Lies always serve the interest of Self. The beneficiary of every lie is Self. Self never lies solely for the benefit of Others. Lies are always self-regarding, self-protecting, self-preserving, or self-promoting. Therefore, the benefit of every lie is to Self. Even the smallest lie maximizes benefit and minimizes harm for Self. This includes even the small lies, sometimes called white lies, exaggerations, stretching the truth, or tall tales.

On careful examination, it is clear that Self is the primary beneficiary of even these small lies. Each example maximizes benefit and minimizes harm for Self. The benefit to Self might be status, reputation, recognition, financial gain, or simply to protect the feelings of Self. However, in each case, the benefit is synonymous with pleasure. The harm avoided for Self may include disapproval, reprimand, punishment, or some other penalty. Each is synonymous with pain or the privation of pleasure for Self. Minimizing or avoiding harm or pain to Self is pleasing or pleasant for Self. Pleasure is associated with minimizing or avoiding pain or the privation of pleasure for Self. Minimizing or avoiding pain for Self does result in a good feeling for "I," "Me." Therefore, "I," "Me" is at the core of every lie and the utility of every lie is always to Self.

The same is true of all other acts or behaviors termed dishonest. For instance, the benefit of every act of cheating is to Self. The benefit of every act of fraud is to Self. The same is the case for every act of deception. It is the same for those acts termed a swindle or a scam. The benefit of these acts or behaviors is always to Self. In every case, the act maximizes benefit and minimizes harm for Self. In every case, benefit is synonymous with pleasure and harm is synonymous with pain or the privation of pleasure for Self.

Beyond those dishonest behaviors, many other acts or behaviors manifest the hedonistic utilitarian component. Many of these outward manifestations are not generally considered hedonistic but, upon closer examination, are manifestations of the hedonistic utilitarian component. Each focus on maximizing benefit and minimizing harm (pain or the privation of pleasure) for Self. An example here is the use of credit and credit cards.

Most people would likely not associate credit and credit cards with the hedonistic utilitarian component. Yet, using credit and credit cards is often tied to pleasure for Self. Credit cards, in particular, are often used to satisfy immediate wants or desires. They often provide the means for self-gratification, instant gratification, self-indulgence, and over-indulgence, each example resulting in pleasure for Self. Credit and credit cards often fuel excess for Self. For instance, they fuel excess consumerism and materialism, which are tied to pleasure for Self. At the same time, credit and credit cards enable Self to minimize or avoid pain or the privation of pleasure for Self. They enable living for today with little or no regard for tomorrow.

Yet, risks are associated with acts and behaviors motivated by the hedonistic utilitarian component. These risks relate to potential harm for Self, as well as potential harm for Others and the collective whole. For instance, the immediate risk of harm to Self associated with a hedonistic lifestyle includes the possibility of contracting socially transmitted diseases (STDs) and even AIDS. It includes the possibility of addiction to drugs or alcohol. It includes the possible loss of employment and even the possibility of incarceration. It includes the possibility of unwanted pregnancies. It includes the possibility of discredit, disgrace, dishonor, and shame. It can include the possibility of bankruptcy and financial ruin. These are all risks of harm for Self. They are harms Self will often ignore to maximize pleasure. However, these same acts and behaviors risk harm for Others and the collective whole.

For instance, a promiscuous lifestyle risks spreading socially transmitted diseases (STDs) or AIDS to Others. It can lead to the transmission of STDs or AIDS throughout a collective whole. It can lead to unwanted pregnancies. Unwanted pregnancies can become a burden to the collective whole. They can become a burden by expanding costs for human services. Likewise, the abuse of drugs and alcohol can result in harm, extending to death, for Others. It can result in harm to employers in the form of impaired performance and absenteeism. It can harm the collective whole as alcohol and drug abuse burden the health care system. Similarly, acts and behaviors that result in obesity also burden the health care system and result in greater health care costs that harm Others and the collective whole.

But there is another set of harms that arise from acts and behaviors that maximize benefit (pleasure) and minimize harm (pain or the privation of pleasure) for Self. This set of harms is perhaps more obvious when we consider acts and behaviors termed dishonest. These harms may well include actual physical harm for Others but may also include emotional or psychological harm for Others. These harms can include the financial ruin of Others or a level of collective whole. However, the greater harm of these acts and behaviors is building distrust, suspicion, insecurity, anxiety, apprehension, uncertainty, and doubt within Others and the collective whole. These harms include building skepticism, cynicism, and pessimism within Others and the collective whole. They include building jealousy, envy, bitterness and resentment within Others and the collective whole. These harms can and do result when each Self acts only to maximize benefit (pleasure) and minimize harm (pain or the privation of pleasure) for Self.

These harms collectively result in a lack of cohesion and unity within a collective whole. They result in dissonance, discord, and disharmony within a collective whole as distrust, suspicion, insecurity, anxiety, apprehension, uncertainty, and doubt spread. They result in dissonance, discord, and disharmony within a collective whole as skepticism, cynicism, and pessimism spread. They result in dissonance and disharmony within a collective whole as jealousy, envy, bitterness, and resentment spread. Dissonance and disharmony within a collective whole encourage competition within the collective whole as each Self seeks to maximize benefit and minimize harm for Self

However, Self minimalizes or ignores these harms so Self can continue to act and behave to maximize benefit and minimize harm for Self. Self minimalizes or ignores these harms and continues to act or behave to serve the interest, welfare, and good of Self. This willingness and ability to minimalize or ignore harm to Others and the collective whole is powered by the third component of the Unevolved Ethic. This willingness and ability to minimalize or ignore harm to Others and the collective whole manifests the rational morality component.

The Rational Morality Component

In this theory of ethics, I use the term "rational" to describe the morality component that encourages and enables the willingness and ability to minimalize or ignore harm that results for Others or the collective whole when Self acts or behaves to maximize benefit and minimize harm for Self. This morality component enables and encourages acts and behaviors that maximize benefit and minimize harm for Self by encouraging and enabling the willingness and ability to minimalize or ignore harm to Others and the collective whole. By minimalize is meant to downplay or marginalize harm to Others or the collective whole. By ignore is meant to overlook, disregard, or neglect harm to Others or the collective whole. This component is very much rooted in the rational ability to reason. It is the ability to reason that leads to my use of the term "rational" to describe the morality component of the Unevolved Ethic.

It is always through reasoning, that Self considers consequences to Self. Self determines the most advantageous act or behavior for Self through reasoning. Through reasoning, Self determines that which serves the interest, welfare, or good of Self. However, through reasoning Self also creates the logical sounding "reasons" that rationalize, justify, explain, and excuse harm to Others and the collective whole. Through reasoning Self creates the often logical sounding "reasons" why Self should benefit and Others and the collective whole should bear the harm. These sometimes very elaborate and logical sounding "reasons" minimalize or ignore harm to Others and the collective whole. Yet, these "reasons" often amount to little more than justifications, rationalizations, explanations and excuses.

The ability to reason provides the rationalizations, justifications, explanations, and excuses Self employs to minimalize or ignore harm to Others or the collective whole when Self acts and behaves to maximize benefit and minimize harm for Self. Self employs these rationalizations, justifications, explanations, and excuses to provide the "reasons" an act or behavior is right, correct, appropriate, or at least acceptable. They become the means for minimalizing or ignoring harm to Others so long as the benefit is to Self.

Yet, in each case, regardless of how elaborately or logically the "reason" is constructed, the benefit is still primarily to Self and resulting harm is still borne by Others or the collective whole. This is the case whether the harm is actual pain or the privation of pleasure for Others or if the harm is the less definable spread of distrust, suspicion, doubt, uncertainty, and insecurity. It is the case if the harm is to spread jealousy, envy, bitterness, and resentment. It is the case if the harm is to spread cynicism, skepticism, and pessimism. Each of these harms can and do result in anger, bitterness, and resentment within the collective whole. Often, these harms result within multiple levels of collective whole. Each of these harms results in dissonance and disharmony within one or more levels of collective whole. Therefore, each is contrary to the best interest, welfare, and good of the collective whole, regardless of the level of collective whole.

For example, the willingness and ability to minimalize or ignore harm to Others and collective whole are seen in the acts and behaviors of those selves who under-report or fail to report income to minimize or avoid payment of income tax. It is seen in the willingness and ability to minimalize or ignore harm in the acts and behaviors of those Selves who employ off-shore accounts to hide taxable income. In addition, it is seen in the willingness and ability to minimalize or ignore harm in the acts and behaviors of those Selves who employ various tax shelters to minimize tax liability. In each case, the act or behavior maximizes benefit and minimizes harm for Self. In each case, Self minimalizes or ignores the harm to Others and the collective whole in the interest, welfare, and good of Self. In each case, Self employs reasoning to rationalize, justify, explain, and excuse this harm to Others and the collective whole.

In this example of under-reporting income or the use of tax shelters, the immediate harm to Others and the collective whole is the resulting lower revenues collected by taxing entities. Governments must reduce budgets, raise taxes, or issue debt when revenues fall short of budget needs. In each instance, there is harm to Others and the collective whole. Reduced budgets often result in reduced services. Harm for Others and the collective whole results when government entities must reduce services. Harm also results for Others and the collective whole when governments must increase taxes. Indeed, this harm often results in Others bearing a disproportionate tax burden. Finally, if a government entity must issue debt to meet budget needs, the harm may actually be to future generations of taxpayers who "inherit" the debt. In each instance, the harm is borne by Others or the collective whole. Lost is the realization that acts and behaviors that serve only the interest of Self seldom occur in total isolation.

It is the case that some acts and behaviors that maximize benefit and minimize harm for Self do not impact Others or a collective whole, but these are exceptions. The majority of acts and behaviors that maximize benefit (pleasure) and minimize harm (pain or the privation of pleasure) for Self do impact Others and one or more levels of the collective whole. The vast majority do carry harm, small or large, for Others and one or more levels of the collective whole. This is the case whether the Others are family members, neighbors, co-workers, team members, employers, friends, or strangers. It is the case whether the collective whole is a family, neighborhood, community, team, or organization. It is the rational morality component that enables and encourages Self to minimalize or ignore this harm in the interest of Self. Self simply employs reasoning to rationalize, justify, explain, and excuse the harm in the interest of Self.

It is, therefore, the rational morality that drives or powers the Unevolved Ethic. It powers the willingness and ability to construct and employ the logical, reasonable-sounding arguments Self utilizes to rationalize, justify, explain, and excuse harm (pain, distrust, insecurity, uncertainty, etc.) to Others or the collective whole, so long as an act or behavior serves the interest, welfare, or good of Self. The rational morality enables and motivates selfish, self-centered, self-protective, self-promoting acts and behaviors that serve the interest, welfare, and good of Self at the expense of harm to Others and collective whole. Therefore, it is reasonable and fair to term this morality component "rational" and tie it to the mind and the ability to reason.

The mind, the source of the ability to reason, is capable of providing an endless stream of logical sounding and sometimes very elaborate "reasons" for acts and behaviors that maximize benefit and minimize harm for Self; acts and behaviors that serve only the interest, welfare, or good of Self. The mind can provide endless rationalizations, justifications, explanations, and excuses for acts and behaviors that maximize benefit _and_ minimize harm for Self. It is capable of an endless stream of rationalizations, justifications, explanations, and excuses intended to deflect or avoid responsibility and accountability for harm that results for Others or the collective whole when Self acts only for the interest, welfare, and good of Self. Deflecting or avoiding responsibility and accountability also maximizes benefit and minimizes harm for Self. Self does not have to accept the pain of responsibility or accountability for harm to Others or the collective whole if Self can successfully rationalize, justify, explain, or excuse that harm.

Accepting responsibility and accountability for acts and behaviors that harm Others or the collective whole can and often does result in pain for Self. It may result in the privation of pleasure for Self. Self does not like pain or the privation of pleasure. So, Self seeks to enjoy the good feelings associated with acts and behaviors that maximize pleasure and minimize pain or the privation of pleasure for Self and then rationalizes, justifies, explains, and excuses the resulting harm for Others and the collective whole. The rational morality enables these attempts to minimalize or ignore harm to Others or the collective whole through deflection or avoidance of responsibility and accountability. The rational morality also enables and encourages the creation of self-deception strategies.

Self-deception strategies are also attempts to deflect or avoid responsibility and accountability for harm to Others and the collective whole. Self will often employ self-deception strategies to mitigate or avoid responsibility and accountability for acts and behaviors that are wrong, incorrect, or inappropriate. Self may also employ a self-deception strategy to rationalize or justify the failure of Self to manifest a right, correct, or appropriate act or behavior. In each instance, the creation and employment of self-deception strategies become a means to mitigate or avoid pain or the privation of pleasure for Self. Further, these strategies are often an attempt to convince both Self and Others that Self is moral despite evidence to the contrary. This is moral hypocrisy.

These strategies take many forms, and there are often variations of a particular strategy. For instance, perhaps one of the oldest self-deception strategies is to blame the devil for wrong, incorrect, or inappropriate acts or behaviors. Self blames the devil and the devil's temptations for selfish, self-centered acts and behaviors that maximize benefit and minimize harm for Self and result in harm for Others and the collective whole. Yet, every act or behavior Self might blame on the devil or the devil's temptations maximizes benefit and minimizes harm for Self. Indeed, it would be fair to suggest the devil is "I," "Me" and the willingness and ability to act and behave to maximize benefit and minimize harm for Self.

Fortunately, in the 21st century, most people raise an eyebrow if Self blames acts or behaviors on the devil. However, Self still needs someone or something to blame for self-interested, self-regarding, self-promoting, and self-aggrandizing acts and behaviors that result in harm to Others and the collective whole. Self still needs strategies to deflect or avoid responsibility and accountability for the acts and behaviors of Self that harm Others and the collective whole. Self still needs strategies to mitigate or avoid pain or the privation of pleasure when Self cannot deflect or avoid responsibility or accountability. So, Self creates and employs rational and, often, logical-sounding self-deception strategies. Some of these strategies and variations are, unfortunately, all too familiar.

For instance, one example of a self-deception strategy is the lost or faded memory strategy. In this strategy, Self cannot recall specific details of an incorrect, wrong, or inappropriate act or behavior. Conversely, Self may be unable to recall why Self did not take a right, correct, or appropriate action. This strategy clearly attempts to sidestep responsibility and accountability by blaming poor memory. It attempts to mitigate or avoid harm for Self by blaming poor memory. Employment of this strategy is usually accompanied by statements such as "I forget," "I don't remember," "I can't recall the specifics," "I'll have to check my records," or similar such phrases. Sometimes, this strategy is referred to as "selective memory".

A second strategy includes shifting or deflecting responsibility and accountability for acts and behaviors to alcohol or drugs, sometimes even gambling or sex. Excuses and explanations employed in this strategy include "I was too drunk (or high)" or "I had too much to drink (or smoke) and can't recall." This strategy may extend to claims of alcohol or drug addiction (as well as gambling, sex, or other addictions) to justify, explain or excuse wrong, incorrect, or inappropriate behavior and mitigate or avoid harm for Self. The obligatory visit to a rehabilitation program or center often accompanies this strategy. Ultimately, the harm to Others or the collective whole often becomes lost in the addiction claims.

A third strategy is the "stonewalling" strategy. This strategy involves refusing to compare acts or behaviors of Self with established codes, standards, or laws. In this strategy, the individual attempts to deflect or avoid responsibility and accountability by simply refusing to accept a comparison between the act or behavior of Self and existing codes, standards, or laws. The strategy may also rely on refusal to admit knowledge of a code, standard, or law. In either case, if successful, Self may mitigate or avoid harm for Self. The harm done to Others and the collective whole is minimalized or ignored.

A variation of this strategy involves refusing to acknowledge an act or behavior is wrong, incorrect, or inappropriate. This variation often relies on demonstrating that an act or behavior is not "technically" wrong, incorrect, or inappropriate. The act or behavior doesn't "technically" violate a code, standard, or law. It often employs the use of extenuating or mitigating circumstances intended to cloud the issue of right or wrong, correct or incorrect, and appropriate or inappropriate. But the intent, as with all self-deception strategies, is to deflect responsibility and accountability and mitigate or avoid harm for Self. Again, harm to Others or the collective whole becomes lost in the strategy.

A fourth strategy is the "victim" strategy. In this strategy, Self seeks to transfer or deflect responsibility and accountability for an act or behavior and the resulting harm to someone else. The intent of this strategy is to appear to be the victim of some other person's or other people's wrong, incorrect or inappropriate behavior. Self argues that responsibility and accountability belong to that other person or those other people since Self is only a victim. If successful, Self can shift blame for the act or behavior and the harm to Others and the collective whole to another person or persons. If successful, Self may deflect responsibility and accountability or, at least, mitigate or avoid harm for Self.

Another self-deception strategy is the complexity strategy. This strategy seeks to demonstrate that situations or circumstances surrounding right or wrong, correct or incorrect, appropriate or inappropriate acts or behaviors were so complex that Self could only act or behave in the manner in which Self did act or behave. This strategy seeks to confuse the issue of right and wrong, correct or incorrect, appropriate or inappropriate by burying the issue under complexity.

By heaping complexity onto a situation or circumstance, the issue of right or wrong, correct or incorrect, and appropriate or inappropriate behavior becomes confused or lost. In addition, the issue of harm to others and the collective whole can also become confused or lost. Yet, if the complexity is stripped away, right or wrong, correct or incorrect, and appropriate or inappropriate become clearer. If the complexity is stripped away, the harm to Others and the collective whole becomes clear. However, if successful, the strategy does permit Self to deflect responsibility and accountability. It does permit Self to mitigate or avoid harm for Self.

One final example of a self-deception strategy is the "wait-and-see" or "sleep-on-it" strategy. This strategy derives its name from a wait-and-see or sleep-on-it approach to right or wrong, correct or incorrect, and appropriate or inappropriate acts or behaviors. The time Self spends "waiting" or "sleeping" on the right, correct, or appropriate action gives Self time to reason the most advantageous course of action for Self. It allows Self the time to reason the course of action that best serves the interest, welfare, and good of Self. It gives Self time to reason the course that maximizes benefit and minimizes harm for Self. It also gives time to create the rationalizations, justifications, explanations, and excuses necessary to avoid responsibility and accountability. As with all self-deception strategies, the aim is to mitigate or avoid harm to Self.

This is, by no means, a complete list of self-deception strategies or variations of strategies. I provide this list only to draw attention to the strategies and how Self employs strategies to deflect or avoid responsibility and accountability and mitigate or avoid harm for Self. In each case, the beneficiary of a self-deception strategy is always Self. In each case, Self employs the strategy to maximize benefit and minimize or avoid harm for Self. Each strategy demonstrates the willingness and ability to minimalize or ignore harm for Others or the collective whole in the best interest, welfare, and good of Self.

Sadly, many of these self-deception strategies are now associated with legal defense strategies. Civil and defense attorneys may rely on one or a combination of these strategies to exonerate clients' wrong, incorrect or inappropriate acts or behaviors. Even more sadly, there seems to be an unending supply of "expert witnesses" willing to lend credibility to these defenses. In each successful case, Self minimizes or avoids harm (pain or the privation of pleasure) for Self and the harm to Others and the collective whole is minimized or ignored. Perhaps even more sadly, successful employment of many of these self-deception/legal strategies give rise to what is commonly called "gray areas."

It is often said that the world does not exist in black and white, right or wrong; it exists in shades of gray. It exists in shades of gray mainly because of the successful employment of self-deception strategies and legal strategies employing self-deception strategies. In a sense, the "grey area" between right and wrong, correct and incorrect, and appropriate and inappropriate is a self-deception strategy. If Self can successfully argue that an act or behavior falls in the "grey area" between right and wrong or correct and incorrect, Self may deflect or avoid responsibility and accountability for the act or behavior and for the resulting harm to Others and the collective whole. In either case, Self successfully maximizes benefit and minimizes harm for Self.

In the process, black and white turn to grey and separating right from wrong becomes a little more difficult. It becomes just a little easier to minimalize or ignore the harm that results for Others and the collective whole. Acts or behaviors once recognized as wrong, incorrect, or inappropriate become more acceptable and less unacceptable. Self then employs rationalizations, justifications, explanations, excuses, and self-deception strategies to deceive Self and Others into believing Self is moral despite evidence to the contrary. That is called moral hypocrisy. The rational morality and the Unevolved Ethic it powers often result in moral hypocrisy.

It is interesting to note that the concept of moral hypocrisy suggests Self wants to view Self as moral despite acts and behaviors that are selfish, self-interested, self-regarding, self-protecting, and self-promoting.[4] It suggests Self wants to view Self as moral despite acting and behaving always to maximize benefit and minimize harm for Self. It suggests that Self wants to view Self as moral despite acts and behaviors that harm Others and the collective whole. Further, it suggests that Self wants Others to view Self as moral. This disposition of Self toward moral hypocrisy is not surprising.

The illusion of being moral is often very important to Self. How Self and Others view Self is tied to self-concept and self-image. Self wants and likes to feel good about Self. Feeling good about Self is benefit (pleasure) for Self. There is pleasure in feeling good about oneself. Conversely, Self does not like to feel bad about Self. Feeling bad about Self is painful to Self. To avoid feeling bad about oneself, Self attempts to avoid responsibility and accountability for acts and behaviors contradicting this self-concept and self-image. Similarly, Self attempts to avoid responsibility and account-ability for harm done to Others or the collective whole by minimalizing or ignoring the harm. The rational morality component encourages and enables this willingness and ability to create and employ rationalizations, justifications, explanations, excuses, and self-deception strategies that minimalize and ignore this harm.

Summary

The formation of the Unevolved Ethic is complete with the addition of the rational morality component to the egoistic and hedonistic utilitarian components. Figure 2-2 depicts the Unevolved Ethic that results when the three components combine into the whole of the Unevolved Ethic.

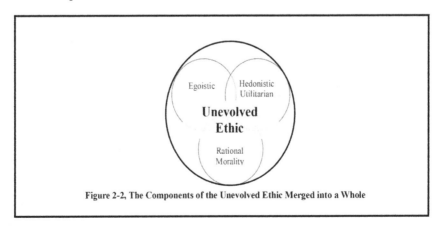

Figure 2-2, The Components of the Unevolved Ethic Merged into a Whole

This ethic guides choices and motivates acts and behaviors that always seek to maximize benefit (pleasure) and minimize harm (pain or the privation of pleasure) for Self and minimalize or ignore the harm that results for Others and any or all levels of collective whole. The ethic encourages and enables Self to act and behave in a manner that maximizes that which is pleasant and minimizes that which is unpleasant for Self and minimalize or ignore any harm that results for Others and any or all levels of collective whole. The ethic encourages and enables Self to act and behave as a free agent – concerned only with the best interest, welfare, and good of Self. It encourages and enables Self to always strive to gain advantage for Self, even if that advantage is detrimental to Others or the collective whole. It encourages and enables Self to minimalize or ignore harm to Others and the collective whole. It does so through the use of the mind, the ability to reason, to create and employ rationalizations, justifications, explanations, excuses, and self-deception strategies. Finally, it encourages and enables moral hypocrisy.

The selfish, self-centered focus and emphasis of this ethic suggests it is right, correct, and appropriate to consider benefit to Self above consideration of harm to Others and the collective whole. It encourages and enables Self to consider the interest, welfare, or good of Others only if and when doing so will gain benefit for Self. It suggests this ethic will motivate an act or behavior that benefits Others only when Self is the primary beneficiary of the act or behavior. However, even appearing to act for the benefit, welfare, or good of Others will result in a felt loss to Self. This felt loss can be thought of as "sacrificing."

Consistent with the selfish orientation of the Evolved Ethic, acting for Others, even when the ultimate beneficiary of the act is Self, will result in a felt loss to Self. Acting for the benefit of Others requires giving up or sacrificing some resource of Self. This loss or sacrifice can often be stated in terms of time, effort, money, or other measurable commodity or resource Self possesses. The sacrifice of a resource Self possesses is a loss to Self and Self will feel that sacrifice. Following this thought, it is easy to conclude that the Unevolved Ethic can only consistently motivate acts and behaviors that range from those termed sacrificing to those termed completely selfish. Figure 2-3 illustrates this range on the Unevolved-Evolved Continuum.

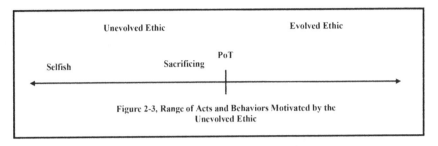

Figure 2-3, Range of Acts and Behaviors Motivated by the Unevolved Ethic

After constructing the Evolved Ethic in Chapter 4, I will place two more words on the continuum. These words describe the range of acts and behaviors guided and motivated by the Evolved Ethic. However, in the next chapter, I will continue the discussion of the Unevolved Ethic. In this further discussion, I will offer many more manifestations and examples of the Unevolved Ethic. Some are specific acts or behaviors, others more general. I will also discuss further manifestations of harm that result from acts or behaviors guided and motivated by the Unevolved Ethic. This additional discussion aims to give the reader further insight into both this ethic and acts and behaviors motivated by the ethic.

CHAPTER 3:
DISCUSSION OF THE UNEVOLVED ETHIC

This chapter provides additional comments, clarifications, examples and manifestations of the Unevolved Ethic. The intent for choosing the examples and manifestations presented is twofold. First, to offer a wide range of manifest acts and behaviors that support and clarify the description of the Unevolved Ethic. In truth, manifestations and examples of the Unevolved Ethic appear in newspapers daily. They are found in the national and local news every day. They are found in the office, at school, at the grocery store, at sporting events, driving down the street or highway, and virtually anywhere one cares to look. Second, the examples and manifestations clarify and support the description of the Unevolved Ethic at various levels of Self, from individual Self, up to and including, the collective level of Self called nation-states. But, before beginning this discussion, I need to mention several cautions.

First, because this book cannot include every possible act or behavior guided and motivated by the Unevolved Ethic, the reader must be able to look beyond the examples cited. The reader must be able to extrapolate the examples provided into other situations, circumstances, and possibilities that are similar but different. The reader should not focus only on the specific acts or behaviors presented but should consider additional acts and behaviors that are not exactly the same but are similar.

Second, some examples and manifestations will seem terribly obvious; others may even seem frivolous. However, it is fair to include these examples. Ethic guides and motivates all acts and behaviors, even the most obvious or frivolous. It would be wrong to assume that ethic motivates only large, more complex, or more damaging acts and behaviors. As such, the discussion includes some of these simpler and more obvious examples.

Third, it is possible to think of both patterns of acts and behaviors guided and motivated by the Unevolved Ethic and individual acts and behaviors as extending from wrong to more wrong, incorrect to more incorrect; and, inappropriate to more inappropriate. Both patterns of acts and behaviors and individual acts and behaviors are always more wrong, incorrect, or inappropriate, to the extent motivated by selfish concern for the best interest, welfare, and good of only Self. They are more wrong, incorrect, or inappropriate to the extent they are self-protecting, self-regarding, and self-promoting. They are more wrong, incorrect, or inappropriate to the extent they maximize benefit and minimize harm only for Self.

Further, they are more wrong, incorrect, or inappropriate to the extent they harm Others or the collective whole. They are more wrong, incorrect, or inappropriate to the extent they are contrary to the interest, welfare, or good of Others or the collective whole. They are more wrong, incorrect, or inappropriate to the extent that Self minimalizes or ignores harm to Others or the collective whole in favor of Self. Even small acts and behaviors are less wrong or more wrong as the motivation for these acts or behaviors is the interest, welfare, or good of Self and Self minimalizes or ignores resulting harm to Others or the collective whole.

A good analogy for this concept of wrong to more wrong is the concept of venial and mortal sin found in Roman Catholicism. A venial sin is a lesser sin. A mortal sin is a more grievous sin. They are all sins. Some are simply considered proportionately less wrong, and others proportionately more wrong. The greater the harm to Others or the collective whole, the more grievous the sin. Extending this analogy of sin, the pattern of acts and behaviors guided and motivated by the Unevolved Ethic is the equivalent of living in a state of sin.

Figure 3-1 illustrates this concept of wrong to more wrong using the Unevolved-Evolved Continuum. Within this illustration the term "wrong" also represents the terms "incorrect" and "inappropriate".

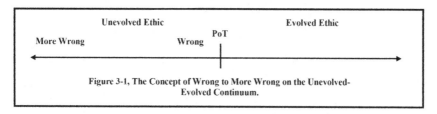

Figure 3-1, The Concept of Wrong to More Wrong on the Unevolved-Evolved Continuum.

After constructing the Evolved Ethic, I will suggest that both the pattern of acts and behaviors guided and motivated by the Evolved Ethic and individual acts and behaviors extend from right to more right, correct to more correct, and appropriate to more appropriate to the extent motivated by concern for the interest of Others and the collective whole. They are more right to the extent they maximize benefit and minimize harm for Others and the collective whole. I will also suggest the pattern of acts and behaviors guided and motivated by the Evolved Ethic is essentially the equivalent of living in a state of grace.

However, and this is a very important caution, isolated acts or behaviors do not necessarily provide insight into motivating ethic. In addition, isolated behaviors do not necessarily give insight into the location of the motivating ethic along the Unevolved-Evolved Continuum. They do not because every Self can manifest isolated acts and behaviors that appear to benefit Others and the collective whole. Every Self can manifest isolated acts and behaviors that appear to benefit the interest, welfare, and good of Others and the collective whole. Likewise, every Self is capable of manifesting isolated acts and behaviors that appear to benefit Self and every Self is capable of manifesting isolated acts and behaviors that appear to benefit the interests, welfare, and good of Self. Therefore, isolated behaviors are neither an indicator of ethic nor an indicator of where ethic lies along the continuum. They are simply isolated acts or behaviors.

To understand this better, consider any act termed a "random act of kindness." For instance, opening a door for someone, helping someone reach an item in a store, or helping someone carry a heavy load could all fit the description of a random act of kindness. Regardless of ethic, any Self might perform any of these or similar acts. But, as an isolated or random act, none of these indicates one's ethic. By contrast, it is just as possible to consider a "random act of meanness or spitefulness".

A mean or spiteful act or behavior can be just as random as an act of kindness. This random act of meanness could be any act or behavior that appears completely selfish, self-centered, self-promoting or self-regarding. It could appear malicious or vicious. The behavior could be as small as a thoughtless, cruel, or condescending comment. It could be as simple as ignoring someone who needs assistance or any other random act that appears guided and motivated by the Unevolved Ethic. Therefore, neither random acts of kindness nor random acts of meanness have value in determining ethic or the location of an ethic along the Unevolved-Evolved Continuum.

To even attempt to determine ethic or estimate the location of ethic along the continuum requires much more than observing isolated or random acts or behaviors. It requires observing patterns of acts and behaviors in various situations and circumstances. It requires observing acts and behaviors for a sufficient period of time to establish ongoing, long-term patterns of acts and behaviors. Ongoing, long-term patterns of acts and behaviors give insight into the motivating ethic. It is ongoing, long-term patterns of acts and behaviors that can give insight into the location of ethic along the Unevolved-Evolved Continuum.

Considering these cautions, it is appropriate to begin this discussion of manifestations and examples of acts and behaviors guided and motivated by the Unevolved Ethic. I will begin with some simple acts and behaviors that all demonstrate a selfish emphasis or focus on Self and the interest, welfare, or good of Self. When part of a pattern of acts and behaviors, each is indicative of the Unevolved Ethic. Each of these is a fairly common example.

For instance, cutting a line is a fairly common example. Littering is another fairly common example. Failing to keep a pet on a leash or cleaning up behind a pet are common examples. Another very common example is failing to listen while someone is speaking. Attempting to speak over someone is yet another fairly common example. Failing to signal turns while driving is a fairly common example. Failing to maintain the appearance of a yard or house is a fairly common example. Tagging or spray-painting graffiti, regardless of the message, is another. Still further is the example of utilizing the express lane in a grocery store with too many items. Swearing in public is yet another example. These example acts and behaviors demonstrate concern or regard for Self and a lack of concern or regard for Others. Each maximizes benefit and minimizes harm for Self. Each demonstrates the willingness and ability to minimalize or ignore harm to Others.

The same can be said of every act or behavior that is thoughtless, inconsiderate, discourteous, impolite, insensitive, or careless of the feelings of Others or the collective whole. The same is true of every act or behavior that disrespects or devalues Others or the dignity of Others. The Unevolved Ethic motivates a pattern of acts and behaviors that disrespect or devalue Others and the dignity of Others. Yet, those Selves whose acts and behaviors are motivated by the Unevolved Ethic often demand consideration, regard, and respect for themselves and the dignity of Self. They will demonstrate a lack of consideration, courtesy, sensitivity, respect, and dignity of Others, yet demand the same for themselves as part of an ongoing pattern of acts and behaviors. Indeed, their pattern of acts and behaviors may even suggest a belief in entitlement or special privilege for Self.

One excellent example of this lack of consideration, courtesy, and respect for Others is the inconsiderate use of cell phones. Cell phones are a convenient technology often used in a manner completely inconsiderate of Others. For instance, calls made or taken in public places such as restaurants, retail stores, meetings, seminars, or other inappropriate locations is inconsiderate. It is impolite and disrespectful of Others and the collective whole to make or take calls in any of these situations. However, Self minimalizes or ignores these harms as Self acts to maximize benefit and minimize harm for Self. Self may offer rationalizations, justifications, excuses, or explanations if confronted. Each rationalization, justification, excuse, or explanation minimalizes or ignores the harm to Others or the collective whole. A further example is the habit of talking on cell phones or texting while driving. These are unsafe behaviors that manifest regard for Self and minimalize or ignore potential harm for every other person on the road. Finally, there is the use of cellphones to take calls, text, use various social media, and check email while at work.

Another inconsiderate and disrespectful manifest act or behavior is the using of racial, ethnic, or religious slurs. The same is true of slurs related to nationality, gender identity or sexual preference. These slurs always carry a demeaning and disrespectful inference. They often carry meaning that is dehumanizing. They suggest that a member of the slurred race, ethnic group, religious affiliation, or nationality is somehow less than a human being. This is disrespectful of the dignity of Others. It devalues Others. This is harm to Others. However, the harm extends beyond members of the slurred race, ethnic group, religion, or nationality.

The harm extends to all Others present and the collective whole. This harm may take the form of pain or the privation of pleasure for Others but extends to the spread of greater harms such as distrust, doubt, misgiving, and insecurity within the collective whole. These slurs spread resentment, bitterness, discord, and acrimony within a collective whole. They are and always will be divisive. This is the case even if the Self using the slur is a member of the slurred group. Therefore, using these slurs when part of an ongoing pattern of acts and behaviors indicates the Unevolved Ethic.

The Unevolved Ethic also motivates all acts and behaviors related to racism, sexism, and ethnic and religious persecution. It motivates all acts and behaviors that result in harassment or persecution based on sexual or gender identity or preference. Further, the Unevolved Ethic motivates all acts and behaviors that enslave or subjugate Others for the interest, welfare, or good of Self. It is the ethic that motivates human trafficking and genocide.

All acts or behaviors that enslave or subjugate Others maximize benefit and minimize harm for Self or a collective form of Self. All acts or behaviors related to human trafficking or genocide maximize benefit and minimize harm for Self or a collective form of Self. All are self-preserving, self-regarding, and self-promoting. All minimalize or ignore harm done to Others and the collective whole. Yet harm does occur and the impact of this harm can be far-reaching. In every case, these harms are always contrary to building cohesion, unity, or harmony and the best interest, welfare, or good of the collective whole. The impact of these harms can span centuries.

Indeed, much of the hostility and enmity that exist in the world today is traceable to acts and behaviors that occurred, in some cases, centuries ago. Much of the tribal, ethnic, religious, and national hatred and hostility that exists today reflects harm for Others that occurred, in many instances, centuries ago. Yet, this harm lingers in the collective memory of tribal, ethnic, and religious groups or nationalities. Even today, these old harms underlie the desire of many Selves or collective forms of Self for vengeance. Even today, these old harms result in the inability to accept and embrace Others. They result in the willingness to demean, dehumanize, and exclude Others.

The Unevolved Ethic always motivates the willingness and ability to demean, dehumanize and exclude. It is always the Unevolved Ethic that motivates patterns of acts and behaviors that demean, dehumanize, and exclude those who are not like "I" "Me" or do not look like "I," "Me" or those who do not speak the same language or practice the same religion.

It motivates patterns of behavior that manifest the willingness to demean, dehumanize, and exclude those who are not in the same race or ethnic group as "I," "Me" or those who do not hold the same beliefs, attitudes, opinions, and ideologies as "I," "Me". Further, it guides and motivates acts and behaviors termed "intolerant" and "tolerant".

While it may be surprising to suggest the Unevolved Ethic motivates "tolerance," I can demonstrate this with a short examination of the words "intolerant" and "tolerant." I can then place these words on the Unevolved-Evolved Continuum.

Intolerance is the unwillingness or inability to endure, abide, or bear Others whose background, religion, ethnic group, language, sexual preference, or nationality is not the same as "Mine." It is the unwillingness or inability to endure, abide, or bear beliefs, attitudes, opinions, and ideologies that are not like "Mine." It can extend to an unwillingness or inability to view Others as equal to Self or deserving of the same consideration, respect, and dignity afforded to Self or Others who are like Self.

Tolerance, on the other hand, is the willingness or ability to endure, abide, or bear Others whose background, race, religion, ethnic group, or nationality is not the same as "Mine." It is the willingness or ability to endure, abide, or bear beliefs, attitudes, opinions, and ideologies that are not like "Mine." It extends to the willingness or ability to bear or abide Others who are not like "I," "Me" as equal to Self and deserving of the same consideration, respect, and dignity afforded to Self or Others like Self.

While it is clear that intolerance carries a very negative connotation, it is perhaps less obvious that tolerance also carries a negative connotation. This negative connotation is contained in the words "endure," "abide," or "bear." Each of these words carries a connotation of loss or felt loss. They carry the connotation of giving up something, a connotation of sacrifice.

Indeed, Self often endures, abides, or bears Others who are not like Self only grudgingly, sometimes very grudgingly, and sometimes only when forced or required to do so by some outside pressure or legal requirement.

In some instances, there is even harm (pain or the privation of pleasure) in the form of a penalty for Self if Self cannot or does not display behaviors that manifest tolerance of Others. In the United States, laws concerning equal rights, equal opportunity for education, equal housing and employment, are all examples of laws that attempt to encourage or enforce tolerance of Others.

This connotation of loss or felt loss, this connotation of sacrifice, places tolerance under the Unevolved Ethic. Tolerance does reside nearer to the PoT and intolerance further away from the PoT, but tolerance still resides under the Unevolved Ethic. Figure 3-2 illustrates the location of "intolerant" and "tolerant" on the continuum.

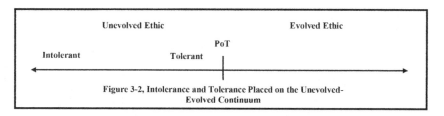

Figure 3-2, Intolerance and Tolerance Placed on the Unevolved-Evolved Continuum

After constructing the Evolved Ethic, I will complete this figure to include the two words that relate to that ethic. For now, I want to return to an example act used earlier to illustrate the hedonistic utilitarian component of the Unevolved Ethic. The example is telling a lie.

In an earlier discussion, I established that every lie maximizes benefit or minimizes harm for Self. With each lie told, Self minimalizes or ignores the harm that results for Others and the collective whole. I also established that the same holds true for every dishonest act or behavior. For instance, when part of a pattern of acts and behaviors, the Unevolved Ethic guides and motivates exaggerating or outright lying on a resume. The same ethic motivates cheating on a partner; test; income taxes, or inflating an expense account. The same ethic motivates cheating on a spouse and all other examples that involve cheating. The same ethic guides and motivates every fraud, scam, swindle, or embezzlement. In each case, Self benefits, in some manner, from the act or behavior. In each case, the behavior maximizes benefit or minimizes harm for Self. In each case, the act or behavior harms Others and the collective whole. In each case, Self minimalizes or ignores this harm to Others or the collective whole in the interest, welfare, and good of Self. Self rationalizes, justifies, explains, and excuses this harm in the interest of Self. It is the same with many other acts and behaviors that maximize benefit and minimize harm to Self.

The Unevolved Ethic guides and motivates the pattern of acts and behaviors that include selling products and services that will not and cannot meet the performance claims of the seller. The Unevolved Ethic motivates the selling of tainted or unsafe products. The Unevolved Ethic motivates cheating or defrauding the elderly or unsuspecting. The Unevolved Ethic always motivates the use of deception and deceit to maximize benefit and minimize harm for Self. The Unevolved Ethic always motivates minimalizing and ignoring the harm to Others and the collective whole. Likewise, the Unevolved Ethic always motivates a pattern of attempts to deflect or avoid responsibility and accountability for harm to Others or the collective whole.

It is also the Unevolved Ethic that motivates the litigious nature of society. It motivates a pattern of acts and behaviors that include filing what are often termed frivolous lawsuits. Further, the ethic motivates false claims for workman's compensation benefits and disability benefits. All too often, Self is willing to pursue fictitious or imaginary claims of injury in an effort to gain benefit through a large monetary settlement for Self. All too often, Self is willing to stretch or embellish the truth or outright lie to gain this benefit for Self. Unfortunately, all too often, there are those who aid and abet this pursuit of benefit for Self. These individuals do so to maximize benefit and minimize harm for themselves.

This group would include personal injury attorneys encouraging questionable lawsuits and questionable or fraudulent claims for disability and social security benefits. This group would also include the expert witnesses who provide testimony supporting the questionable lawsuits or questionable or fraudulent claims for benefits. In each case, the personal injury attorneys and expert witnesses attempt to maximize benefit and minimize harm for themselves and minimalize or ignore the harm to Others and the collective whole. A related act is the filing of bankruptcy.

Filing bankruptcy is an act that maximizes benefit and minimizes harm for Self. It is an attempt to deflect or avoid responsibility and accountability for the accumulated debts of Self. If successful, bankruptcy does result in harm to Others and the collective whole. Self minimalizes or ignores this harm in the interest of Self. Unfortunately, filing bankruptcy, an act once considered unacceptable, has become far more acceptable. As the pursuit of pleasure and the avoidance of pain or the privation of pleasure for Self has grown, bankruptcy has become far more acceptable as a means of deflecting or avoiding responsibility and accountability for the debts of Self.

This ethic is also apparent in the acts and behaviors of those who fail to provide support for children, as well as acts and behaviors associated with child abuse, domestic abuse, and sexual abuse. In each instance, the acts or behaviors maximize benefit or minimize harm for Self. In each instance, there is harm to Others and the collective whole. In many instances, this harm involves actual physical pain, but it can also result in emotional or psychological pain for Others. In each instance, harm results for the collective whole since each is contrary to the best interest, welfare, and good of the whole. Each act results in the spread of fear, doubt, uncertainty, and distrust. Each spreads acrimony, bitterness, resentment, and anger. Each is usually accompanied by rationalizations, justifications, explanations, and excuses intended to minimize the harm, or the harm is simply ignored.

But this is also the ethic that motivates fits of anger or rage and crimes of passion. This ethic motivates acts and behaviors that stem from possessiveness, jealousy, and envy. Jealousy and envy are emotions, emotions are tied to feelings, and feelings are always tied to Self. Emotions are always concerned with "I," "Me." Often, emotional acts and behaviors result in harm to Others or the collective whole. This is especially true of acts and behaviors associated with negative emotions, such as anger or rage, as well as temperamental acts. Acts and behaviors that demonstrate emotion, especially strong emotion, always maximize benefit and minimize harm for Self. Self then minimalizes or ignores any harm that results for Others or the collective whole.

As an example, sorrow is an emotion. Sorrow is a word used to describe emotion tied to a felt loss. Perhaps it is the felt loss that results from the death of a loved one or a favorite pet. "I," "Me" feels sorrow or feels sorrowful at the loss to Self. Sorrow is therefore focused on "I," "Me." It is often expressed through grief. Grief is a behavioral response to the felt loss. Grief is, therefore, a self-interested behavior. It is a behavior that maximizes benefit for Self. Self does not grieve for the loved one or the favorite pet; Self grieves over the felt loss to Self. Regardless of the emotion, when Self acts from emotion, Self is acting out the feelings of Self.

An extreme example that illustrates acting out the feelings and emotions of Self is suicide. Suicide is an act that is always self-regarding. It is an act that minimizes pain or the privation of pleasure for Self. It is also an act that minimalizes or ignores harm to Others. It manifests a lack of regard for harm to Others. This harm is, generally speaking, pain for Others. Suicide is, therefore, always wrong, incorrect, and inappropriate. It is always tied to the emotions and feelings of Self. The same is true when Self acts from superstition or fear.

Both superstition and fear are very individual and always felt by "I," "Me". Superstition and fear can be very powerful. Like other feelings and emotions, superstition and fear are very subjective. This is the case even in situations where the same or a similar superstition or fear affects large numbers of people at the same time or is shared by many individuals. Self still feels superstition or fear. "I," "Me" is superstitious or feels fearful. As a result, acts or behaviors that manifest superstition and fear always manifest concern or regard for Self.

These acts or behaviors are often tied to concern for the survival of Self regardless of whether the fear results from a clear and present physical danger or a less well-defined and non-physical danger. The acts and behaviors that stem from superstition and fear are self-protecting, self-preserving, and self-promoting. These acts or behaviors maximize benefit and minimize harm for Self. The same is true of acts and behaviors associated with the biases and prejudices of Self.

Biases and prejudices are subjective. The term bias refers to the preferences of Self. It refers to the tendencies and inclinations of Self. These preferences, tendencies, and inclinations are all very subjective. They are all tied to "I," "Me." They are tied to that which "I," "Me" likes or dislikes. They are tied to that which "I," "Me" favors or disfavors and that which "I," "Me" enjoys or abhors. The prejudices of Self are similar. Self is prejudiced in favor of or against something or someone based on preconceived feelings, beliefs, attitudes, or opinions. Prejudices are not based on knowledge or fact. Like the biases of Self, the prejudices of Self can and often do result in acts and behaviors that harm Others and the collective whole.

Acts and behaviors manifesting Self's prejudices as part of an ongoing pattern of acts and behaviors can and do harm the best interest, welfare, and good of the collective whole. They spread dissonance and disharmony within a collective whole. As a result, they are always contrary to the best interest, welfare, and good of the collective whole. As such, acts and behaviors associated with the biases and prejudices of Self are manifestations of the Unevolved Ethic. They maximize benefit and minimize harm for Self. Similarly, acts and behaviors based on grudges also indicate the Unevolved Ethic.

Self may hold a grudge because feelings or pride are injured. Perhaps Self holds a grudge because Self or Self's honor has been damaged or injured. Honor, in this context, is simply another word for pride. Self holds a grudge because Self feels pain. Self may seek to alleviate that pain through revenge. Self will feel better if Self can get even and Self likes to feel good. So, Self holds a grudge and seeks an opportunity to avenge hurt feelings, pride, or honor. Therefore, all acts and behaviors associated with holding a grudge maximize benefit and minimize harm for Self. They are all wrong, incorrect, and inappropriate. However, in each case, Self will rationalize, justify, explain, and excuse the harm that results for Others or the collective whole in the interest of benefit for Self. But there are still many other manifestations of the Unevolved Ethic.

For instance, the Unevolved Ethic guides and motivates the deliberate use or manipulation of wealth or power to benefit Self or self-interest. Likewise, the Unevolved Ethic motivates the deliberate use or manipulation of position, for instance, a public position, to benefit Self. This is the case whether Self refers to an individual Self or a collective form of Self such as a corporation or nation-state. In any case, using or manipulating wealth, power, or position is an attempt to maximize benefit and minimize harm for Self or self-interest.

This use of wealth, power, or position to maximize benefit and minimize harm for Self is self-regarding and self-promoting. In each instance, there is harm to Others and the collective whole. This harm may be physical or non-physical. It can take the form of spreading dissonance and disharmony. It can and often does result in competition. Indeed, the Unevolved Ethic motivates all acts and behaviors that encourage and enable competition. However, to understand this assertion requires a short examination of competition.

I will start this examination by stating that competition always focuses on "I," "Me". It is always "I," "Me" who wins a competition. Conversely, it is always "I," "Me" who loses a competition. It is not a different "I," "Me", who wins or loses, it is the same "I," "Me" who wins or loses any competition. Therefore, winning and losing both refer to the same Self or collective form of Self. Competition is not "I" win and "you" lose or "you" win and "I" lose. The correct interpretation of competition is "I" win or "I" lose.

The significance of "I" win or "I" lose extends back to the discussion of pleasure and pain or the privation of pleasure. Winning feels good to Self. Losing does not feel good to Self. Winning is pleasant for Self. Losing is not pleasant for Self. Winning is pleasure. Losing is pain or the privation of pleasure. Therefore, winning is benefit and losing is harm for Self. Therefore, acts and behaviors that manifest competition are tied directly to benefit (pleasure) and harm (pain or the privation of pleasure) for Self. When Self competes, Self is acting to maximize benefit and minimize harm for Self. This is the case regardless of whether Self refers to an individual Self or a collective form of Self.

In all its forms, competition is guided and motivated by the Unevolved Ethic. This is the case when two or more individuals compete or two or more teams compete. It is the case when two or more cities, states, or nation-states compete. Competition is always an attempt to maximize benefit and minimize harm for Self or a collective form of Self. In addition, competition always results in harm for Others and the collective whole. It always results in the harms previously identified. Competition is always divisive. It results in dissonance and disharmony within the collective whole. As each competitor competes for the benefit, welfare, and good of Self, jealousy, envy, resentment and enmity increase within the collective whole. As each competitor seeks advantage and opportunity for Self, dissonance and disharmony increase within the collective whole. This is not in the best interest of the collective whole.

The level of competition extends from contention to conflict. In some instances, competition manifests as contention between the best interest, welfare, and good of two or more Selves. In other instances, competition manifests as the more extreme conflict between the best interest, welfare, and good of two or more Selves. All competition then falls within the range between and including contention and conflict. In the worst case, conflict can and does escalate to armed conflict, even war. Figure 3-3 illustrates this range of competition using the Unevolved-Evolved Continuum.

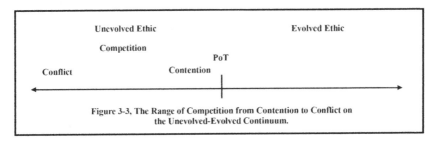

Figure 3-3, The Range of Competition from Contention to Conflict on the Unevolved-Evolved Continuum.

I place contention near the Point of Transcendence (PoT). I place conflict further away from the PoT to indicate that conflict is the more extreme level of competition. However, whether competition manifests as contention or conflict, competition is always wrong, incorrect, and inappropriate. It is wrong, incorrect, and inappropriate because it seeks to maximize benefit and minimize harm for Self. It is wrong, incorrect, and inappropriate because it harms Others and the collective whole. Competition is, therefore, always contrary to the best interest, welfare, and good of the whole.

As an example, there is always harm that results from competition in the business or corporate world. For instance, there is the cost of competition for resources. Competition for resources increases demand for a resource. Increased demand then increases the price of the resource. This results in additional costs for the end product. The additional costs pass through to the consumer of the product. This additional cost is harm to the consumer. A related example is the competition for knowledgeable, talented, and skilled workers. This competition increases the cost of recruiting and sustaining a workforce. In addition, there is a cost for advertising and marketing products and services. Each of these costs of competition pass through to the consumer of the product or service. The costs pass to the individual consumer and the collective whole composed of all consumers of a product or service. Therefore, it is the consumer who bears the harm of this competition.

But those who promote competition minimalize or ignore that harm to Others and the collective whole in the interest of Self. Those who promote competition as right, correct, and appropriate rationalize, justify, explain, and excuse the harm. They construct rational and logical-sounding "reasons" that rationalize, justify, explain, and excuse harm to Others and the collective whole. They construct the very rational "reasons" that suggest it is right, correct, and appropriate for Others and the collective whole to bear this harm.

A related example that illustrates the presence of the Unevolved Ethic within the corporate or business arena is the growing number of "working poor." The term "working poor" describes those who struggle to make ends meet on inadequate pay or compensation. It is a term that describes those whose time, effort, knowledge, skills, talents, and abilities contribute to the profitability of a business, enterprise, or corporation in exchange for pay and compensation often inadequate to meet essential needs. It describes those whose labor contributes to company executive's often lavish compensation packages in exchange for pay and compensation that fails to recognize this contribution. This is the case since many company executives' compensation packages are tied to the performance and profitability of the business, enterprise, or corporation.

The tie of executive compensation packages to performance and profitability motivates corporate executives to act and behave to maximize benefit and minimize harm for Self. It motivates acts and behaviors that result in harm for Others and the collective whole. It results in payment of a wage or salary that qualifies Others to wear the title "working poor." It results in job loss for some and additional workload for Others as corporate executives enact downsizing strategies to improve profitability. It results in job loss as the ever-expanding implementation of robotics and other technologies replace people. It results in the ever-widening gap between the wage and compensation at the bottom of a business, enterprise, or corporation and the wage and compensation of those at the top. However, in each instance, these acts maximize benefit and minimize harm for those executives in a position to enact these policies and practices. The harm for Others and the collective whole is minimalized or ignored.

These harms are minimalized or ignored through use of reasonable and often elaborate-sounding rationalizations, justifications, explanations, and excuses. Indeed, "competition" or "improved competitiveness" is often cited to justify acts and behaviors that maximize benefit and minimize harm for Self and minimalize or ignore harm for Others and the collective whole.

It should be clear that these comments are not intended to demonize technology. Technology is only a tool or means to an end. As a means, technology is essentially neutral. It is neither good nor bad. It is employment of the means, the employment of technology, that is good or bad. If the use of technology maximizes benefit and minimizes harm only for Self and harms Others or the collective whole, this is wrong, incorrect, or inappropriate. It is a selfish, self-centered, self-regarding, and self-promoting use of technology. However, technology is often a means to benefit Others and the collective whole. This would be a right, correct, and appropriate use of technology. So, these comments are not intended to demonize technology, but only to highlight acts and behaviors motivated by the Unevolved Ethic which maximize benefit and minimize harm for Self and minimalize or ignore harm to Others and the collective whole.

Further, I do not mean to infer that every contribution by every Self within an organization is equal and should be compensated equally. I recognize that levels of responsibility and accountability merit consideration in determining fair compensation. There are skills, talents, abilities, and knowledge that merit consideration in determining fair compensation. Further, there are simply those who work harder and contribute more toward the success of any organization or corporation and others who contribute less.

However, this discussion does suggest that the increasingly wide differential in compensation is often no longer based on an objective assessment of contribution. It does suggest that the differential is more often motivated by the ethic that motivates all self-interested, self-regarding, self-promoting, and self-aggrandizing acts and behaviors. It does suggest the differential is now based far more on the willingness and ability to maximize pleasure and minimize pain or the privation of pleasure for Self. Unfortunately, this willingness and ability to maximize pleasure and minimize pain or the privation of pleasure on the part of corporate executives has another far-reaching consequence. This is the impact the ethic of corporate executives has on organizational ethic and culture.

The term "organizational culture" is certainly not new. Essentially, it is the collective behavior of those individuals within an organization and the meaning given to that behavior. It is seen in how individuals interact with other individuals within and outside of the organization. It includes the organization's values, principles, beliefs, ideology, and philosophy. It can be seen in the organization's customs, rules, symbols, language, traditions and habits. Every organization, including every institution and corporation, has a culture. This culture influences the acts and behaviors of all employees or members of the organization. It influences the relationships that form and exist within an institution or organization. It influences relationships between the organization and other organizations. It influences the relationships between an organization and its customers, suppliers, and stakeholders. However, it is the organizational ethic that guides and motivates the acts and behaviors that comprise the organizational culture. Finally, it is the organizational ethic that guides and motivates the values, principles, beliefs, attitudes, goals, customs, rules, traditions, policies, and practices that become the culture. Understanding this assertion, requires a brief examination of the term "organizational ethic."

Each organization, corporation, or institution is composed of individuals. Each individual represents one Self. Each Self has an ethic that lies somewhere along the Unevolved-Evolved Continuum. The organizational ethic represents the cumulative, collective ethic of all employees or members of the organization, corporation, or institution. If the cumulative, collective ethic of all or the majority of employees or members is the Unevolved Ethic, the organizational ethic will manifest the Unevolved Ethic. By extension, the organizational culture will then reflect this ethic. This culture will favor acts and behaviors that maximize benefit and minimize harm for the collective Self which is the corporation, organization, or institution. Further, this culture will demonstrate the willingness and ability to minimalize or ignore harm for Others and the collective whole. Finally, the organizational culture will encourage deflection or avoidance of responsibility and accountability for harm to Others or the collective whole.

While the organizational ethic is the cumulative, collective ethic of all employees or members of a corporation, organization, or institution, the acts and behaviors of senior managers, corporate executives, and directors carry the greatest influence in setting this ethic. If the acts and behaviors of senior managers, executives, and directors maximize benefit and minimize harm for Self, the example set will influence the organizational ethic. The organizational ethic will then guide and motivate the acts and behaviors that underlie the organizational culture. If the acts and behaviors of senior managers minimalize or ignore harm to Others (including employees) or the collective whole, the example set will influence the organizational ethic. The ethic will then influence the acts and behaviors that underlie the organizational culture. If the acts and behaviors of senior managers are self-preserving, self-regarding, self-promoting, and self-aggrandizing, the organizational ethic will follow this lead and the culture will manifest this focus on the best interest, welfare and good of Self.

It is possible to identify the influence of the Unevolved Ethic in the organizational ethic and culture of many different organizations, corporations and institutions. For instance, it is evident in the ethic and culture of those companies and corporations that demand tax concessions or abatements from communities and states. It is likewise evident in those companies and corporations that employ power and fear to bully suppliers into ever-lower prices and quality. It is evident in the ethic of those that produce and sell products of dubious quality, products that quickly find their way into landfills but guarantee repeat customer purchasing. Indeed, it is often evident in the labor practices of organizations, institutions, and corporations. However, and not surprisingly, it is also present in the acts and behaviors of organized labor. Organized labor often manifests acts and behaviors which also seek to maximize benefit and minimize harm for Self.

Continuing, it is in the ethic and culture of companies or corporations that pollute the air, water, and land only to maximize benefit and minimize harm for Self. It is in the ethic and culture of those that then minimalize the harm to Others and the collective whole. In this case, Others can include all sentient beings and the planet itself. However, it is also in the ethic and culture of companies and corporations that attempt to circumvent regulations intended to protect consumers (Others) and the collective whole, including the environment. It is not surprising that many of these same companies and corporations fight attempts to enact regulations of industry.

It's not surprising since the regulation of any industry, much like any other code, standard, or law is an attempt to restrain or constrain the ethic of those working in the industry. It is an attempt to restrain or constrain acts and behaviors that maximize benefit and minimize harm for Self. It attempts to restrain or constrain acts or behaviors that harm Others or the collective whole. In other instances, these regulations encourage or force acts or behaviors that benefit Others or the collective whole.

Therefore, when a government moves to regulate or increase regulation of an industry, it is not regulating the industry. It is regulating the ethic of those individual Selves working or operating in the industry. It is regulating ethic to limit the ability of those working in the regulated industry to maximize benefit and minimize harm for individual Self or the collective Self represented by the industry. So, it is no surprise these individuals and industries seek to limit government regulation. They are simply demonstrating the willingness and ability to maximize benefit and minimize harm for Self.

The same willingness and ability to maximize benefit and minimize harm for Self are present in all predatory and exploitive acts or behaviors. This is the case whether the predatory or exploitative act is attempting to snare an unsuspecting teenager on the internet or a check cashing company using advertising to snare an unsuspecting customer into high-interest, short-term, payday loans. It doesn't matter whether the predatory or exploitative act is committed by a pedophile attempting to lure a child with candy or a car dealer attempting to lure an unsuspecting consumer with promises of easy credit terms and low interest rates; terms and rates that often hold the potential of financial disaster for the consumer. It doesn't matter whether it is the predatory or exploitative practices of a drug dealer or pimp or those who wear the finest suits and ties and work on Madison Avenue. In nature, predators come in many forms, sizes, and shapes. The human species is no different. Human predators also come in all forms, sizes, and shapes.

This is not to suggest that all predation or exploitation is illegal. That would certainly not be the case. Many examples of predation or exploitation are clearly legal. There are many examples of predation or exploitation considered acceptable. However, predation and exploitation always indicate the willingness and ability to maximize benefit and minimize harm for either Self or a collective form of Self. Predatory and exploitive acts and behaviors always serve the interest, welfare, or good of the predator or exploiter first and foremost. Therefore, predation and exploitation always range from wrong to more wrong. This is the case at the level of individual Self or the collective level of Self represented by a business, corporation, industry or even nation-state.

Both predation and exploitation result in harm to Others or the collective whole. In the case of predation, there is often a clear victim of the predator. There is benefit only to the predator and harm is born by the victim and, often, the collective whole. Regardless of who or what the predator is, the benefit of a predatory act is to Self only. Therefore, harm is always born by the victim. On the other hand, there is not always a clear victim in the case of exploitation.

There is not always a clear victim in cases of exploitation because there is at least the appearance of benefit to the exploited Self. There is, to some degree, the appearance of mutual benefit. However, exploitive acts and behaviors always maximize benefit and minimize harm primarily for the exploiter. While the exploited Self may appear to benefit, this benefit is secondary to the benefit gained by the exploiter. Perhaps this is most easily illustrated by examining the marketing of products or services to consumers.

Any marketing campaign aims to create and build demand for a product or service. A marketing campaign builds demand by creating a felt want or desire for a product or service. To create this felt want or desire, marketers appeal to the ethic of the target audience. Regardless of the medium employed, marketing campaigns target the consumer's willingness and ability to maximize pleasure and minimize pain or the privation of pleasure for themselves. They often target the want or desire for that which is pleasing or pleasant for the consumer. The focus of some marketing campaigns is maximizing pleasure for the consumer, and the focus of other marketing campaigns is minimizing pain or the privation of pleasure for the consumer. In either case, there is the appearance of benefit for the consumer. They always emphasize this benefit for the consumer. The harm that results for Others and the collective whole is then minimalized or ignored in the interest of the advertising Self or collective form of Self.

Perhaps the greatest harm from exploitation by marketing campaigns is excessive consumerism or materialism. It takes raw materials to manufacture the products Self wants, desires and craves. The manufacture of these products depletes the natural resources of the planet. It depletes the natural resources available to every future generation. This is the case whether the focus is on the depletion of fossil fuels that power manufacturing or the depletion of the many other natural resources necessary to manufacture products. This is harm to all future generations of human beings. It is harm that Self chooses to minimalize or ignore in the interest of benefit for Self.

It takes a long-range view to see the coming day when resources deplete. It takes the willingness and ability to project into the future to see the day when natural resources deplete. Unfortunately, for both the planet and future generations of human beings, the Unevolved Ethic encourages only a short-range view. It only encourages a short-range view of maximizing benefit and minimizing harm for Self. It cannot and does not encourage a long-range view that includes Others yet to be born. This is because the short-range view serves Self and the interest, welfare, and good of Self.

It is the short-range view that motivates the wants, desires, or cravings for more, bigger, and better for Self. It is the short-range view of Self that minimalizes or ignores harm to future generations of human beings. Unfortunately, this short-range view is apparent in the acts and behaviors of individuals, corporations, and even nation-states. The same view is evident in acts and behaviors that contribute to climate change.

For over 60 years scientists have warned of the harmful effects of pollution on the planet. Pollution contributes to the "greenhouse effect," resulting in climate change. Yet, each time Self chooses to drive a personal vehicle, Self contributes to the pollutants in the atmosphere and the overall impact of pollution on the environment. Self chooses in a manner that carries harm to future generations and every creature that does or will inhabit the planet. Self chooses to maximize benefit and minimize harm for Self and minimalizes or ignores harm to the future. Self then minimalizes the harm by employing rationalizations, justifications, explanations, and excuses.

For instance, Self may rationalize that science or improved technology will overcome the harmful effects of climate change. These rationalizations and justifications suggest that science or technology will find solutions that enable Self to continue acting or behaving to maximize benefit for Self. Self may justify or excuse not utilizing public transportation by employing any number of other reasonable-sounding explanations or reasons. Then Self or a collective form of Self demands government policies and practices that continue to supply fuel as cheaply as possible so Self can continue to maximize benefit and minimize harm to Self. But this willingness and ability to act or behave to maximize benefit and minimize harm for Self is certainly not limited to individual Selves or to businesses and corporations. It is often also evident in the policies and practices of the collective form of Self called nation-states.

Like corporations, nation-states also have a cumulative, collective ethic. Like every organization or institution, nation-states are also composed of individuals. Each member of a nation-state has an ethic. The cumulative, collective ethic of the members of a nation-state influences the national ethic. The degree or extent to which the collective ethic of a nation-state is the Unevolved Ethic, the acts and behaviors of the nation-state will reflect this ethic. The acts and behaviors of the nation-state will seek to maximize benefit and minimize harm for the collective Self that is the nation-state. Similar to the discussion of corporations, those individuals who rule or govern nation-states most influence the national ethic. Further, it is the ethic of those ruling or governing that most influence and motivate the nation-states domestic and foreign policy.

For instance, it is the ethic of those ruling or governing that most influences and motivates policies and practices that encourage or defend acts and behaviors that oppress segments of a population, whether this oppression is tribal, racial, ethnic, political, or religious. It guides and motivates policies and practices that endorse or support acts of genocide. It guides and motivates policies and practices that restrict the freedoms of individuals or groups of individuals based on tribal, racial, ethnic, political, or religious beliefs. Finally, it guides and motivates policies and practices that favor any one population segment over another. Generally speaking, the ethic of those ruling or governing often guides and motivates policies and practices that encourage or support persecution. This is the case regardless of the type and form of government.

There are essentially three types of governments; autocracy, oligarchy, and democracy. An autocracy is rule or governance by one; an oligarchy is rule or governance by a few and democracy is rule or governance by all. These three types of government can and do take many forms. For instance, autocracy can take the form of both a monarchy or a dictatorship. An oligarchy can take the form of a plutocracy or theocracy. Democracy can also take different forms, including direct or indirect representation. Clearly, the form of government impacts the level or degree to which those ruling or governing influence the national ethic.

The ethic of those ruling or governing an autocracy or oligarchy will greatly influence the national ethic of a nation-state. The ethic of those ruling in an autocracy or oligarchy will determine the extent or degree to which the policies and practices of the nation-state seek to maximize benefit and minimize harm for Self and the collective form of Self. Further, the ethic or collective ethic of those ruling or governing in an autocracy or oligarchy will determine the extent or degree to which those ruling or governing will employ force or the threat of force to remain in power. It will determine the degree or extent to which those ruling or governing will employ fear to remain in power. It will determine the degree or extent to which those ruling or governing will employ arbitrary imprisonment, torture, and death to remain in power. In addition, the ethic or collective ethic of those ruling or governing will determine how much bribery, graft, and other forms of corruption are encouraged or permitted. It will determine the degree or extent to which acts and behaviors will maximize benefit and minimize harm for Self. However, this is even the case in a democracy.

Democracy is often viewed as the type of government that best serves the interest, welfare, and good of the collective whole represented by the citizens it governs. Democracy is often viewed as the type of government that exists to maximize benefit and minimize harm to the collective whole of its citizens. As such, the domestic use of force to remain in power is generally not associated with a true democracy. Using arbitrary imprisonment, torture, and death to remain in power is not generally associated with a true democracy. Similarly, confiscating property and political, ethnic, or religious persecution are not generally associated with a true democracy.

This would, of course, not include democracies that are, in reality, oligarchies or autocracies thinly disguised as democracies. It would not include those democracies in which one individual, family, or political party is willing and able to employ fraud, fear, and manipulation to maintain power. It would not include examples of democracy in which arbitrary imprisonment, torture, and death ensure continued power. However, even in the finest examples of democracy, it is possible to identify acts and behaviors guided and motivated by the Unevolved Ethic.

For instance, if part of an ongoing pattern of acts and behaviors, the Unevolved Ethic motivates acts and behaviors associated with "pork barrel politics." This includes the use of "earmarks" to funnel federal taxpayer money into a home district or state. "Pork" and "earmarks" both maximize benefit and minimize harm for both the politician and the collective form of Self represented by the home district or state. The collective whole composed of all taxpayers, districts, and states bear the resulting harm. These harms may take the form of increased tax burden, or they may take the form of increased national debt. However, they may also include increased competition as other politicians, districts, or states vie for their share of the "pork" or "earmarks." It may increase contention and conflict as politicians, districts, and states seek to maximize benefit and minimize harm for Self. This manifests the Unevolved Ethic.

The Unevolved Ethic also motivates the bartering, trading, buying, and selling of votes to influence legislation. It motivates all attempts to influence legislation through lobbying. It motivates the extent or degree to which lobbying by individuals or special interest groups ultimately does influence legislation. Indeed, legislation may only favor the interest, welfare, or good of one special interest group over the interest, welfare, or good of the collective whole. This does not result in government of the people, by the people, for the people. Instead, it results in government of the people, by special interest groups, for special interest groups.

In this situation, the government no longer exists to maximize benefit and minimize harm for the collective whole of its citizens. It no longer exists to maximize benefit and minimize harm for the best interest, welfare, and good of its citizens. Now, it exists to maximize benefit and minimize harm for politicians and special interest groups. Now, it exists to serve the best interest, welfare, and good of politicians and special interest groups. Now, it serves to further the special interest group's beliefs, attitudes, and opinions. Both the special interest groups and politicians then minimalize or ignore the harm to the collective whole or the good of the whole. The special interest groups and politicians rationalize, justify, explain, and excuse the harm to the good of the whole so long as benefit is to Self. The same is equally true of acts and behaviors termed "partisan politics."

"Partisan politics" is the attempt to advance a belief, attitude, opinion, or ideology of Self; even if that Self is a collective form of Self, such as a political party. It involves all manner of rationalizations, justifications, explanations, and excuses to advance the beliefs, attitudes, opinions, or ideology of Self or a collective form of Self. These rationalizations and justifications often take the form of very elaborate, very rational arguments. At other times, these rationalizations and justifications clearly stem from emotions and feelings. At still other times, the rationalizations and justifications appear based on biases, prejudices, superstitions, and fears. The harm that results from "partisan politics" is born by the collective whole. Indeed, due to "partisan politics," it is often difficult to even determine that which serves the best interest, welfare, or good of the collective whole.

Competition within and among the political parties is always divisive. It always builds distrust, insecurity, and uncertainty. It builds resentment, bitterness, acrimony, hostility, and resentment within the collective whole. As more extreme beliefs, attitudes, opinions, and ideologies move to the forefront, both government and the collective whole become increasingly polarized. This results in even more discord and disharmony within the collective whole as each party attempts to maximize benefit and minimize harm for Self.

However, this divisiveness is often evident within the collective whole composed of all nation-states. The same discord, disharmony, and competition, exist between and among all the nation-states. This discord and disharmony result when one or more nation-states acts and behaves to maximize benefit and minimize harm for Self.

Historically, self-interest characterizes the interactions of nation-states with other nation-states. Throughout history, this focus on the best interest, welfare, and good of Self repeatedly demonstrated itself through power struggles, wars of conquest, and, in many cases, the subjugation of one nation-state or entire regions of the world by more powerful nation-states (empire building and colonialism). The quest for and use of power to project national self-interest and manipulate other nation-states' behavior to benefit Self has continued since the rise of nation-states. Looking far deeper into human history, the interest, welfare, and good of Self lay at the heart of many of the interactions between the various collective levels of Self that preceded nation-states.

As human beings organized into ever larger collective levels of Self, the interest, welfare, and good of the collective level of Self was and remains the primary motivator of the behavior of these progressive collective levels of Self. As humans organized into collective levels of Self, such as clans, tribes, and later city-states, principalities, kingdoms, and empires, the cornerstone of interaction remained maximizing benefit and minimizing harm for Self. The result is that interactions were and still are characterized by competing self-interest and the willingness to use cunning, force, and power to serve the interest, welfare, and good of Self. The resulting history of competition, contention and conflict, is a history of competing self-interest between these various levels of collective Self. This is still the case today.

Today, the prevailing doctrine of international relations is known as realism. The doctrine of realism rests on the very rational position that the goal of each nation-state is its own survival and continued existence. Therefore, the doctrine of realism promotes and defends the position that each nation-state should and must act and behave in a self-interested, self-protecting, self-regarding, and self-promoting manner. It further holds that each nation-state should favor another nation-state's interest only if there is benefit to Self for doing so. A nation-state should act for the benefit of another nation-state only to the degree or extent necessary to maximize benefit and minimize harm for Self. As such, it is easy to conclude that the doctrine of realism is essentially a manifestation of the Unevolved Ethic at the level of nation-states. While it is possible to look for historical acts and behaviors that evidence the influence of the Unevolved Ethic at the level of nation-states, it is not all that necessary. This influence is readily seen in the workings of the United Nations.

It is evident in the unwillingness and inability of the collective whole of nation-states, represented by the United Nations, to set aside national self-interest in favor of that which benefits the collective whole of nation-states. It is evident in the manner in which nation-states align or realign in order to maximize benefit and minimize harm for Self. It is evident in how each nation-state votes its own national interest, welfare, or good. It is evident in deliberations and votes in the Security Council and the General

Assembly that favor each voting nation-state's interest, welfare, and good. As is always the case, the resulting harm to the collective whole, represented by the community of nations, is minimalized or ignored in favor of benefit for Self.

Unfortunately, in the case of nation-states, the pursuit of national self-interest can and often does collide with the self-interest of other nation-states, and competition ensues. This competition, like all competition, may range from contention to conflict. This conflict may extend to outright war. Enormous harms result from this level of competition between rival national self-interests. Certainly, the building of discord and disharmony results within and among the collective whole of nation-states.

But often, conflict at the level of warfare between two or more nation-states results in far more immediate and real harms. It can take the form of human misery and suffering. It can take the form of death and the destruction of property. It can take the form of refugee camps, and starvation and disease within these camps. It can take the form of the cost required to maintain large militaries and the cost of arms development and procurement. It can take the form of production and storage of chemical and biological weapons. It can even take the form of nuclear proliferation. However, these harms to the collective whole are rationalized, justified, explained, and excused or simply ignored, often in the interest of national pride.

Based on this discussion, it is easy to conclude that all war, like all competition, is wrong, incorrect, and inappropriate. This would be the case since competition, including the extreme example of warfare, is motivated by the Unevolved Ethic. However, it would also be the case that war is more wrong for an aggressor nation-state and less wrong for a nation-state waging war only to defend itself from an aggressor. It is more wrong for a nation-state acting to maximize benefit for Self and less wrong for a nation-state acting to minimize harm for Self. However, it is also the case that war will likely continue as long as competition exists between and among the nation-states. War results from competition. The higher or broader the level of competition, the greater and more widespread the harm that results for Others and the collective whole.

The acceptance of competition as right and correct is the acceptance of contention and conflict. The acceptance of competition is acceptance of harm for Others and the collective whole. As long as human beings view competition as right, correct, appropriate or even acceptable, contention and conflict will mark interactions between Selves and collective forms of Self at all levels. As long as the acts and behaviors of each Self and collective form of Self act and behave to maximize benefit and minimize harm for Self, there will always be contention and conflict. There will always be the risk of war.

Further, as long as Selves, whose ethic is the Unevolved Ethic, are in a position to influence the foreign policy of nation-states, there will always be competition at that level. As long as those who would subjugate Others and a collective whole to maximize benefit for Self are in a position to influence the foreign policy of nation-states, there will be war. It will be necessary for other nation-states to defend themselves. It will be necessary for other nation-states to wage war to minimize harm to Self. Failure to defend Self only encourages aggressor nation-states. This can clearly be seen in history.

Success by aggressor nations, and the Selves who rule them, only encourages more aggression. For instance, the conquests of the Roman Empire, the Mongol Empire, and the conquests of virtually all empires suggest that an aggressor's success leads only to further aggression. More recently, this is easily seen in the case of Nazi Germany in the years leading up to and including World War II. Success encourages and enables acts and behaviors that maximize benefit for Self. It encourages minimalizing and ignoring resulting harm to Others and the collective whole. This will remain true as long as the dominant ethic in the world is the Unevolved Ethic.

It is equally true that many of the other largest and most severe problems affecting the global community of nation-states will also continue to exist. These problems will remain unsolved as each nation-state attempts to maximize benefit and minimize harm for Self. They will remain unsolved so long as each nation-state continues to minimalize or ignore the harm that results when Self acts and behaves to maximize benefit and minimize harm for Self. They will remain unsolved so long as the acts and behaviors of nation-states seek only to serve the interest, welfare, and good of Self. The resulting harm is buried in rationalizations, justifications, explanations, and excuses. Responsibility and accountability are deflected or avoided, and harm to Self is mitigated by employing self-deception strategies such as the complexity strategy.

There are a great many issues or problems said to be too complex to solve. For instance, the problems of both poverty and hunger are said to be complex. As a result, people die of starvation and malnutrition each year. Millions live in abject poverty and misery each year. The problem of inadequate healthcare for millions is also said to be complex. As a result, people, even in the more advanced countries, die of treatable diseases. There are children, many in this country, who are denied the opportunity for a quality education. Many children, in this country and others, are denied the fair opportunity to grow and develop their knowledge, skills, talents, and abilities. But these problems remain unsolved and the harm that results for Others and the collective whole is minimalized or ignored. It is buried in complexity.

This is also often the result when moral relativism is used to rationalize, justify, explain, and excuse the failure to solve the same or similar problems and issues. Moral relativism suggests there is no one way to treat all peoples of the world. It holds that moral standards of behavior in various cultures and societies are so different that treating all people the same would be wrong, incorrect, or inappropriate. While it is true that cultures and societies practice many different traditions and customs, I believe there is a fundamental manner in which all people want to be treated.

All people want to live free of pain and fear. All people want to live free of doubt, uncertainty, and insecurity. People want to live a full and useful life, free from fear of persecution, torture, and death, free of hunger and disease, free from fear of having property confiscated, and free to practice religious beliefs without fear of harassment or persecution. In short, people, regardless of gender identity, race, ethnic group, religion, nationality, sexual preference, or any other difference, want to be treated with respect and dignity. People do not want to be marginalized or ignored. They do not want to be left to wither and die. These are very fundamental, even universal, ways in which all people want to be treated.

But these are not universally recognized or practiced. They are not, nor can they be, so long as Self or the various collective forms of Self, up to and including nation-states, are willing and able to act and behave only to maximize benefit and minimize harm for Self. They are not, nor can they be, as long as Self and the various collective forms of Self are willing and able to minimalize or ignore the harm that results for Others and the collective whole. They are not, nor can they be, so long as Self and collective forms of Self are willing and able to invoke rationalizations, justifications, explanations, and excuses to deflect or avoid responsibility and accountability for failing to give respect and dignity to all Others.

The willingness and ability to act and behave only for the best interest, welfare, and good of Self will always lead to inequity, inequality, and injustice. It will always lead to pain and suffering. It will always lead to hopelessness, and perhaps this is the greatest harm of the Unevolved Ethic: the absence of hope for a better day for millions worldwide. Such is the legacy and future of a world dominated by the Unevolved Ethic.

In the next chapter, I will introduce the Evolved Ethic. I will introduce the ethic that does not guide and motivate acts and behaviors that maximize benefit (pleasure) and minimize harm (pain or the privation of pleasure) for Self and that result in harm for Others and the collective whole. I will introduce the ethic that does not rely on rationalizations, justifications, explanations, and excuses to minimalize or ignore harm to Others and the collective whole. It is the ethic that does not guide and motivate the willingness and ability to deflect and avoid responsibility and accountability for the acts and behaviors of Self. I will introduce the ethic that does not rely on self-deception strategies to mitigate or avoid responsibility for wrong, incorrect, and inappropriate acts and behaviors. It is the ethic that does not result in moral hypocrisy.

Instead, it is the ethic that guides and motivates right, correct, and appropriate acts and behaviors. The ethic that guides and motivates acts and behaviors that maximize benefit and minimize harm to Others and the collective whole. It is the ethic that minimalizes or ignores harm to Self in the interest of Others and the collective whole. The ethic that guides and motivates acts and behaviors that build trust, certainty, security, and confidence. The ethic that guides and motivates acts and behaviors that build unity and community. The ethic that holds the possibility of a better day; a day in which no human being is left behind. It is the ethic that holds the possibility of a better day for all future generations. This is the Evolved Ethic.

CHAPTER 4:
THE EVOLVED ETHIC

The Evolved Ethic is the focus of this and the next chapter. This chapter introduces the ethic, and the next chapter further discusses it. The Evolved Ethic is the ethic that guides choices and motivates acts and behaviors that consistently demonstrate concern for the interest, welfare, and good of Others and the collective whole. It guides and motivates acts and behaviors that consistently place the interest, welfare, and good of Others and the collective whole above the interest, welfare, and good of Self. The pattern of acts and behaviors motivated by the Evolved Ethic manifests consistent regard and consideration for Others and the collective whole. This ethic guides choices and motivates right, correct, and appropriate acts and behaviors even when no one is watching.

Acts and behaviors motivated by this ethic are not selfish, self-centered, egotistical, vainglorious, or narcissistic. They are not self-important, self-absorbed, self-preserving, self-regarding, self-promoting, or self-righteous. Acts and behaviors motivated by this ethic do not maximize benefit and minimize harm for Self. Rather, acts and behaviors motivated by this ethic maximize benefit and minimize harm for Others and the collective whole. These acts and behaviors do not result in harm for Others or the collective whole that Self then minimalizes or ignores. Instead, these acts and behaviors often result in harm (pain or the privation of pleasure) for Self. They often result in harm that Self must be willing and able to minimalize or ignore.

Like the Unevolved Ethic, the Evolved Ethic is a composite. Like the Unevolved Ethic, three components make up the whole. The first or foundational component is the virtue component. The second component is the pluralistic utilitarian component. The final component, the Transcendent Morality, is the morality component that powers the Evolved Ethic. The Evolved Ethic components in each case contrast the Unevolved Ethic's three components.

As in Chapter 2, this chapter includes a sampling of manifest acts and behaviors to illustrate or represent each component. However, much of the discussion of manifest acts and behaviors motivated by the Evolved Ethic occurs in the next chapter. The purpose in this chapter is to introduce the components and discuss how the components combine to form the whole. Therefore, the focus is on the whole and not the components. Figure 4-1 illustrates the three components of the Evolved Ethic.

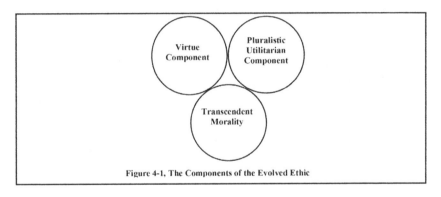

Figure 4-1, The Components of the Evolved Ethic

The Virtue Component

The idea of virtue as a basis or foundation for right, correct, and appropriate behavior is certainly not new. The virtue ethic is generally associated with early Greek philosophers such as Aristotle. While many of the virtues described by Aristotle are now considered values, in the same sense that Mill used the term, some of the virtues mentioned by Aristotle appear as virtues in this theory of ethics. However, in this theory, virtue is only the foundation upon which the remaining two components build. However, before proceeding too far with this discussion, it might be helpful to establish what the term virtue means.

Unfortunately, the English language is not always exact. Many words in the English language have multiple meanings, many different words have the same or similar meaning, and, there is often confusion over the use of a specific word. This is very true of words that describe virtues and emotions. Words that describe virtues are often used to describe emotions and vice versa. To clarify one from the other, drawing a line that delineates virtues from emotions is necessary. Fortunately, it is possible to draw that line.

In the discussion of the Unevolved Ethic, I tied emotions to feelings which are always directly tied to Self. As such, emotions are always subjective. Emotions are always concerned with "I," "Me" and what "I," "Me" is feeling or experiencing. The emotion of sorrow was used to illustrate this point. "I," "Me" feels sorrow or feels sorrowful. Grief is a behavioral response to the felt emotion of sorrow. Acts or behaviors that manifest sorrow maximize benefit and minimize harm for Self.

Virtue is just the opposite. The beneficiary of acts and behaviors based in virtue is Others. Acts and behaviors based in virtue serve Others. They serve the interest, welfare, or good of Others. Because these acts and behaviors focus on benefit for Others, they also serve or benefit the best interest, welfare, and good of the collective whole. Said differently, acts and behaviors manifesting virtue cannot be self-serving or self-interested. They cannot serve the interest, welfare or good of Self.

As an example, the virtue compassion is not and cannot be self-serving or self-interested. Acts or behaviors manifesting compassion always serve someone or something outside of "I," "Me." Therefore, compassionate acts and behaviors always focus on Others. These acts always focus on benefit for Others and, by extension, the collective whole. Self may manifest compassion through acts and behaviors that comfort, console, soothe, calm, share, and give. Self may demonstrate a wide range of behaviors that are outward manifestations of the virtue compassion. Each manifestation will convey consideration, thoughtfulness, kindness, and caring. However, Self can only demonstrate compassionate acts or behaviors to benefit Others. Self cannot be self-compassionate. Self cannot act or behave compassionately for Self.

Any attempt to act or behave self-compassionately would only result in a self-serving, self-interested behavior. It would only result in an act or behavior that maximizes benefit for Self. Therefore, self-compassion would have a different name. This name might be self-pity. It might also be self-indulgence. Self-pity and self-indulgence both focus on benefit for Self. Acts and behaviors manifesting self-pity or self-indulgence maximize benefit and minimize harm for Self. It is the Unevolved Ethic that motivates acts and behaviors that manifest self-pity or self-indulgence as part of a pattern of acts or behaviors.

This is still the case if Self acts from the emotion pity. Self may feel pity for Others. Feelings of pity for Others may result in an act or behavior that benefits Others. However, pity is still an emotion. Pity is still oriented to "I," "Me". Self feels pity. Self may act from feelings of pity, but the primary beneficiary of the act is still Self. The benefit to Others is only a secondary benefit of an act intended to benefit Self. The benefit to Self is to remove the feeling of pity. There is no "feel good" for Self in feelings of pity. The "feel good" for Self comes when Self acts to remove the feelings of pity. The act or behavior that removes the feeling of pity may benefit Others, but the primary beneficiary is Self when the feelings of pity are removed. The same is true for all acts and behaviors that manifest emotions similar to pity. It is different with acts and behaviors based in virtue.

Self acts for Others from virtue. Self does not feel the virtues. Acts and behaviors that manifest virtue are not based on feelings. Therefore, virtues are not emotions. They are not felt as Self feels emotions. For instance, Self does not feel compassion; Self acts from the virtue compassion. Therefore, acts and behaviors that manifest virtues are not emotional responses. Further, acts and behaviors that consistently manifest the virtues require the setting aside of Self and self-interest. This is in sharp contrast to the foundational component of the Unevolved Ethic, the egoistic component. The focus of the egoistic component of the Unevolved Ethic is always Self and the interest, welfare, and good of Self, first and foremost. By contrast, the focus of the virtue component is always Others and the best interest, welfare, and good of Others, first and foremost.

This is the case for all the virtues associated with the virtue component of the Evolved Ethic. For instance, honesty and loyalty are virtues associated with this component. Others are the beneficiary of acts and behaviors that manifest honesty and loyalty. When Self acts from the virtues of honesty and loyalty, Self acts for Others. The same is the case with each of the other virtues. When Self acts from virtue, Self acts and behaves for the interest, welfare and good of Others and, by extension, the collective whole.

However, like the egoistic component of the Unevolved Ethic, the virtue component may develop with an emphasis on either maximizing benefit _or_ minimizing harm for Others. The emphasis of this component may be maximizing benefit for Others. However, the emphasis may also be minimizing harm for Others. Regardless of which emphasis develops, Others are still the beneficiaries of these acts and behaviors. The best interest, welfare, and good of Others benefit when Self acts and behaves to minimize harm _or_ maximize benefit for Others.

Which emphasis the virtue component manifests will depend greatly on how the component develops. It will depend on how Self learns and practices the virtues. It will depend on how parents or other significant adults teach and model the virtues. It will also depend on how Self perceives this teaching and modeling. The emphasis of the virtue component on either maximizing benefit _or_ minimizing harm follows the learning and practice of the virtues. However, discussion of the development of the virtue component comes in a later chapter. For now, it is more appropriate to continue discussing the component itself.

Regardless of the emphasis of the virtue component that develops, the component infers that it is right, correct, and appropriate for Self to focus on that which serves the interest, welfare, and good of Others and, by extension, the collective whole. It infers that it is right, correct, and appropriate to act and behave in a manner that serves Others and the collective whole. It infers that it is right, correct, and appropriate to manifest regard and concern for Others and the collective whole. Further, the virtue component infers that it is right, correct, and appropriate to act and behave in a manner that preserves, protects, and promotes the interest, welfare, and good of Others and the collective whole. It places Others and the collective whole above Self.

In all, there are twelve virtues I associate with the virtue component. Ten of these virtues are covered in this discussion of the virtue component. Two additional virtues are covered later in this chapter. The two additional virtues come later because they play a different role in forming the Evolved Ethic. The ten listed here represent what I term the lesser feminine and lesser masculine virtues. It should be understood that using the masculine and feminine labels to categorize virtues does not infer that males should learn one set of virtues and females the other. The masculine and feminine labels serve only as convenient terms to categorize the lesser virtues. However, before listing the lesser feminine and masculine virtues, I would like to make a point concerning the list of virtues.

When developing this theory of ethics, it became apparent that I would need to provide a list of virtues. I also realized there are many, many words in the English language that could fit the description of a virtue. Therefore, there are many words and synonyms for words that I could include. To keep the list short and easy to recall, I chose twelve words that seem to cover the widest range of acts and behaviors that maximize benefit _or_ minimize harm for Others and the collective whole. Ten of these words appear in this discussion of the virtue component. These ten words are compassion, empathy, generosity, modesty, patience, honesty, bravery, loyalty, moderation, and perseverance.

I combine compassion, empathy, generosity, modesty, and patience together to form the subset of lesser feminine virtues. I then combine honesty, bravery, loyalty, moderation, and perseverance to form the lesser masculine virtues subset. In each case, Others are the beneficiary of acts and behaviors that manifest these virtues. The beneficiary of the act or behavior is Others and, by extension, the collective whole. Any benefit to Self that results is secondary to the benefit for Others and the collective whole. Acts or behaviors manifesting these ten virtues serve the best interest, welfare, and good of Others and one or more levels of collective whole.

For instance, I've already mentioned the lesser feminine virtue of compassion. I established that Self can only manifest compassion for Others and the collective whole. The beneficiary of acts and behaviors that manifest compassion is Others and the collective whole. I also established that Self cannot be self-compassionate. Any attempt to act compassionately for Self would benefit only Self. This is similar to all the other virtues listed. Any attempt to manifest a virtue for Self results in selfish, self-centered, self-promoting, or self-protecting acts or behaviors that maximize benefit or minimize harm for Self. A brief review of each virtue illustrates this point. I will begin with the lesser masculine virtue of honesty.

Others and the collective whole are always the beneficiaries of acts and behaviors that consistently manifest honesty. Acts and behaviors that manifest honesty always serve the interest, welfare, or good of Others and the collective whole. This benefit may take the form of pleasure for Others, but pleasure is not the critical benefit of acts and behaviors that manifest honesty. The critical benefit is building trust, confidence, reliance, certainty, assurance, and security. It includes building optimism, concord, and harmony within a collective whole. It is the building of community within a collective whole.

These benefits contrast the harms resulting from acts and behaviors manifesting the opposite of honesty or dishonesty. Dishonesty builds distrust, suspicion, doubt, uncertainty, and insecurity. It builds jealousy, envy, resentment, and bitterness. It builds skepticism, cynicism, and pessimism. It builds discord, and disharmony. It encourages competition. This is the same for each virtue and the opposite or contrast of the virtue. Each opposite or contrast of virtue maximizes benefit for Self and results in harm for Others and the collective whole. This can be seen again through a short examination of the virtue of loyalty and its contrast, disloyalty.

Acts and behaviors that consistently manifest loyalty benefit Others and the collective whole. These acts or behaviors also build trust, confidence, reliance, certainty, assurance, and security. They build optimism, concord, and harmony or community within the collective whole. By contrast, disloyalty benefits only Self and always harms Others and the collective whole. However, as with honesty, Self cannot manifest loyalty for Self. Any attempt to act or behave in a self-loyal manner results in a selfish, self-centered, self-regarding, or self-promoting act. Self can, however, manifest acts and behaviors that manifest loyalty for a friend, a companion, or a spouse. Self can manifest acts and behaviors that manifest loyalty for a team, a club, an organization, a community, or many other examples of collective whole. In each instance, the beneficiary of acts or behaviors that manifest loyalty is Others and the collective whole. The lesser masculine virtue of bravery is similar.

When discussing bravery it should be clear that bravery as a virtue is not the same as battlefield bravery. Acts of bravery on a battlefield may be self-preserving, self-protective, or self-regarding acts. From these acts, benefit to Others may only be secondary to benefit for Self. When used as a virtue, bravery refers to acts or behaviors that demonstrate the willingness and ability to face or endure difficulties or hardship in the interest, welfare, and good of Others or the collective whole. It refers to acts and behaviors that demonstrate the willingness and ability to face or endure hardships while preserving, defending, and protecting Others and the collective whole. This could include battlefield bravery; however, this would also include acts or behaviors demonstrated in any situation in which Self manifests the willingness and ability to act on behalf of Others or the collective whole. It could include acts or behaviors that carry the risk of harm for Self but benefit for Others and the collective whole.

Like honesty and loyalty, Self cannot demonstrate bravery only for Self. Acts or behaviors that demonstrate bravery for Self are self-preserving, self-protecting, self-regarding, or self-promoting. In each case, Self is the primary beneficiary of the act or behavior. In each case, these acts or behaviors maximize benefit for Self. As a virtue, Self can only demonstrate bravery for Others or the collective whole. The next lesser masculine virtue, perseverance, is similar still.

Self can only persevere or manifest perseverance for Others or a collective whole. Like loyalty and bravery, Self may manifest perseverance for a friend, a companion, or a spouse. Self may manifest perseverance for a team, an organization, or a community. Self may even manifest perseverance for a project or cause that benefits Others or the collective whole. This virtue often manifests itself in acts or behaviors termed resolute, steadfast, or purposeful. In each case, Others and the collective whole benefit from acts and behaviors that manifest perseverance. However, one must be very careful when examining perseverance. As a virtue, perseverance requires that acts and behaviors benefit Others or the collective whole. Perseverance must serve the best interest, welfare, or good of Others or the collective whole. As such, perseverance should not be confused with persistence.

Self does not manifest persistence for Others or the collective whole. Self manifests persistence for Self. Persistence serves the best interest, welfare, or good of Self. Acts and behaviors manifesting persistence are often termed stubborn, obstinate, or inflexible. Persistence may also take the form of rigidity or inflexibility. Acts and behaviors manifesting persistence maximize benefit and minimize harm for Self. Persistence does not benefit, and may well result in harm for Others and the collective whole. Perseverance is different. Perseverance serves the interest, welfare, and good of Others and the collective whole. This is again similar to the lesser masculine virtue of moderation.

Others and the collective whole benefit from acts and behaviors that manifest moderation. For instance, moderation in the choice of language maximizes benefit or minimizes harm for Others and the collective whole. It is considerate and respectful of Others. As another example, moderation in the use of alcohol serves the interest, welfare, and good of Others. Likewise, moderation in consumerism is also considerate of Others and the collective whole. In this case, Others and the collective whole can be thought of as both present and future generations as well as all sentient beings and the planet Earth itself.

The reverse of moderation is immoderation or excess. Excess was addressed when discussing the Unevolved Ethic. Immoderation or excess often takes the form of self-gratification, instant gratification, self-indulgence, and over-indulgence. Each term infers immoderation or excess and Self is always the beneficiary of excess. The benefit (pleasure) of excess, regardless of how manifest, is to Self. Immoderation or excess always maximizes benefit and minimizes harm for Self. The reverse of excess is moderation, and moderation is a virtue.

When taken together, the lesser masculine virtues describe integrity. Clearly, integrity encompasses honesty, loyalty, perseverance, moderation, and bravery. Overall, acts and behaviors that manifest the lesser masculine virtues manifest integrity. Further, they indicate what might be termed good character or honor. In this usage, both good character and honor are synonymous with integrity. Acting and behaving with good character, honor, and integrity builds trust. It builds certainty, assurance, confidence, and security. It builds concord and harmony within the collective whole. These all serve the best interest, welfare, and good of Others and every level of collective whole.

However, manifesting the virtues that comprise integrity only when someone is watching is an illusion of integrity. It is an illusion of good character and honor. Manifesting integrity only when Self benefits in some manner or fashion is not true integrity. It is only a false illusion of integrity that serves the best interest, welfare, or good of Self. It is an illusion that maximizes benefit and minimizes harm for Self. It is an illusion tied very directly to moral hypocrisy. It is tied very directly to the desire of Self to believe Self is more moral than evidence would support. Further, it is tied to the desire of Self for Others to view Self as moral. It is the Unevolved Ethic that motivates this public illusion of integrity. True integrity serves the best interest, welfare, and good of Others and the collective whole.

This is equally true of the five virtues termed the lesser feminine virtues. Each of the lesser feminine virtues also serve the best interest, welfare, and good of Others and, by extension, the collective whole. The first of these five is the already identified virtue compassion. The second lesser feminine virtue is patience.

Like all lesser virtues, Self manifests patience for Others and the collective whole. Self does not manifest patience for Self. Much like persistence, Self manifests impatience for Self. When Self manifests impatience, Self manifests self-importance, self-absorption, self-regard, and self-interest. When Self manifests impatience, Self acts and behaves in a self-centered, self-important, and conceited manner. When Self manifests impatience, Self manifests selfishness to some extent or degree. Often, acts and behaviors that manifest impatience also manifest emotions like frustration and anger. These acts and behaviors are generally thought to be unpredictable and erratic. Acting out these emotions only serves to make Self feel better. There is a "feel good" or self-satisfaction for Self in acts and behaviors that manifest impatience.

Patience does not result in unpredictable or erratic acts or behaviors. When Self manifests the virtue patience, Self remains calm and composed. Self does not become frustrated or angry. Self does not become aggressive or belligerent. Acts and behaviors remain calm, passive, and composed. The benefit of remaining calm, passive, and composed is to Others and the collective whole. It is not to Self. This benefit is similar to all the lesser feminine virtues, including generosity.

Generosity refers to acts and behaviors that manifest giving or sharing of the resources of Self to benefit Others or the collective whole. It refers to using the resources of Self to benefit Others. These resources could include money, but may include other possessions of Self. For instance, it can include both time and effort. These resources can also include Self's knowledge, skills, abilities, and talents. It can include the wisdom of Self. The giving or sharing of these resources benefits Others and the collective whole. When Self consistently manifests generosity, it helps build trust, assurance, confidence, and security. Self helps build optimism and community.

However, to manifest the virtue generosity, Self must consistently give or share resources freely and without regard for Self. Self must be willing and able to give or share the resource without consideration of benefit for Self. If Self gives or shares a resource of Self only to gain benefit for Self, the act or behavior is still self-serving and self-interested. Sacrifice or selfishness is associated with giving or sharing only to receive. Self may bear this sacrifice to gain some benefit and avoid some harm for Self. But, the concept of giving or sharing to receive is covered in the next chapter, for now it is more appropriate to move to the next lesser virtue, modesty.

Like compassion, patience, and generosity, Self manifests the virtue of modesty for Others and not for Self. Modesty maximizes benefit or minimizes harm for Others and the collective whole. This is the case in any situation or circumstance in which acts and behaviors of Self consistently manifest modesty. Self manifests modesty in dress or appearance for Others or the collective whole. Self manifests the reverse of modesty, immodesty, for Self.

Similarly, Self manifests modesty in comments and references to Self or the accomplishments of Self for Others and the collective whole. Self brags or boasts about Self only to promote or aggrandize Self. Likewise, Self manifests modesty in items like jewelry, homes, and vehicles for Others or the collective whole. Self manifests immodesty in these same choices only for Self.

Self often manifests immodesty in acts and behaviors termed ostentatious or prideful. Ostentatious means acts and behaviors that flaunt or show off wealth, knowledge, skill, talents, abilities or any other resource possessed by Self. These acts or behaviors may also be termed pretentious, conspicuous, overdone, garish, outlandish, and sometimes even gaudy or vulgar. Each of these acts and behaviors manifests immodesty which always serves only the interest, welfare, and good of Self. It always maximizes benefit and minimizes harm for Self.

But immodesty does harm Others and the collective whole. Immodesty practiced by Self often results in jealousy and envy. It results in hurt feelings and hurt pride, and the emotions that arise from hurt feelings and pride. It results in resentment, bitterness, and hostility. It results in competition leading to discord and disharmony within the collective whole. However, Self minimalizes or ignores this harm in the interest of benefit for Self. Self then minimalizes or ignores this harm through rationalizations, justifications, explanations, and excuses.

On the other hand, practicing the virtue modesty reduces or eliminates these harms. Acts and behaviors that manifest modesty reduce jealousy and envy. They reduce resentment, bitterness, and hostility. They reduce competition. They reduce discord and disharmony and encourage concord and harmony within the collective whole. Thus, acts and behaviors that manifest the virtue of modesty benefit Others and the collective whole. This is also the case with the final lesser feminine virtue. This is the virtue empathy.

Empathy is understood to mean affinity and rapport. It means understanding, connection, and even camaraderie. Acts and behaviors that manifest empathy include those that are attentive, responsive, considerate and thoughtful. It includes acts and behaviors that are respectful, courteous, and deferential. It also includes acts and behaviors that manifest caring and concern. Finally, it includes acts and behaviors that are accepting of Others. Acts or behaviors that manifest empathy in all its many forms benefit Others and the collective whole.

However, it should be clear that empathy does not refer to sympathy. Like pity, sympathy is an emotion and not a virtue. When Self acts from the emotion sympathy, Self is acting primarily for Self. When Self acts out of sympathy, the benefit is primarily to Self. Further, sympathy, like other emotions, leads to acts and behaviors that are often inconsistent, unreliable, erratic, and irregular. The virtue empathy, as well as the other lesser virtues, motivates more consistent and reliable acts and behaviors. These acts or behaviors do not stem from emotion and are not an emotional response.

When taken together as a subset, the lesser feminine virtues account for acts and behaviors often described as nurturing. Other terms that might apply include cultivating, fostering, developing, and promoting. As these terms apply to this discussion, they refer to nurturing, cultivating, fostering, developing, and promoting the best interest, welfare, and good of Others and the collective whole. In each case, acts and behaviors manifesting these terms benefit Others and the collective whole.

Acts and behaviors that manifest the opposite or contrast of the virtues manifest the egoistic component of the Unevolved Ethic. These are acts and behaviors that manifest vices. For each virtue, there is a corresponding vice. For instance, I already mentioned the vice that is the opposite of the virtue loyalty. This is disloyalty. Disloyalty always maximizes benefit or minimizes harm for Self. The vice of disloyalty results in harm for Others. The harm may include feelings of betrayal, infidelity, or unfaithfulness. This harm may be physical, emotional, or psychological pain for

Others. However, the greater harm is building distrust and the other harms mentioned previously. It is the building of pessimism, cynicism, and skepticism. It is the building of discord, disharmony, and competition within Others and the collective whole. The Unevolved Ethic motivates acts and behaviors that consistently manifest the vices to some extent or degree. Appendix 1, which follows the final chapter, lists the ten lesser virtues and their corresponding vices.

I will revisit the discussion of the vices in the next chapter. For now, returning to the discussion of the virtue component is more appropriate. I want to do so by pointing to the relationships that exist among and between the lesser masculine and feminine virtues.

Acts and behaviors can and often do manifest more than one lesser virtue, either feminine or masculine. This suggests a close relationship exists between and among the lesser virtues. For instance, it is often possible to draw a relationship between loyalty and bravery or loyalty and perseverance. Likewise, it is often possible to draw a relationship between compassion and empathy, as well as empathy and generosity. However, it is also often possible to draw a relationship between the lesser masculine virtue of perseverance and the lesser feminine virtue of patience. The two often go hand-in-hand. A final example is the relationship between the lesser masculine virtue of moderation and the lesser feminine virtue of modesty. Similar relationships exist among and between the other lesser virtues. For this reason, learning and practicing all virtues, both the lesser masculine and lesser feminine, is critical to developing the virtue component and the Evolved Ethic.

It is important that Self learn and practice all the virtues. Further, Self must learn and practice the virtues to the point that virtuous acts and behaviors become habits. Self must practice the lesser virtues to the point of habituation to these acts and behaviors. In addition, Self must practice virtuous acts and behaviors to the point of habituation in various situations and circumstances. The learning and practice of virtue, to the point of habituation, in various situations and circumstances is essential to developing both the virtue component and the Evolved Ethic as a whole.

While it is not appropriate to discuss the development of the Evolved Ethic in this chapter, it is important to stress that learning and practicing the lesser virtues should begin at the earliest possible time. The ethic of each Self begins developing at birth. It begins with developing the foundational component of either the Unevolved or the Evolved Ethic. This means that either the egoistic or virtue component begins developing at birth. As such, the alternative to learning and practicing the virtue component is the learning and practice of the egoistic component of the Unevolved Ethic. However, developing the virtue component requires learning all the lesser virtues, not just the lesser masculine or lesser feminine virtues. It requires balance in the learning and practice of the virtues. This balance is important for two reasons.

First, learning and practicing one virtue or subset of virtues, to exclude other virtues will result in inconsistent, irregular acts and behaviors. For instance, if Self learns and practices only the lesser masculine virtues, Self might be capable of acts and behaviors that manifest honesty or bravery, but will likely find it difficult to demonstrate compassion or empathy. On the other hand, if Self learns and practices only the lesser feminine virtues, Self might be capable of demonstrating generosity or modesty but find it difficult to demonstrate loyalty or perseverance. Therefore, balancing the learning and practice of the lesser masculine and feminine virtues is essential.

Second, balance in the learning and practice of the lesser masculine and feminine virtues will impact the growth and development of the two virtues not yet introduced. These are the two enabling virtues that, when combined, form the third component of the Evolved Ethic: The Transcendent Morality. But before discussing the enabling virtues and the Transcendent Morality component of the Evolved Ethic, I first need to introduce the second component, the pluralistic utilitarian component.

The Pluralistic Utilitarian Component

When introducing the components of the Unevolved Ethic, I indicated that the second component of that ethic was the hedonistic utilitarian component. I indicated that the hedonistic utilitarian component builds from and includes the egoistic component. I further indicated this component continues to guide choices and motivate acts and behaviors that maximize benefit (pleasure) *and* minimize harm (pain or the privation of pleasure) for Self.

To continue the construction of the Evolved Ethic, I now require a utilitarian component that contrasts the hedonistic utilitarian component. This component must build from and include the virtue component. It must be a utilitarian component that guides and motivates acts and behaviors that maximize benefit *and* minimize harm for Others and the collective whole. The pluralistic utilitarian component meets this requirement.

By its name, this component infers more than one. The word plural means more than one. It can mean many. For this theory of ethics, the interpretation of plural is Others and the collective whole. From this interpretation, the pluralistic utilitarian component becomes the opposite or contrast of the hedonistic utilitarian component. Where the focus of the hedonistic utilitarian component is Self, the focus of the pluralistic utilitarian component is Others and the collective whole. Where the hedonistic utilitarian component guides and motivates Self to act and behave to maximize benefit *and* minimize harm for Self, the pluralistic utilitarian component guides and motivates Self to act and behave to maximize benefit *and* minimize harm for Others and the collective whole.

Just as was the case with the hedonistic utilitarian component of the Unevolved Ethic, the focus of the pluralistic utilitarian component is the beneficiary of the acts and behaviors of Self and resulting consequences. In other words, the focus is on who or what benefits from acts or behaviors and who or what is harmed. If Self is consistently the beneficiary of the acts and behaviors of Self, then it is the hedonistic utilitarian component. The benefit to Self may be pleasure, or it may be the avoidance of pain or the privation of pleasure. If Others and the collective whole are consistently beneficiaries of the acts and behaviors of Self, then it is the pluralistic utilitarian component.

However, it is important to note that the benefit for Others or the collective whole associated with the pluralistic utilitarian component is not inferred to be pleasure. Likewise, harm for Others associated with the pluralistic utilitarian component is not inferred to be pain or the privation of pleasure. The benefit for Others may include pleasure, but pleasure is not the primary benefit of acts and behaviors associated with the pluralistic utilitarian component. Similarly, the harm minimized for Others may include pain or the privation of pleasure, but minimizing pain or the privation of pleasure is not the primary harm minimized by acts and behaviors associated with this component.

The primary benefits of acts and behaviors associated with this component are the same as those that result from acts and behaviors that manifest the virtue component. These benefits include building trust, confidence, assurance, and security. They building optimism, concord and harmony within the collective whole. They are the building of cohesion and unity within the collective whole; the building of community. These are the primary benefits that result and accrue when Self consistently and evenly manifests acts and behaviors that maximize benefit for Others and the collective whole.

The primary harms minimized for Others and the collective whole are, of course, the building of distrust, doubt, apprehension, anxiety, suspicion, insecurity, and fear. It is the building of skepticism, cynicism, and pessimism. It is the building of resentment, bitterness, jealousy, and acrimony. It is the building of discord, disharmony, disunity, and competition. Each of these harms is contrary to the best interest, welfare, and good of Others and the collective whole. When Self acts and behaves to minimize harm for Others and the collective whole, Self minimizes each of these harms to some extent or degree.

Since the pluralistic utilitarian component includes the foundational virtue component, this component remains focused on the best interest, welfare, and good of Others and the collective whole. It encourages a focus and viewpoint of Others and the collective whole first and foremost. It simply adds the second or complimentary emphasis of the utilitarian component. If the emphasis of the virtue component that developed is maximizing benefit for Others and the collective whole, the pluralistic utilitarian component adds emphasis on minimizing harm for Others and the collective whole. If the emphasis of the virtue component that developed is minimizing harm for Others and the collective whole, the pluralistic utilitarian component adds emphasis on maximizing benefit for Others and the collective whole. As with the hedonistic utilitarian component, the emphasis subtly shifts from "_or_" to "_and._" With the addition of the second or complimentary emphasis, the pluralistic utilitarian component maximizes benefit _and_ minimizes harm for Others and the collective whole.

To illustrate the pluralistic utilitarian component, I can point to the telling of truth. The telling of truth contrasts with the telling of a lie, which was used to illustrate the hedonistic utilitarian component of the Unevolved Ethic.

Consistently telling the truth serves the best interest, welfare, and good of Others. By extension, the telling of truth serves the best interest, welfare, and good of the collective whole at every level. The beneficiary of acts and behaviors that result in telling the truth is always Others and the collective whole at every level. Consistently telling the truth builds trust, confidence, assurance, security, and the other benefits mentioned above. However, consistently telling the truth minimizes or eliminates the harms mentioned earlier. It minimizes or eliminates harms contrary to the best interest, welfare, and good of Others and the collective whole. Therefore, consistently telling the truth maximizes benefit and minimizes harm for

Others and the collective whole. As such, this component encourages cooperation and collaboration within the collective whole.

Cooperation and collaboration require acts and behaviors that maximize benefit and minimize harm for Others and the collective whole. They require acts and behaviors that maximize trust and minimize distrust. They require acts and behaviors that maximize certainty and minimize doubt. They require acts and behaviors that maximize security and minimize insecurity. Going further, they require acts and behaviors that maximize optimism and minimize skepticism and pessimism. Therefore, they require acts and behaviors that enable and encourage community and discourage acts and behaviors that enable and encourage competition.

Community does not occur without acts or behaviors that are cooperative and collaborative. Community does not occur without acts or behaviors that maximize benefit and minimize harm for Others or the collective whole. Community only occurs when each Self consistently acts and behaves to maximize benefit and minimize harm for Others and the collective whole. Therefore, in this theory of ethics, "Community" becomes the opposite of "Competition." Likewise, the words "Cooperation" and "Collaboration" become the contrasts of "Contention" and "Conflict". Figure 4-2 places "Community," "Cooperation," and "Collaboration" on the Unevolved-Evolved Continuum to illustrate this contrast.

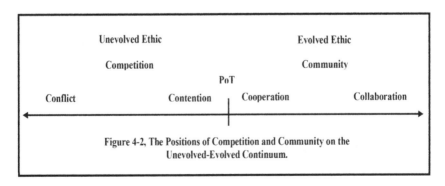

Figure 4-2, The Positions of Competition and Community on the
Unevolved-Evolved Continuum.

With the addition of "Community," as well as "Cooperation" and "Collaboration," to the Unevolved-Evolved Continuum, there is one additional point to make concerning the pluralistic utilitarian component of the Evolved Ethic. This point is one I must acknowledge. It is that consistently and evenly acting or behaving to maximize benefit and minimize harm to Others and the collective whole can and often does result in harm for Self. Consistently and evenly placing the interest, welfare, and good of Others and the collective whole above the interest, welfare, and good of Self can and often does result in pain or the privation of pleasure for Self.

It is the third component of the Evolved Ethic that powers this willingness and ability to minimalize or ignore these harms for Self. It is this third component that powers the willingness and ability to minimalize or ignore these harms for Self when acting or behaving for the best interest, welfare, and good of Others and the collective whole. This third component is the Transcendent Morality.

The Transcendent Morality

This morality is called" transcendent" because it powers the willingness and ability to minimalize or ignore harm (pain and the privation of pleasure) for Self that results when Self acts or behaves to maximize benefit and minimize harm for Others and the collective whole. The willingness and ability to minimalize or ignore harm for Self requires transcendence of concern or regard for Self. It requires transcendence of the best interest, welfare, and good of Self in favor of the best interest, welfare, and good of Others and the collective whole.

The term "transcendent" suggests the willingness and ability to rise above Self and the interest, welfare, and good of Self in favor of the interest, welfare, and good of Others and the collective whole. This contrasts with the rational morality which enables and encourages the willingness and ability to minimalize or ignore harm to Others and the collective whole in favor of Self. Figure 4-3 illustrates this contrast using the Unevolved-Evolved Continuum.

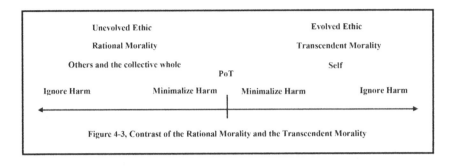

Figure 4-3, Contrast of the Rational Morality and the Transcendent Morality

Further, the Transcendent Morality component enables and encourages right, correct, and appropriate acts and behaviors, even in the face of harm for Self. This component enables and encourages right, correct, and appropriate manifest acts and behaviors regardless of situation or circumstance. It enables and encourages right, correct, and appropriate manifest acts and behaviors even when no one is watching or observing.

This morality has its basis in the growth and development of the two enabling virtues I did not introduce in the earlier discussion of the virtue component. The term "enabling" not only separates these two virtues from the lesser virtues but also suggests their role in powering the willingness and ability to minimalize or ignore harm for Self. It is the combined, integrated, strength of these two enabling virtues that is the Transcendent Morality.

The two enabling virtues are Love and Courage. These are the two virtues that rise above the ten lesser virtues. They transcend, but include the lesser masculine and lesser feminine virtues. Throughout the remainder of this discussion of ethic, I will always capitalize these two virtues to distinguish their role in forming the Transcendent Morality. However, both Love and Courage are words that can have multiple meanings. Both can have different meanings when used in different contexts. I will briefly describe each to better understand the use of the words in the context of this theory of ethics.

As I use the word Courage, it does not describe bravery. Bravery is a lesser masculine virtue. Neither does it describe battlefield courage. In this theory of ethics, Courage is the enabling virtue that, when combined with Love, enables Self to consistently manifest acts and behaviors that are right, correct, and appropriate regardless of situation and circumstance. When combined with Love, it is the virtue that enables the willingness and ability to minimalize or ignore harm that results for Self when Self acts and behaves to maximize benefit and minimize harm for Others and the collective whole. When combined with Love, it is the virtue that enables the willingness and ability to accept pain or the privation of pleasure for Self when acting for the interest, welfare, and good of Others or the collective whole.

For example, it takes Courage to consistently manifest acts and behaviors associated with the lesser masculine virtue honesty, especially when these acts and behaviors may result in harm for Self. It takes Courage to consistently manifest acts and behaviors associated with loyalty, perseverance, bravery, and moderation especially when they may result in harm for Self. It takes Courage to consistently act with integrity. But it also takes Courage to manifest acts and behaviors associated with each of the lesser feminine virtues when these acts or behaviors may result in harm (pain or the privation of pleasure) for Self. In each case, Courage powers or enables the willingness and ability to minimalize or ignore this harm for Self. In the absence of Courage, Self will simply act to maximize benefit and minimize harm for Self and minimalize or ignore the harm to Others and the collective whole. The same is the case with the enabling virtue of Love.

As the word Love is used in this context, it does not mean emotional love. It also does not mean romantic love. It is not a felt love. This is not the love that makes the heart pound when a loved one is present. It is not the love that can result in jealousy or other negative emotions nor is it the lust sometimes called love. That love is clearly tied to feelings and emotions. As such, emotional love is associated with Self and the feelings of Self. Emotional love is associated with pleasure and, sometimes, pain for Self. The enabling virtue of Love is not tied to feelings and emotions.

The enabling virtue Love is a higher Love. It is an unconditional Love for Others, an unconditional Love for humanity. A Greek word is very useful for describing this higher Love. The word is agape. Agape is defined as "unselfish, platonic love of one person for another; brotherly love." This is not the same as emotional love.

This higher Love is not confined or restricted only to those Others with whom Self shares an emotional bond. This Love is not confined to only those Others who are like "I," "Me." The many labels or categories that separate and divide humanity do not confine or restrict it. Each of these labels and categories represents forms of collective wholes and, at the same time, collective forms of Self. Each of these labels and categories represents both a form and level of "We," "Us" and, at the same time, a form and level of "I," "Me." Each label and category exclude Others who do not fit that label or category. This Love is not confined or restricted by those labels and categories. This Love is inclusive, not exclusive. It transcends differences to find commonality or sameness. It recognizes that each Self is one with the whole of humanity.

As such, this Love does not see race or ethnicity. It does not hear differences in language. It is unaware of borders or nationalities and holds all religions and religious sects equal. It doesn't know age or gender and looks beyond disability, appearance, dress, culture, and custom. This Love sees "We," "Us," "Our," and "Ours." This Love knows only people – other human beings. At its highest level of development, this unselfish, plutonic Love is absolutely unconditional.

When combined with Courage, this Love enables the willingness and ability to consistently minimalize or ignore harm for Self in the interest, welfare, and good of Others and the collective whole. It is this Love that, when combined with Courage, enables Self to consistently manifest acts and behaviors that are right, correct, and appropriate and to minimalize or ignore harm that results for Self.

For instance, it takes Love to consistently manifest acts and behaviors based in compassion, generosity, empathy, modesty, and patience, especially when these acts or behaviors may result in pain or the privation of pleasure for Self. But it also takes Love to manifest acts or behaviors based in the lesser masculine virtues when these acts or behaviors may result in pain or the privation of pleasure for Self. Without the enabling virtue of Love, Self will simply act to maximize benefit and minimize harm for Self and minimalize or ignore resulting harm for Others and the collective whole.

The development of the two enabling virtues, Love and Courage, differs from the development of the lesser masculine and feminine virtues. It is different in that the development of the two enabling virtues depends on the development of the lesser virtues first. It is further dependent on the development of the pluralistic utilitarian component, which develops from but incorporates, the virtue component. The willingness and ability to minimalize or ignore harm to Self is directly tied to first learning to act for the benefit of Others and the collective whole. It depends on learning to act and behave to maximize benefit and minimize harm for Others and the collective whole. Self can only learn to minimalize or ignore pain or the privation of pleasure for Self if Self has first learned to act or behave to maximize benefit and minimize harm for Others or the collective whole. One necessarily precedes the other.

Therefore, the development of Love and Courage depends on learning and practicing the lesser virtues. However, Self must learn all the lesser feminine virtues, not just one or two or three of them. If one or more are absent, Love will not completely develop. The same is true for Courage. Self must learn all the lesser masculine virtues. If one or more are absent, Courage will not completely develop. It will remain underdeveloped. Unfortunately, if Love or Courage fails to develop, the lesser feminine or masculine virtues will likely remain underdeveloped as well. This is because of the generative nature of virtue. The generative nature of virtue is fairly easy to grasp.

When I say virtue is generative, I mean the practice of one or more virtues encourages the development and strengthening of another virtue. The practice of the second virtue then encourages the further growth and development of the first virtue or virtues. Putting this in terms of the enabling and lesser virtues, it suggests that the learning and practice of the lesser virtues encourages the development, growth, and strengthening of the enabling virtues. The development, growth, and strengthening of the enabling virtues then encourage the further practice and development of the lesser virtues. This further practice and development of the lesser virtues then encourage the further development, growth, and strengthening of the enabling virtues and the cycle repeats. Through this generative cycle, Self becomes habituated to acting and behaving from the virtues. But, the development, growth and strengthening of the two enabling virtues depend on first learning and practicing the corresponding lesser virtues.

The development, growth, and strengthening of the enabling virtue Love depends directly on the learning and practice of the lesser feminine virtues. Love then encourages the continued practice and development of the lesser feminine virtues. If lesser feminine virtues are absent, Love remains underdeveloped.

However, Love cannot encourage the continued practice and development of a lesser feminine virtue that is not present. For instance, the learning and practice of the lesser feminine virtue of patience encourages the development and strengthening of Love. The development and strengthening of Love then promote the further practice and development of patience, which, in turn, further strengthens Love. But, if patience is absent, Love cannot encourage the further practice of patience. The same generative relationship exists between the development of each lesser feminine virtue and Love. But this same generative relationship between the lesser masculine virtues and Courage also exists.

Courage's development, growth, and strengthening directly depends on learning and practicing the lesser masculine virtues. Courage promotes the continued development and practice of the lesser masculine virtues. It encourages habituation to the practice of the lesser masculine virtues. If any of the lesser masculine virtues are absent, Courage remains underdeveloped. In turn, Courage cannot promote or encourage the development and practice of a lesser masculine virtue that is absent.

However, it is also important to note that Love cannot promote or encourage the further development and practice of the lesser masculine virtues. Likewise, Courage cannot promote or encourage the further development and practice of the lesser feminine virtues. The development, growth, and strengthening of the two enabling virtues depend on the learning and practice of the corresponding subset of lesser virtues. Ultimately, the strength of the Transcendent Morality directly depends on the development, growth, and strength of the two enabling virtues.

The Transcendent Morality is the combined, integrated strength of the two enabling virtues. The combined, integrated strength of Love and Courage powers the willingness and ability to minimalize or ignore harm for Self when acting for the benefit of Others or the collective whole. The absence of lesser masculine or feminine virtues lessens the strength of the corresponding enabling virtue. Without either Love or Courage, the Transcendent Morality will fail to develop. This again suggests the need for balance in the learning and practice of both the lesser virtues and, now, the enabling virtues.

Balance suggests that no lesser virtue is more important than another. All are necessary for the development and strengthening of the corresponding enabling virtue. Balance further suggests that neither of the two enabling virtues is more important than the other. Courage and Love are equal in importance and position within the Transcendent Morality component. Both are necessary to develop, grow, and strengthen the Transcendent Morality component. Both are necessary to enable and power the willingness and ability to minimalize or ignore pain or the privation of pleasure for Self when acting or behaving to maximize benefit and minimize harm for Others and the collective whole.

If the Transcendent Morality fails to develop, the rational morality will develop instead. Self will learn to minimalize or ignore the harm that results for Others and the collective whole when acting or behaving to maximize benefit and minimize harm for Self. If the Transcendent Morality is absent, Self will be unable or unwilling to consistently minimalize or ignore pain or the privation of pleasure for Self. Self will instead minimalize or ignore harm that results for Others and the collective whole when Self acts for the benefit of Self. Self will employ the rationalizations, justifications, explanations, and excuses needed to minimalize or ignore that harm. Self will learn to construct and utilize self-deception strategies. Self will employ reasoning to construct the rationalizations, justifications, explanations, excuses, and self-deception strategies necessary to deflect or avoid responsibility or accountability for the harm to Others and the collective whole. This is all consistent with the rational morality component of the Unevolved Ethic.

In the earlier discussion of the Unevolved Ethic, I associated the rational morality component with the mind and the ability to reason. It is centered in the mind and is reasoning-based. It encourages and enables Self to act and behave with primary consideration of consequence (utility) for Self. It encourages and enables Self to act and behave with primary consideration for the best interest, welfare, and good of Self. It encourages and enables Self to act and behave in a manner that is self-preserving, self-protecting, self-regarding, self-promoting, and even self-aggrandizing. The rational morality component encourages and enables acts and behaviors that maximize benefit and minimize harm for Self.

However, I have now described a morality component that does not encourage consideration of consequences for Self. I have now described a morality that powers the willingness and ability to transcend or rise above consideration of consequence for Self. It encourages and enables Self to minimalize or ignore the harm to Self that results from acts and behaviors that maximize benefit and minimize harm for Others and the collective whole. It does not rely on rationalizations, justifications, explanations, excuses or self-deception strategies. It does not result in moral hypocrisy. It is not, therefore, centered in the mind and is not reasoning-based. Thus, it is not a rational morality. However, neither is it an irrational morality.

The irrational is generally associated with feelings and emotions. The irrational is associated with impulses and urges. As such, an irrational morality would be centered in the heart. The heart is traditionally associated with feelings and emotions. An irrational morality component would, therefore, be heart-centered and feelings-based. But, feelings, emotions, impulses, urges, superstitions, fears, biases, and prejudices all focus on Self. They all focus on "I," "Me," "My," and "Mine" and what "I," "Me" is feeling. They result in acts and behaviors that are often inconsistent and erratic. These acts and behaviors are often termed irrational.

Regardless of how irrational an act or behavior may appear when it occurs, Self is attempting to maximize benefit or minimize harm for Self. When harm results for Others or the collective whole, it is still through reasoning that Self attempts to minimalize or ignore this harm. Through reasoning, Self still creates and employs the rationalizations, justifications, explanations, and excuses that minimalize or ignore harm for Others and the collective whole. It is still through reasoning that Self creates and employs self-deception strategies to mitigate or avoid harm for Self. Therefore, the morality component associated with irrational acts and behaviors remains the rational morality component of the Unevolved Ethic.

However, the rational morality cannot account for acts and behaviors that consistently transcend concern or regard for Self. It cannot account for acts and behaviors that consistently maximize benefit and minimize harm for Others and the collective whole. These acts and behaviors are neither rational nor irrational. They are transrational. They are acts and behaviors that transcend the rational. Therefore, transrational acts and behaviors require a transrational morality component. This is the Transcendent Morality. As such, the Transcendent Morality is not centered in the mind or the heart. Rather, the center or seat of the Transcendent Morality is the soul.

I should be very clear that in the context of this theory of ethics, the term soul does not carry a religious connotation. It does not carry the connotation of an everlasting or immortal soul. Nor does it carry the connotation of oneness with a God or God-like deity. In this theory of ethics, the soul simply provides a center or seat for the Transcendent Morality. It provides a center that is transrational, a center that transcends both the irrational heart and the rational mind.

This usage is, however, in keeping with the notion of the soul as the center or seat of goodness. It is in keeping with the notion that a good soul acts for the benefit of Others and the collective whole. Often, a good soul is identified with acts and behaviors that maximize benefit and minimize harm for Others and the collective whole. A good soul acts for the benefit of Others and the collective whole without regard for consequences to Self. In short, a good soul minimalizes or ignores harm that results for Self when acting for the benefit of Others and the collective whole. This usage of the term soul is then consistent with the Transcendent Morality component of the Evolved Ethic. The Transcendent Morality component is not based in thinking or reasoning. It is not based in feeling. Instead, it is based in "sensing".

It is based in "sensing" that which is right and wrong, correct or incorrect, or appropriate and inappropriate. This "sense" of right and wrong, correct and incorrect, or appropriate and inappropriate stems from habituation to acts and behaviors that maximize benefit and minimize harm to Others and the collective whole. Right, correct, or appropriate means the extent or degree an act or behavior maximizes benefit and minimizes harm for Others and the collective whole. Wrong, incorrect, or inappropriate means the extent or degree an act or behavior maximizes benefit and minimizes harm for only Self. This is a morality capable of encouraging and enabling acts and behaviors that consistently and evenly place the interest, welfare, and good of Others and the collective whole above that of Self. It is a morality I can and will associate with a higher level of consciousness, a level of consciousness that transcends only Self.

Consciousness means awareness or sentience. A higher level of consciousness means awareness or sentience that transcends awareness or sentience of only Self. This awareness transcends consideration of the best interest, welfare, and good of only Self. This awareness transcends the feelings, emotions, urges, impulses, superstitions, fears, biases, and prejudices of Self. It is awareness or sentience of the interest, welfare, and good of Others and the collective whole. Further, it is awareness or sentience of the harm that results for Others and the collective whole when Self acts only to maximize benefit and minimize harm for Self.

This higher level of consciousness or sentience develops as the Evolved Ethic develops. It develops as Self learns to act and behave to maximize benefit and minimize harm to Others and the collective whole. It develops as Self learns to minimalize or ignore the harm for Self. It develops as the components of the Evolved Ethic develop. If the Evolved Ethic does not develop, this higher level of consciousness or sentience will also fail to develop and the level of awareness or sentience will remain at the level of Self.

Summary

Therefore, the Transcendent Morality component, the combined integrated strength of Love and Courage, completes formation of the Evolved Ethic. The Transcendent Morality becomes the vital third component that powers the willingness and ability to minimalize harm (pain or the privation of pleasure) for Self. It is the component that powers the willingness and ability to minimalize harm that result for Self when Self acts or behaves to maximize benefit and minimize harm for Others and the collective whole.

With the addition of this component, Figure 4-4 illustrates the three components merged to form the Evolved Ethic.

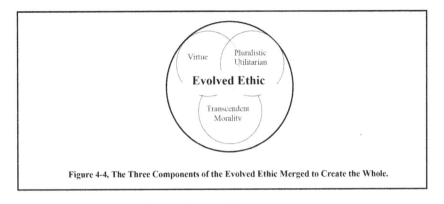

Figure 4-4, The Three Components of the Evolved Ethic Merged to Create the Whole.

This ethic encourages and enables consistently manifesting right, correct, and appropriate acts and behaviors. It encourages and enables manifesting right, correct, and appropriate acts and behaviors regardless of harm for Self. It encourages consistently doing the right thing, even when no one is watching. The ethic enables sensing that which is right, correct, and appropriate and that which is wrong, incorrect, and inappropriate. The ethic encourages and enables transcending or rising above the interest, welfare, and good of Self in favor of the interest, welfare, and good of Others and the collective whole.

As such, this ethic consistently motivates acts and behaviors termed "self-sacrificing" and "selfless." Self-Sacrificing is voluntarily giving up concern for one's own interest, welfare, and/or good in the interest of Others. It is voluntarily giving up of concern for one's own interest, welfare, and good in the interest of the collective whole. Selfless is essentially a disregard or indifference for the interest, welfare, and good of Self in favor of the interest, welfare, and good of Others and the collective whole.

Neither self-sacrificing nor selfless carries a connotation of felt loss when acting or behaving for the interest, welfare, or good of Others and the collective whole. As such, these words are useful to describe the range of acts and behaviors associated with the Evolved Ethic. These words then contrast the words "sacrificing" and "selfish" previously associated with the Unevolved Ethic. Much as the difference between "sacrificing" and "selfish" is in degree only, the difference between "self-sacrificing" and "selfless" is also in degree only.

For this discussion of ethics, "selfless" simply resides further along the Unevolved – Evolved Continuum than "self-sacrificing". In both cases, Self is acting for the benefit, interest, welfare, or good of Others and the collective whole. In one instance, Self is freely and voluntarily giving up the interest, welfare, and good of Self in favor of the interest, welfare, and good of Others and the collective whole. In the other instance, Self disregards the interest, welfare, and good of Self in favor of the interest, welfare, and good of Others or the collective whole. Figure 4-5 illustrates proper placement of "self-sacrificing" and "selfless" on the Unevolved-Evolved Continuum.

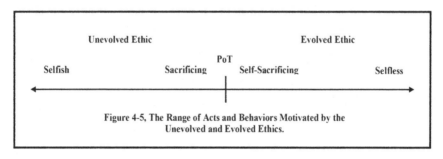

Figure 4-5, The Range of Acts and Behaviors Motivated by the Unevolved and Evolved Ethics.

Earlier, in the discussion of the Unevolved Ethic, I indicated acts and behaviors that are wrong, incorrect, and inappropriate or more wrong, incorrect, and inappropriate to the degree or extent they maximize benefit and minimize harm only for Self. They are wrong or more wrong to the degree or extent they serve only the interest, welfare, or good of Self. Further, they are wrong or more wrong to the degree or extent they result in harm for Others and the collective whole. Finally, I indicated one could think of the Unevolved Ethic as living in a state of sin.

At this time, I will assert that acts and behaviors are right to more right to the degree or extent they maximize benefit and minimize harm for Others and the collective whole. Similarly, they are more correct and more appropriate to the degree or extent they maximize benefit and minimize harm for Others and the collective whole. They are right to more right to the extent they serve the interest, welfare, and good of Others and the collective whole. Finally, acts and behaviors are right or more right to the degree or extent they result in harm only for Self. From this, one can think of the Evolved Ethic as living in a state of grace.

Figure 4-6 incorporates this concept of right to more right and the state of grace to the previous depiction of the concept of wrong to more wrong and the state of sin.

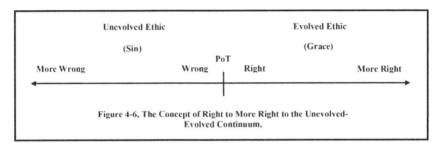

Figure 4-6, The Concept of Right to More Right to the Unevolved-Evolved Continuum.

In the next chapter, I will continue discussion of the Evolved Ethic. I will offer additional comments, examples, and manifestations of the Evolved Ethic. Included among the various subjects addressed in the next chapter is a discussion of giving or sharing to receive. In addition, there is discussion of the values that derive from the lesser virtues. These are the values consistent with the Evolved Ethic. But this portion of the chapter also covers the contrasting values consistent with the Unevolved Ethic. Further, there is a discussion of conscience and the subjects of objectivity and subjectivity. The chapter concludes with an examination of the relationship between Happiness and the Evolved Ethic.

CHAPTER 5:
DISCUSSION OF THE EVOLVED ETHIC

To begin this chapter, I will provide some examples of acts and behaviors that may indicate the Evolved Ethic when part of a consistent, long-term pattern. Some of these are remarkably simple acts and behaviors. Yet, they are examples that are not necessarily widespread or commonplace. I will then broaden the discussion to incorporate the concept of giving or sharing to receive. I first mentioned this concept in the last chapter. Giving or sharing to receive will lead to discussing values derived from virtues and vices. Aligning one set of values with the Evolved Ethic and one set with the Unevolved Ethic is possible.

Following the discussion of values is a short discussion of objectivity and subjectivity and a discussion that revisits the higher-level of consciousness I associate with the Evolved Ethic but also includes a discussion of conscience. I will also include a discussion of contrition and forgiveness. Finally, the chapter concludes with a discussion of Happiness, Unhappiness, and the privation of Happiness.

It might seem that this is an ambitious agenda for one chapter. However, this is not really case. Each of the subjects covered in the chapter has its basis in the distinction between the two ethics. So long as the distinction between the two ethics is understood, it is not difficult to cover these subjects with a relatively brief discussion.

The Unevolved Ethic guides and motivates acts and behaviors that maximize benefit and minimize harm for Self. The Evolved Ethic guides and motivates acts and behaviors that maximize benefit and minimize harm for Others and the collective whole. The Unevolved Ethic is powered by a morality component that encourages and enables the willingness and ability to minimalize or ignore harm that results for Others and the collective whole when Self acts and behaves to maximize benefit and minimize harm for Self. The Evolved Ethic is powered by a morality component that encourages and enables the willingness and ability to minimalize or ignore harm that results for Self when Self acts and behaves to maximize benefit and minimize harm for Others and the collective whole. With these distinctions in mind, it is relatively easy to provide examples of acts or behaviors that might indicate the Evolved Ethic when part of a long-range pattern of acts and behaviors.

For instance, acts and behaviors that consistently manifest kindness, politeness, and thoughtfulness are often simple acts that maximize benefit and minimize harm for Others. Acts and behaviors that are respectful, courteous, considerate, and helpful of Others are also often simple. These acts and behaviors are no more difficult than greeting Others or sharing a smile with Others. They are no more difficult than holding a door for someone or offering to help someone carry a heavy load. They are no more difficult than stopping to be polite or exchanging pleasantries with Others. They can be as simple as refraining from the use of profanity both in private and especially in public.

These are simple acts and behaviors, yet all benefit Others and the collective whole. All minimize harm for Others and the collective whole. All nurture the interest, welfare, and good of the collective whole. Each of these, and so many more similar acts and behaviors, demonstrate concern for the dignity of Others. They recognize and respect the dignity of other human beings. Further, they recognize the common bond between all human beings, regardless of differences.

But it takes time and effort to practice courtesy, politeness, kindness, thoughtfulness, and consideration for Others. It takes the willingness and ability to give and share the moment of time it takes to recognize and acknowledge the existence of Others, to recognize and acknowledge the dignity of Others. That time and effort are forever lost to Self. This loss of time and effort is pain for Self. This is harm Self must be willing and able to minimalize or ignore in order to consistently act or behave for the benefit of Others.

When Self is unwilling or unable to minimalize or ignore this loss of time or effort, Self will fail to consistently manifest even the smallest acts and behaviors that maximize benefit and minimize harm for Others and the collective whole. Similarly, when Self cannot or will not rise above the beliefs, opinions, and attitudes of Self, Self will fail to demonstrate the simple acts and behaviors that benefit Others. When Self cannot or will not rise above the biases, prejudices, superstitions, and fears of Self, Self will again fail to manifest the acts and behaviors that respect the dignity of Others. Giving respect and dignity to Others is right, correct, and appropriate.

When Self chooses to withhold the right, correct, and appropriate behavior, the result harms Others and the collective whole. Cooperation and collaboration, community, cannot exist where Self is willing and able to withhold respect or ignore the dignity of Others. Withholding the right, correct, and appropriate acts or behaviors maximizes benefit and minimizes harm for Self. The same is the case if we examine acts and behaviors that enrich or improve the lives of Others. Many of these are also relatively simple acts and behaviors.

Certainly, acts and behaviors that enrich and improve the lives of Others serve the best interest, welfare, and good of Others. Acts and behaviors that enrich and improve the lives of Others build trust, assurance, confidence, security and optimism. They encourage community and there are many ways Self can enrich and improve the lives of Others. For instance, Self can tutor, teach, mentor, or coach Others. Self can help Others develop their knowledge, talents, skills, and abilities. However, it takes time and effort to tutor, teach, mentor, and coach Others. It takes time and effort to help Others develop knowledge, talents, skills, and abilities. It takes time and effort to help Others to learn, grow, and develop.

That time and that effort are lost to Self. The loss of that time and effort for Self is harm. Because there is a loss to Self, it also takes the willingness and ability to give and share time and effort to benefit Others without regard for that loss to Self. It takes the willingness and ability to minimalize or ignore that harm for Self.

In addition to the time and effort required, tutoring, teaching, mentoring, and coaching Others often takes the willingness and ability to give and share knowledge, skills, talents, and abilities of Self with Others. It takes the willingness and ability to share the accumulated wisdom of Self with Others. It is not wisdom that is the virtue. Wisdom is only the accumulated learning, knowledge, and experiences each Self possesses. The willingness and ability to freely give and share wisdom has its basis in virtue. The virtuous act is the giving and sharing of wisdom to maximize benefit and minimize harm for Others. It is the act of freely and voluntarily giving and sharing any resource of Self without regard for consequence to Self that is the virtuous act. It is the act of freely giving and sharing any resource of Self that enables independence and a fuller life for Others. This serves the best interest, welfare, and good of the collective whole at every level.

In this context, independence means not being dependent or reliant on Others to meet basic needs, even basic survival needs. With independence comes dignity. This is dignity in the context of adequately providing for oneself and one's family. It is dignity in the context of prospering and contributing to the fullest extent of one's knowledge, talents, skills, and abilities. Independence gives worth and value to Others. Acts and behaviors that help Others become more independent and less dependent honor the dignity of Others. These acts and behaviors give respect to Others. As such, they maximize benefit and minimize harm for Others and the collective whole.

On the other hand, the failure to act and behave in a manner that recognizes the worth, dignity, and value of Others results in harm for Others and the collective whole. It results in pain. Lack of independence and reliance on Others can be painful. However, it also results in the other harms already mentioned at length. Each of these harms is contrary to the best interest, welfare, and good of Others and every level of collective whole. Each contributes to discord and disharmony, as well as competition. But Self often fails to recognize these harms. Self fails to recognize these harms because Self is unaccustomed to examining the impact of acts and behaviors beyond the benefit or harm for Self. Instead, Self acts and behaves to maximize benefit and minimize harm for Self. Yet opportunities to improve and enrich the lives of Others through tutoring, mentoring, teaching, and coaching are plentiful.

These opportunities are found in a wide variety of situations and under a wide variety of circumstances. They are found in the workplace, in schools, and communities. They are found through non-profits and civic organizations. These opportunities exist every day and take an infinite variety of forms. Many do not require much time and even less effort. Clearly, others require more time and more effort. Self has only to see these opportunities and then be willing and able to act without regard for Self and self-interest. Self must be willing to act freely and unencumbered by concern for the interest, welfare and good of Self.

The Evolved Ethic motivates this willingness and ability to consistently and freely give and share the resources of Self to benefit Others and the collective whole without regard for consequence to Self. The Evolved Ethic guides and motivates the willingness and ability to consistently give and share without regard or concern for receiving some benefit for Self. But the Unevolved Ethic guides and motivates giving or sharing to receive.

Giving or sharing to receive some benefit for Self is just another expression of the willingness and ability to maximize benefit and minimize harm for Self. When giving or sharing only to receive, Self gives or shares a resource of Self, but only in anticipation of gaining some benefit and reducing or avoiding some harm for Self. In this instance, Self is still the primary beneficiary of the act or behavior. Others may benefit from the act or behavior, but that benefit for Others is secondary to the benefit for Self. A good example of giving to receive is charitable gifts or donations.

Often a charitable gift or donation is given only with the intent to receive some benefit for Self. In these circumstances, the gift becomes a means to an end for Self. That end is benefit for Self. The benefit to Self might be a tax deduction for Self. It might be advancing an attitude, belief, or opinion of Self. It might be recognition, publicity, status, or prestige for Self. It might be enhanced reputation or community standing for Self. It might even be memorializing Self. In any of these instances, the act or behavior of giving or sharing is a means of gaining a reward for Self. Reward feels good to Self. A reward is pleasant for Self. Therefore, Self is the primary beneficiary of the act or behavior. However, since self is the primary beneficiary, the act or behavior is really not giving or sharing at all.

Indeed, giving or sharing to receive is actually a buying or purchasing behavior. It is an act or behavior that seeks to buy or purchase some reward for Self. This is the case whether examining giving or sharing to receive at the level of individual Self or a collective form of Self such as a corporation or even a nation-state. While there is utility (benefit) in the gift or donation for the recipient organization or cause receiving the gift or donation, the motivation for the gift or donation is benefit for Self. Therefore, the intent of the gift or donation is to buy or purchase a benefit for Self and the gift is only a means to that end.

The difference between giving and sharing or buying and purchasing hinges on intent. Suppose Self manifests an act or behavior that appears to be sharing or giving but could also be buying behavior. In that case, one cannot be certain which it is. Like ethic itself, it is not possible to physically examine intent or intention. Only an observed, long-range pattern of acts and behaviors gives insight into possible intent. Only observation of acts and behavior over a sufficiently long period and under various situations and circumstances can shed light on the intent or intention behind an act or behavior. This is the case since intent or intention is tied to the guiding and motivating ethic of Self or a collective form of Self.

To further illustrate this discussion of both intent and giving to receive, I can examine the giving of gifts to a young child. When a child receives a gift from an adult, the child is the recipient of the gift. There is utility (benefit) for the child. However, the real beneficiary of the act or behavior may be the adult who provides the gift. This is the case if the intent behind the gift is to gain a favorable response for the adult giving the gift. For instance, the sought-after response may be the child's reaction to the gift. It may be the child's smile, laugh, excitement or other emotional response to the gift. The child's emotional response is reward. It is a benefit (pleasure) for the adult providing the gift. The child's emotional response results in a good feeling for the adult, and the adult may well provide additional gifts to recapture the good feeling for Self.

In this instance, the act or behavior is not a giving behavior but a buying or purchasing behavior. Providing the gift is an attempt to buy or purchase the child's emotional reaction and the accompanying "feel good" for the adult. This is an example of using a gift as a means to an end, an end that results in benefit (pleasure) for Self. Similarly, an adult may provide gifts in an attempt to buy the preference of a child.

Often, a child demonstrates acts or behaviors that show a preference for an adult who provides gifts. A child will often prefer the adult or adults most likely to provide benefit (pleasure). This preference, on the part of the child, may be the sought-after reward for the adult providing the gifts. Being the preferred parent, grandparent, aunt, or uncle feels good. There is pleasure for the adult in being the preferred parent, grandparent, aunt, or uncle. This preference can be bought; however, a child will likely not hesitate to seek benefit from another adult if the preferred adult fails to provide a sought-after benefit. Unfortunately, attempts by adults to buy the preference of a child can and do influence the developing ethic of the child.

As stated previously, ethic begins developing at birth. Development of either the egoistic or virtue components of the two ethics is very strongly influenced by the teaching and example of parents and other significant adult influences in a child's early life. Which of the two components of ethic develops during these earliest years is strongly influenced by the manifest acts and behaviors of parents and other significant adults in a child's early life. A constant stream of gifts may teach a child to seek benefit (pleasure) for Self. A child may learn to pursue that which makes Self feel good. In addition, a child may learn to want, desire, crave and obsess over material objects. There is pleasure for the child in possessing material objects; more material objects equal more pleasure.

However, this same discussion of gifts as a means to an end for Self often applies to providing gifts to a girlfriend, boyfriend, spouse, or significant other. Self often gives gifts in anticipation of receiving a benefit or minimizing harm for Self. Self often gives these gifts in anticipation of reward for Self. The sought-after reward may only be a smile or a thank you, but that is still a reward for Self. In other instances, the sought-after reward may be a preference for the gift giver. That preference is still a reward for Self. If the anticipated reward is not forthcoming, emotions may engage. If the anticipated reward is not received, feelings of rejection, frustration, resentment, anger, and even rage may occur. These feelings occur because Self did not get the reward Self intended to buy or purchase with the gift.

From this discussion of giving to receive, it becomes apparent that giving or sharing to receive always benefits primarily Self. Giving to receive is always a means to a desired end for Self. It is always an effort to maximize benefit (pleasure) and minimize harm (pain or the privation of pleasure) for Self. As such, giving or sharing to receive is always associated with the

Unevolved Ethic. This is the same when giving to receive is practiced at the level of corporations and even nation-states.

For instance, many companies and corporations attempt to buy or purchase consumer loyalty through reward programs. These programs ostensibly reward customers for exhibiting behaviors that mimic loyalty. However, the primary beneficiary of these programs is not the consumer; it is the sponsoring company or corporation. There is a secondary benefit to the consumer; however, the program intends to maximize benefit (in the form of consumer spending) and minimize harm (reduced consumer spending or lost customers) for the sponsoring company or corporation. The intent is to exploit the consumer's desire to maximize benefit and minimize harm for Self. Therefore, these programs are a form or variation of giving or sharing to receive.

However, these programs always favor the sponsoring company or corporation's best interest, welfare, and good. They are always self-preserving, self-regarding, and self-promoting. Any harm (cost) associated with offering or maintaining the reward program passes through to the consumer. Even the cost of promoting the programs through advertising passes to the consumer. This is harm to the collective whole represented by the consumers. But the sponsoring company or corporation minimalizes or ignores this harm to the collective whole in the interest of Self. The company or corporation rationalizes, justifies, explains, and excuses this harm in the interest of competition or competitive advantage. All of which is consistent with the Unevolved Ethic.

Even nation-states engage in behaviors that appear as giving or sharing but are little more than attempts to buy or purchase benefit for Self. Nation-states engage in buying behaviors to buy the preferences of other nation-states. They engage in buying behaviors to gain and maintain friends and allies. Nation-states engage in buying or purchasing behavior to gain recognition, status, prestige, or position within the community of nation-states. They engage in buying behavior to gain and maintain approval within the community of nation-states. This giving or sharing to gain benefit for Self is consistent with the doctrine of realism mentioned earlier. It is a buying behavior intended to maximize benefit and minimize harm for the collective Self that is the nation-state. It is giving or sharing to receive.

In the context of this theory of ethics, an act or behavior only constitutes true giving or sharing if manifested with no regard or sought-after reward for Self. An act or behavior only constitutes true giving or sharing if performed free of concern for the benefit, welfare, or good of Self. A gift is only given or shared without intent to receive. It is given or shared only to the extent it is given or shared to maximize benefit and minimize harm for Others. It is given or shared only to the extent or degree Self is willing and able to minimalize or ignore resulting harm for Self. This is the case regardless of whether the level of Self is an individual Self or a collective level of Self, such as a club, organization, corporation, or nation-sate. Only when Self or a collective Self consistently and freely gives and shares resources of Self, without regard or concern for Self, would the act or behavior suggest the act is guided and motivated by the Evolved Ethic.

This discussion of giving or sharing to receive suggests a modification to what is commonly referred to as the "Golden Rule." This discussion suggests a Golden Rule that reads, "Do for Others without regard for Self." This restatement contrasts the more commonly stated Golden Rule, "Do for Others as you would have them do for you." Clearly, the current version incorporates consideration or regard for Self. Clearly, it infers doing or giving in anticipation of receiving. It infers a benefit for Self is and should be the motivation for doing for Others. This is a rational version of the Golden rule that is consistent with the Unevolved Ethic. "Do for Others without regard for Self" carries no such inference of sought-after benefit for Self. It suggests self-sacrificing and selfless acts and behaviors. It is a transrational restatement of the Golden Rule that is more consistent with the Evolved Ethic.

Freely giving and sharing to maximize benefit and minimize harm for Others takes the willingness and ability to transcend Self. It takes the willingness and ability to set aside Self and the interest, welfare, and good of Self. It takes the willingness and ability to forego the convenience of Self in the interest of Others. Sometimes, it takes the willingness and ability to step outside the comfort zone of Self. It takes the willingness and ability to rise above the fears, superstitions, biases, and prejudices of Self to act for the benefit of Others and, by extension, the collective whole. However, this willingness to rise above regard or concern for Self in the best interest, welfare, and good of Others is also evident in the values consistent with the Evolved Ethic.

Values consistent with the Evolved Ethic demonstrate regard for Others and the collective whole at all levels. These values demonstrate concern for the best interest, welfare, and good of Others and the collective whole at every level. Acts and behaviors manifesting these values maximize benefit and minimize harm for Others and the collective whole.

In the context of this discussion of values, the word "value" is intended to mean a trait, quality, or characteristic desirable as an end in itself and as a means to a desirable end. There are values that derive from each of the lesser masculine and feminine virtues associated with the virtue component and the overall Evolved Ethic. In each case, these values are desirable qualities and characteristics in themselves. However, these values are also the means to desirable ends.

For example, the qualities and characteristics associated with the virtue honesty include truthfulness, forthrightness, genuineness, and straightforwardness. Each of these qualities or characteristics is desirable in itself. However, these qualities and characteristics are also means to desirable ends. These desirable ends are the benefits already associated with acts and behaviors that maximize benefit and minimize harm for Others and the collective whole. Therefore, acts and behaviors that manifest values derived from honesty serve the best interest, welfare, and good of Others and the collective whole at every level.

On the other hand, qualities and characteristics also derive from the vice contrasting the virtue honesty. This is the vice dishonesty. These qualities and characteristics include untruthfulness, unfairness, disingenuousness, deceptiveness, deviousness, and unscrupulousness. The qualities and characteristics that derive from dishonesty are associated with terms such as perfidy, chicanery, cunning, duplicity, and trickery. Each of these qualities and characteristics is generally considered undesirable. Further, each of these is a means to undesirable ends. These ends include the building of each of the harms already mentioned. Yet, acts and behaviors manifesting these values maximize benefit and minimize harm for Self. The harms that result for Others and the collective whole are minimalized or ignored by Self in the interest of Self. If necessary, Self creates and employs rationalizations, justifications, explanations, and excuses to minimalize or ignore these harms.

In each case, the qualities and characteristics that derive from the lesser virtues are desirable. Also, in each case, these qualities and characteristics are the means to desirable ends. The reverse is equally true. The qualities and characteristics derived from the vices are all considered undesirable. Likewise, the qualities and characteristics derived from the vices are all means to undesirable ends. Therefore, the values derived from the lesser virtues are desirable, and those from the contrasting vices are undesirable. The result is something of a paradox. How can qualities and characteristics considered undesirable be called values? Further, how can qualities and characteristics that are the means to undesirable ends be called values? The answer to both these questions lies in the moral hypocrisy of the Unevolved Ethic. The answer lies in the moral hypocrisy of the ethic that guides and motivates Self to maximize benefit and minimize harm for Self.

The pattern of acts and behaviors guided and motivated by the Unevolved Ethic suggests these undesirable qualities and characteristics are indeed desirable to maximize benefit and minimize harm for Self. They are desirable as they serve the best interests, welfare, and good of Self. They are desirable as they protect, preserve, and promote Self. To minimalize or avoid the paradox of valuing undesirable qualities and characteristics, Self often professes to practice values that derive from virtue but, in reality, to some extent or degree, practices values that derive from vices. This is consistent with the Unevolved Ethic and the moral hypocrisy associated with this ethic.

As I cover the remainder of the lesser virtues and the values that derive from the virtues, I will also present the contrasting vice and the values that derive from those vices. In each case, the traits and characteristics that manifest the values associated with the vices benefit Self. A list of the ten lesser virtues and the values that derive from these virtues is in Appendix 2. A list of the corresponding vices and the values that derive from the vices is in Appendix 3. However, before continuing this discussion of values, I want to offer two short cautions. The first concerns values and patterns of acts and behaviors.

From the beginning of this discussion of ethics, I have indicated that patterns of acts and behaviors serve as indicators of guiding and motivating ethic. This same caution applies when considering values associated with virtues and vices. Patterns of acts and behaviors give insight into the values of Self. Patterns of acts and behaviors bear witness to the values of Self. Just as they do not give insight into ethic, isolated or random acts or behaviors do not bear witness to the values of Self. For instance, if the pattern of acts and behaviors manifests values that derive from the vice of dishonesty, the pattern is consistent with the Unevolved Ethic. The pattern indicates that, to some extent or degree, Self finds the qualities and characteristics that derive from dishonesty desirable as a means to maximize benefit and minimize harm for Self. The same is the case if the pattern of acts and behaviors indicates that, to some extent or degree, Self finds the qualities and characteristics that derive from the remaining vices desirable as a means for maximizing benefit and minimizing harm for Self. An act or behavior that is isolated or random to the ongoing, long-term pattern does not give evidence that Self finds these qualities and characteristics desirable. It is always the pattern of acts and behaviors that give insight into the guiding and motivating ethic and the values of Self.

The second caution concerns harm for Self when Self acts and behaves in a manner that manifests values associated with the virtues and the Evolved Ethic. Much like acts and behaviors that manifest the virtues, acts and behaviors that manifest values derived from virtue may also result in harm for Self. This is pain or the privation of pleasure that Self must be willing and able to minimalize or ignore consistently. The Transcendent Morality component of the Evolved Ethic powers the willingness and ability to consistently minimalize or ignore this harm for Self. This is the case with each virtue and the values that derive from each virtue.

For instance, the values that derive from the virtues of loyalty and bravery are trustworthiness, faithfulness, steadfastness, staunchness, boldness, directness, candidness, and fearlessness. They include realness and frankness. These are all qualities or characteristics further associated with terms like sincerity, authenticity, allegiance, fidelity, dependability, and reliability. Each word represents traits, qualities, or characteristics desirable in themselves. Still, each also represents qualities and characteristics that are means to desirable ends. These desirable ends maximize benefit and minimize harm to Others and the collective whole.

On the other hand, acts and behaviors that manifest the opposite or contrast to loyalty and bravery are associated with the vices of disloyalty and cowardice. The qualities and characteristics that derive from disloyalty include unfaithfulness, falseness, faithlessness, craftiness, deceitfulness, and even ruthlessness. Qualities and characteristics that derive from the vice cowardice include fearfulness, faintheartedness, feebleness, weakness, and spinelessness. The qualities and characteristics that derive from disloyalty and cowardice are further associated with terms such as infidelity, betrayal, adultery, treachery, and treason.

As a result, the qualities and characteristics derived from the vices of disloyalty and cowardice are generally considered undesirable. However, each of these qualities and characteristics is also the means to undesirable ends when viewed from the standpoint of Others and the collective whole. This is because each harms Others and the collective whole at all levels. However, acts and behaviors that manifest these qualities and characteristics manifest concern or regard for the protection, preservation and promotion of Self.

Acts and behaviors that manifest values that derive from cowardice and disloyalty maximize benefit and minimize harm for Self at the moment of the act or behavior. Therefore, these acts and behaviors are desirable as a means to maximize benefit and minimize harm for Self. They are desirable as they serve the best interest, welfare, and good of Self. Any harm that results for Others is minimized or ignored by Self. If the pattern of acts and behaviors manifests these values, this would indicate that Self finds these qualities and characteristics desirable as they serve Self.

The next pair of virtues for discussion are perseverance and patience. The desirable qualities and characteristics that derive from perseverance include earnestness, resoluteness, decisiveness, and firmness. Acts and behaviors manifesting these values are often termed committed, dedicated, devoted, unswerving, and unwavering. The desirable qualities derived from patience include calmness, quietness, coolness, unobtrusiveness, even-temperedness, and levelheadedness. Acts and behaviors that manifest these values are said to be unruffled, poised, collected, composed, dignified, restrained, and controlled.

In addition, these desirable traits, qualities, and characteristics often demonstrate control or restraint over the feelings and emotions of Self. They manifest control or restraint over the impulses and urges of Self. In each case, these are all desirable qualities and characteristics. They are all desirable as ends in themselves and as means to desirable ends. Acts and behaviors that manifest these values maximize benefit and minimize harm to Others and the collective whole.

The contrasting values that derive from both the vice ambivalence and the vice impatience maximize benefit and minimize harm for Self. The values that derive from ambivalence include indecisiveness, irresoluteness, tentativeness, apprehensiveness, and impulsiveness. Acts and behaviors that manifest these values are often termed hesitant, uncertain, wavering, vacillating, irresolute, indecisive, and uncommitted. The values that derive from the vice impatience include rashness, hastiness, recklessness, carelessness, tempestuousness and hotheadedness. Acts and behaviors that manifest these values are termed excited, agitated, provoked, irritated, turbulent, and even violent. Many acts and behaviors that manifest values derived from impatience demonstrate a lack of self-control or self-restraint. However, these values do maximize benefit and minimize harm for Self. This is the same with the values that derive from both the vice immoderation and the vice immodesty.

The values that derive from the vice immoderation include intemperateness, excessiveness, insensibleness, unreasonableness, rapaciousness, injudiciousness, and voraciousness. Acts and behaviors that manifest these values are often termed gluttonous, voracious, covetous, and insatiable. The traits, qualities, and characteristics that derive from the vice immodesty include boastfulness, brashness, cockiness, affectedness, pretentiousness, snobbishness, and pompousness. The qualities and characteristics associated with the vice immodesty associate well with words like egotistical, conceited, vainglorious, prideful, ostentatious, gaudy, arrogant, and narcissistic. These values are also associated easily with terms like loud, showy, presuming, and even indecency.

Acts and behaviors that manifest values associated with both immoderation and immodesty all manifest disregard and consideration for Others and the collective whole. These acts and behaviors manifest a lack of self-control and self-restraint. Acts and behaviors that manifest these qualities and characteristics are often self-promoting and self-aggrandizing. Each of these traits, qualities, and characteristics is generally considered undesirable. Yet, the pattern of acts and behaviors of many Selves suggest that Self does indeed find these qualities and characteristics desirable as a means to an end for Self. That end is to maximize benefit (pleasure) and minimize harm for Self. Self will then rationalize, justify, explain, and excuse or simply ignore any harm that results.

On the other hand, the values that derive from both moderation and modesty are generally thought desirable. These are qualities and characteristics that maximize benefit and minimize harm for Others and the collective whole. The values that derive from moderation include reasonableness, sensibleness, temperateness, soundness, and judiciousness. The qualities and characteristics that derive from modesty include demureness, naturalness, unaffectedness, humbleness, genuineness, and unpretentiousness. These qualities and characteristics also associate well with terms like unassuming, reserve, reticence, respectability, and decency. Acts and behaviors that manifest values that derive from both moderation and modesty demonstrate self-control and self-restraint. Acts and behaviors that manifest all of these values maximize benefit and minimize harm to Others and the collective whole at all levels.

The same is the case when examining the lesser feminine virtues of empathy and compassion. The values that derive from empathy are responsiveness, receptiveness, pleasantness, friendliness, attentiveness, and openness. The values that derive from compassion are kindheartedness, thoughtfulness, gentleness, and tenderness. Like the other values that derive from the lesser virtues, they are desirable as both ends and means to ends. These acts and behaviors might be termed considerate, attentive, sensitive, benevolent, and humane.

The contrast or opposite of empathy is the vice indifference. The contrast or opposite of compassion is the vice apathy. The values that derive from indifference include thoughtlessness, carelessness, inattentiveness, and impassiveness. The values that derive from apathy include heartlessness, coldness, callousness, harshness, and mercilessness. In addition, both indifference and apathy can spawn qualities and characteristics termed malicious, spiteful, vindictive, hateful, and vicious. To those can be added negligent. Acts and behaviors that manifest any or all of these qualities and characteristics always result in harm for Others and the collective whole. However, Self minimalizes or ignores this harm to Others and the collective whole in the interest of Self.

On the contrary, the values that derive from the lesser feminine virtue of generosity include unselfishness, openhandedness, evenhandedness, fair-mindedness and kindness. These values are associated with terms that include benevolence, munificence, humaneness, self-sacrifice, and selflessness. Acts and behaviors that manifest these qualities benefit Others and the collective whole. These acts and behaviors do build the benefits previously mentioned. They do contribute to the building of community. In contrast, it is the qualities and characteristics that derive from the contrast of generosity that result in harm for Others and the collective whole.

The vice that contrasts generosity is voracity. The values that derive from voracity include selfishness, self-centeredness, greediness, miserliness, stinginess, rapaciousness, and avariciousness. Acts and behaviors that manifest these qualities and characteristics all serve only Self and the interest, welfare, and good of Self. Therefore, these qualities and characteristics become desirable only as means to ends that maximize benefit and minimize harm for Self. Then Self simply minimalizes and ignores the harm that results for Others and the collective whole. Indeed, Self often professes to practice the values associated with the virtue generosity but actually practices the values associated with the vice voracity and then creates and employs the rationalizations, justifications, explanations, and excuses that minimalize or ignore the harm to Others and the collective whole.

It is fair to suggest that, taken together, the values that derive from the lesser feminine and masculine virtues constitute what are commonly referred to as "family values." Family values are generally always thought desirable. The reverse, the set of values that derive from the vices are all generally described to be undesirable. Yet, the pattern of acts and behaviors of so many Selves suggests the values that derive from the vices are indeed desirable as they maximize benefit and minimize harm for Self.

Interestingly, this paradox is often most evident in the pattern of acts and behaviors of those Selves most likely to employ the phrase "family values." However, it takes the willingness and ability to objectively examine the acts and behaviors of Self to see the evidence of this paradox. But then objectivity itself requires that Self be both willing and able to set aside the best interest, welfare, and good of Self in the interest of Others and the collective whole. This is because objectivity requires the absence of Self.

Indeed, objectivity is the absence of Self and self-interest. It is the absence of concern or regard for the interest, welfare, and good of Self. Absolute objectivity is the absolute absence of Self and self-interest. Absolute objectivity is, therefore, absolutely selfless. Objectivity maximizes benefit and minimizes harm for Others and the collective whole. Objectivity builds the same benefits previously mentioned in this discussion of ethics. It builds trust, certainty, assurance, and security. It builds optimism, concord, harmony and community. However, objectivity also requires that Self be willing and able to minimalize or ignore harm for Self.

Conversely, subjectivity always indicates the presence of Self or self-interest. It always indicates concern or regard for the best interest, welfare, and good of Self. Subjectivity maximizes benefit and minimizes harm for Self. Absolute subjectivity is the absolute presence of Self and self-interest. Therefore, absolute subjectivity is absolutely selfish. As such, subjectivity does not serve the best interest, welfare, or good of Others or the collective whole. Quite the reverse is the case. Subjectivity results in the harms previously listed. It contributes to distrust, uncertainty, ambiguity, and doubt. It contributes to pessimism and skepticism, as well as discord and disharmony. It contributes to competition. Figure 5-1 illustrates the positions of subjectivity and objectivity on the Unevolved-Evolved Continuum. Subjectivity aligns under the Unevolved Ethic, and objectivity aligns under the Evolved Ethic.

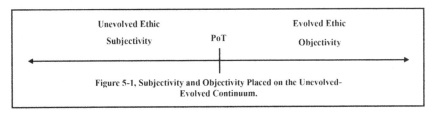

Figure 5-1, Subjectivity and Objectivity Placed on the Unevolved-Evolved Continuum.

Truth and untruth align similarly and for the same reasons. Truth is the absence of Self and Self-interest. Truth is the absence of concern or regard for the interest, welfare, and good of Self. Therefore, truth is objective. Absolute truth is the absolute absence of Self and self-interest. It is absolutely objective. As such, absolute truth is absolutely selfless. Untruth is the reverse. Untruth always indicates the presence of Self and self-interest. It always indicates concern or regard for Self and the interest, welfare, and good of Self. Therefore, untruth is subjective. Absolute untruth is the absolute presence of Self and self-interest. It is absolutely subjective. Therefore, absolute untruth is absolutely selfish.

Truth maximizes benefit and minimizes harm for Others and the collective whole. Untruth maximizes benefit and minimizes harm for Self. Truth requires the willingness and ability to minimalize or ignore harm for Self and untruth requires only the willingness and ability to minimalize or ignore harm for Others and the collective whole. Therefore, truth aligns under the Evolved Ethic and untruth under the Unevolved Ethic on the Unevolved-Evolved Continuum. Figure 5-2 illustrates this alignment.

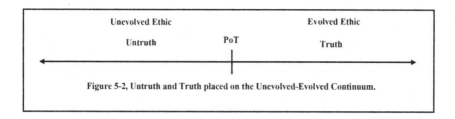

Figure 5-2, Untruth and Truth placed on the Unevolved-Evolved Continuum.

Further, it is possible to demonstrate the same alignments when considering subjective and objective reality. Subjective reality aligns under the Unevolved Ethic. Objective reality aligns under the Evolved Ethic.

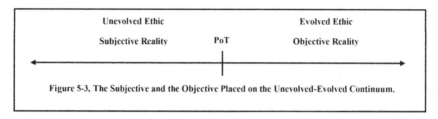

Figure 5-3, The Subjective and the Objective Placed on the Unevolved-Evolved Continuum.

With this alignment, shown in Figure 5-3, it is clear that acts and behaviors that manifest subjective reality maximize benefit and minimize harm primarily for Self. Acts and behaviors that manifest objective reality maximize benefit and minimize harm for Others and the collective whole. Subjective reality serves the best interest, welfare, and good of Self. Objective reality serves the best interest, welfare, and good of Others and the collective whole. Self minimalizes or ignores harm that results for Others and the collective whole when acts or behaviors consistently manifest subjective reality. On the other hand, Self minimalizes or ignores harm that results for Self when acts or behaviors consistently manifest objective reality.

Right, correct, and appropriate acts and behaviors are those that consistently manifest objectivity and truth. They are acts and behaviors that consistently manifest objective reality. Acts and behaviors that consistently manifest objectivity, truth, and objective reality place the interest, welfare, and good of Others and the collective whole above the interest, welfare, and good of Self. They build trust, assurance, confidence, certainty, security, and optimism. They encourage community. They respect, preserve, and promote the collective whole. They respect, preserve, and promote the "We," "Us," "Our," and "Ours" represented by the collective whole. This is the case regardless of the level or form of the collective whole.

Subjectivity and untruth can only motivate acts and behaviors that are, to some extent or degree, wrong, incorrect, and inappropriate. Likewise, subjective reality will only motivate acts and behaviors that are, to some extent or degree, wrong, incorrect, and inappropriate. They are wrong, incorrect, or inappropriate to the extent these acts place the interest, welfare, and Self above the interest, welfare, and good of Others and the collective whole. Acts and behaviors that consistently manifest subjectivity, untruth, and subjective reality are self-preserving, self-regarding, self-promoting, and self-aggrandizing. They are acts and behaviors that result in harm for Others and the collective whole. This harm to Others and the collective whole is minimalized or ignored by Self in the interest of Self. Consistent with the Unevolved Ethic, Self employs rationalizations, justifications, explanations, and excuses to minimalize or ignore these harms.

Often, Self may also employ these same rationalizations, explanations, and excuses to ease the conscience of Self. Conscience is an integral part of the next discussion of the higher level of consciousness associated with the Evolved Ethic.

In the last chapter, I associated the Transcendent Morality component of the Evolved Ethic with a higher level of consciousness. I indicated consciousness means awareness or sentience. By higher level of consciousness, I mean awareness or sentience that transcends awareness or sentience of only Self. I further indicated this level of awareness or sentience transcends consideration of the best interest, welfare, and good of only Self. It is awareness or sentience that transcends the feelings, emotions, urges, impulses, superstitions, fears, biases, and prejudices of Self. It is awareness or sentience of the interest, welfare, and good of Others and the collective whole. It is awareness or sentience of the harms that result for Others and the collective whole when Self acts always to maximize benefit and minimize harm for Self.

This higher level of consciousness is consistent with a Native American rule of thumb that indicates Self should consider the impact of actions, the consequences of actions, out seven generations. This rule of thumb requires consideration of impact or consequence not just in the present, but also far into the future. It requires consideration of impact far beyond the interest, welfare and good of only Self. It requires consideration of impact far beyond maximizing benefit and minimizing harm for Self. Further, it requires consideration of the impact of acts and behaviors of Self on all sentient beings as well as the impact on the very planet on which future generations will live.

Clearly, this higher level of consciousness requires a long-range view of consequences, benefits or harms. It requires the willingness and ability to recognize the ripple effects that result from the acts and behaviors of Self. For instance, it requires the willingness and ability to recognize the ripple effect of benefit for Others when Self acts or behaves to maximize benefit and minimize harm for Others and the collective whole. However, it also requires the willingness and ability to recognize the ripple effect of harm that results for Others and the collective whole when Self acts and behaves to maximize benefit and minimize harm only for Self.

Consistent with this higher level of consciousness is the willingness and ability to accept responsibility and accountability for the harms that result from the acts and behaviors of Self. Accepting responsibility and accountability for acts and behaviors that result in harm for Others or the collective whole often results in pain or the privation of pleasure for Self. However, and consistent with this higher level of consciousness, this willingness and ability to accept accountability and responsibility often manifests before Self acts or behaves. This accountability and responsibility often manifest before Self acts or behaves in a manner that harms Others or the collective whole. It does so by anticipating harm for Others and the collective whole before harm occurs. As such, this level of responsibility and accountability minimizes the possibility of harm for Others and the collective whole. This level of accountability and responsibility is consistent with the higher level of consciousness. It is consistent with the level of consciousness, awareness, and sentience that focuses on Others and the collective whole.

This higher level of consciousness associated with the Evolved Ethic sharply contrasts the lower level of consciousness associated with the Unevolved Ethic. It sharply contrasts the lower level of awareness or sentience that focuses on Self and the best interest, welfare, and good of Self. It sharply contrasts the narrow, short-term view that focuses on maximizing benefit and minimizing harm for Self.

This lower level of consciousness minimalizes or ignores the ripple effect of harm that results for Others and the collective whole when Self consistently acts and behaves to maximize benefit and minimize harm for Self. It ignores the ripple effect of harms that build discord and disharmony within the collective whole at many levels. It minimalizes and ignores these harms as well as those that accrue when Self employs rationalizations, justifications, explanations, and excuses to deflect or avoid responsibility and accountability for the acts and behaviors of Self. Further, this lower level of consciousness is consistent with the creation and employment of self-deception strategies to minimize or avoid harm for Self.

This discussion of a higher and lower level of consciousness is very much related to the subject of conscience. Conscience is defined as "the sense of what is right or wrong in one's conduct or motives, impelling one toward right action. The ethical and moral principles that control or inhibit the actions or thoughts of an individual."

Based on this definition, one could easily conclude that this entire discussion of ethics is a discussion of conscience. However, the use of the word "sense" in this definition warrants closer examination. This examination reveals that this "sense" of right and wrong develops differently as the two ethics develop. As a result, this "sense" of right and wrong functions differently depending on the level of consciousness that develops in concert with ethic.

Indeed, "conscience" is a reflection of the level of consciousness associated with each ethic. The two levels of consciousness result in distinct differences in conscience. This difference is so distinct that I will describe one form of conscience as thoughts and feelings based and the other form as based on sensing. This distinction would then be consistent with earlier comments regarding the two ethics.

Previously, I associated both reasoning and feeling with the Unevolved Ethic. However, I associated sensing with the Evolved Ethic. This distinction results in one form of conscience that is reasoning and feeling-based and in a different form of conscience that is sensing-based. To really understand this difference requires discussing conscience not in terms of right and wrong, correct and incorrect, or appropriate and inappropriate, but rather in terms of benefit and harm.

The Unevolved Ethic guides choices and motivates acts and behaviors that manifest regard and consideration of benefit and harm for Self. This consideration of benefit and harm for Self is tied very directly to the form of conscience that develops in concert with the Unevolved Ethic. This is especially true of consideration of harm for Self. Therefore, this form of conscience is less concerned with issues of right and wrong, and far more concerned with issues of benefit and harm for Self.

This suggests a form of conscience that functions as a form of risk assessment. It suggests a form of conscience that weighs potential risk (harm) against potential reward (benefit) for Self. This assessment of risk and reward provides a further tie to reasoning. It is through the ability to reason that Self conducts this risk/reward assessment. A telltale sign of this assessment of risk and reward for Self is fear, and Self feels fear.

This consideration or assessment of potential harm for Self often results in fear and a fear response. This fear is not concerned with issues of right and wrong. It is concerned with the consideration of harm for Self. This fear often results in visible, physical responses. For instance, this fear often results in physical changes in the body. It often results in higher heart rate and a spike in blood pressure. It may result in perspiration and reddening of the skin. It may result in changes in voice volume or tone. It may result in the voice cracking.

This fear and the accompanying physical response may be lower or less intense in instances in which the potential harm for Self is not high. On the other hand, this fear and the accompanying physical responses will likely be greater or more intense if the potential harm for Self is high. This fear may also be lower in instances in which experience has taught that the harm for Self may be mitigated or avoided through the employment of rationalizations, justifications, explanations, excuses, or self-deception strategies. Finally, the strength of this fear and the accompanying physical indicators may be far less if Self is habituated to wrong, incorrect, and inappropriate acts and behaviors. In this instance, it might be suggested that Self has no conscience. The same may be said if Self is so strongly habituated to benefit for Self that consideration of harm for Self does not seem to occur. It might be said that this Self also has no conscience.

Interestingly enough, this fear and fear response also seem to fade with the repeated success of a particular wrong, incorrect, or inappropriate act or behavior. As an act or behavior is repeated without negative consequence (harm) for Self, the fear of potential harm becomes less. If the act or behavior is repeated enough to become a habit, the fear of harm for Self may disappear completely. The fear response may reappear only in a circumstance in which the possibility of harm for Self suddenly increases.

As an example, many people habitually drive faster than posted speed limits, even though this act or behavior could result in a traffic citation. The traffic citation represents harm (pain or the privation of pleasure) for Self. Yet, because Self is habituated to exceeding speed limits, Self often speeds without fear of consequence for Self. This rapidly changes if Self sees a police cruiser in the rear-view mirror. Under this circumstance, the fear of harm for Self returns instantly and Self reduces speed to the posted limit. Self does not do so out of consideration of right or wrong, but only to reduce or eliminate potential harm for Self.

It is the assessment of potential harm and fear of harm for Self that may motivate Self to demonstrate a right, correct, and appropriate act instead of a wrong, incorrect, or inappropriate act. More often, it will simply deter Self from manifesting a wrong, incorrect, or inappropriate act or behavior. If Self determines the risk of harm for Self is high or the possibility of benefit for Self is low or does not justify the risk of harm, Self will not act. By contrast, if Self determines that the potential benefit to Self outweighs the potential harm, Self will often demonstrate a wrong, incorrect, or inappropriate act. If Self determines the risk of harm for Self is low or the possibility of benefit for Self is high, Self will often act to maximize that benefit for Self. This consideration still does not concern issues of right and wrong. It concerns only consequences, benefit or harm, for Self. The familiar example of telling a lie illustrates this.

Most children and adults learn that telling a lie is wrong, incorrect, and inappropriate. Yet people, regardless of age, tell lies. Further, people will exaggerate, embellish, and stretch the truth. Each of these is also a lie. So, it is clear that prior knowledge of right and wrong are insufficient to deter these acts or behaviors. This is because, in each instance, the lie, exaggeration, embellishment, and stretch, regardless of how big or small, maximizes benefit and minimizes harm for Self. In each instance, prior knowledge of right and wrong has failed to deter the lie, exaggeration, embellishment, or stretch of the truth. In each case, the risk/reward assessment that is this form of conscience has determined that the potential benefit for Self outweighs the potential harm for Self. Because this form of conscience encourages and enables maximizing benefit and minimizing harm for Self, it is the form of conscience associated with the lower level of consciousness or awareness that develops with the Unevolved Ethic. It is the form of conscience associated with feeling and reasoning.

There is, however, a second form of conscience. This form of conscience is associated with the higher level of consciousness that develops with the Evolved Ethic. This is the form of conscience that more completely fits the definition of a "sense" of what is right or wrong in one's conduct or motives that impels Self toward right action. To support this assertion also requires an examination of benefit and harm. In this case, it also includes consideration of right, correct, and appropriate.

The Evolved Ethic guides choices and motivates acts and behaviors that manifest regard and consideration of benefit and harm for Others and the collective whole. This consideration of benefit and harm for Others and the collective whole results in acts and behaviors that maximize benefit and minimize harm for Others and the collective whole. Therefore, these acts and behaviors extend from right to more right. In addition, they extend from correct and appropriate to more correct and more appropriate. It is the willingness and ability to act and behave to maximize benefit and minimize harm for Others and the collective whole that results in the second form of conscience.

This form of conscience anticipates the harms that result for Others and the collective whole when Self acts and behaves only for the best interest, welfare, and good of Self. It is this anticipation that best fits the "sense of right and wrong" alluded to in the definition of conscience. This sensing of right and wrong is actually a sensing of benefit and harm to Others and the collective whole. As such, this form of conscience is not an assessment of risk and reward for Self. It is not an assessment of potential benefit and potential harm for Self. It is, therefore, not based on either feeling or reasoning. It is the sensing of right to the extent or degree the act or behavior maximizes benefit for Others and the collective whole. It is the sensing of right to the extent or degree an act or behavior minimizes harm for Others and the collective whole. It is the sensing of wrong to the extent or degree an act or behavior maximizes benefit and minimizes harm for Self and results in harm for Others and the collective whole.

This is the form of conscience that develops with the Evolved Ethic. It is the form of conscience associated with the higher level of consciousness. It is the form of conscience that develops along with the willingness and ability to minimalize or ignore harm for Self. However, this form of conscience will only develop if the Evolved Ethic develops.

If the Unevolved ethic forms, the form of conscience that develops will focus on the assessment of risk (harm) and reward (benefit) for Self. It is this form of conscience that develops with the Unevolved Ethic that is most closely associated with acts of contrition. Sometimes, acts of contrition are even tied to a desire on the part of Self to "ease a guilty conscience." Yet, on examination, it is often clearly apparent that the act of contrition intends to avoid greater harm (pain or the privation of pleasure) for Self.

Self often expresses contrition only when a wrong, incorrect, or inappropriate act or behavior of Self becomes known. In other instances, Self may express contrition when Self cannot avoid detection of a wrong, incorrect, or inappropriate act or behavior. Regardless of circumstances, Self rarely expresses contrition or says, "I'm sorry," before there is the possibility of harm for Self. Further, acts of contrition are often accompanied by justifications, rationalizations, explanations, or excuses for wrong, incorrect, or inappropriate acts or behaviors. In other instances, an act of contrition may include the employment of a self-deception strategy to further mitigate, reduce, or avoid harm for Self. In each instance, these justifications, rationalizations, excuses, explanations, or self-deception strategies seek to mitigate or avoid harm for Self.

As a result, it is easy to suggest that acts of contrition are always self-preserving, self-regarding, and self-promoting. They are always an attempt to minimize harm or reduce the possibility of greater harm for Self. Therefore, acts of contrition, if part of a pattern of acts and behaviors that maximize benefit and minimize harm for Self, are guided and motivated by the Unevolved Ethic. However, it may be less clear that acts of forgiveness are also guided and motivated by the Unevolved Ethic.

Understanding that acts of forgiveness are guided and motivated by the Unevolved Ethic also requires an examination of benefit and harm. More specifically, it requires examining who primarily benefits from an act of forgiveness. In other words, for whom does an act of forgiveness maximize benefit and minimize harm?

Consistent with this theory of ethics, it is always Self that primarily benefits from an act of forgiveness. Acts of forgiveness always maximize benefit and minimize harm for the forgiving Self. Self says, "I forgive." It is always Self, "I," "Me" who forgives. Self may forgive for a wide variety of reasons; however, each of those reasons ultimately manifests concern or regard for Self. Self forgives in situations and under circumstances in which Self is the primary beneficiary of the act. An act of forgiveness may also result in benefit for the contrite Other; however, this is secondary to the benefit for Self. However, this becomes even clearer by examining the reverse situation. In other words, by examining those situations in which Self fails to forgive.

Self fails to forgive when Self determines forgiving is not in the best interest, welfare, or good of Self. Self fails to forgive when forgiveness does not maximize benefit or minimize harm for Self. Self fails to forgive when Self determines that the benefit to Self is insufficient. This is consistent with the notion that Self should forgive only when the benefit or reward for Self justifies forgiving. It also suggests a risk/reward assessment very similar to the risk/reward assessment associated with the lower form of conscience.

In each situation requiring forgiveness, there is an assessment of the benefit and harm for Self in giving or failing to give forgiveness. "I," "Me" chooses to forgive or not to forgive. "I," "Me" will not forgive if "I," "Me" does not believe it is in the best interest, welfare, and good of Self to forgive. "I," "Me" will not forgive if withholding forgiveness benefits Self more than forgiving. Said differently, Self fails to forgive when Self believes not forgiving or withholding forgiveness maximizes benefit and minimizes harm for Self. This includes those instances in which the failure to forgive is based on strong emotion or hurt feelings or when failure to forgive is tied to pride. This is still very consistent with the discussion of the Unevolved Ethic. Therefore, neither acts of contrition nor acts of forgiveness are generally associated with the Evolved Ethic. On the other hand, acceptance is associated with the Evolved Ethic.

Acceptance means the willingness and ability to minimalize or ignore harm for Self that results from the acts and behaviors of Others. Acceptance does not mean forgiveness. Acceptance is not based on an assessment of benefit or harm for Self. Acceptance is not based on consideration or regard for Self or the best interest, welfare, and good of Self. Further, acceptance does not require forgiveness. Neither does it require an act of contrition on the part of Others. Therefore, acts and behaviors that manifest acceptance of Others are consistent with the Evolved Ethic. It is associated with the willingness and ability to rise above or transcend harm for Self in the interest of Others and the collective whole.

This willingness and ability to rise above harm for Self in the interest of Others is consistent with a broader willingness and ability to accept and embrace the interest, welfare, and good of Others and the collective whole above the interest, welfare, and good of Self. It is consistent with a broader willingness and ability to accept and embrace all Others who do not look like "I," "Me" or who do not sound like "I," "Me" when they speak. It is consistent with a broader willingness and ability to accept and embrace all Others who do not practice the same religion, belong to the same political party, carry the same passport, or live in the same neighborhood or community as "I," "Me."

This broader willingness and ability to accept and embrace is very consistent with the Evolved Ethic. It is consistent with the ethic that guides and motivates this willingness and ability to accept and embrace all Others regardless of the categories that separate and divide. As such, the words

"Accept" and "Embrace" align under the Evolved Ethic. These words contrast the words "Intolerant and "Tolerant" previously associated with the Unevolved Ethic.

When discussing the Unevolved Ethic, I indicated that even the term "tolerant" implies the giving up of something; it implies a loss or a feeling of loss to Self. It implies sacrifice. I associated this feeling of loss or sacrifice with the Unevolved Ethic. However, the words "accept" and "embrace" imply no such feeling of loss or sacrifice. Neither term implies a feeling of giving up something. Figure 5-4 illustrates the inclusion of "accept" and "embrace" under the Evolved Ethic.

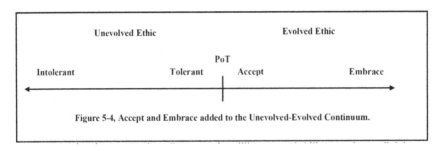

Figure 5-4, Accept and Embrace added to the Unevolved-Evolved Continuum.

I am using the term "embrace" to mean the willingness and ability to embrace all Others equally, individually and collectively. It means the willingness and ability to embrace regardless of differences, whether these differences are physical characteristics, language, race, ethnicity, religion, or nationality. It means the willingness and ability to embrace regardless of beliefs, attitudes, opinions, philosophies, and ideologies.

Placed at the extreme end of the continuum, "embracing" infers the willingness and ability to selflessly embrace all Others without condition. It implies the willingness and ability to embrace the whole of humanity without condition. This unconditional embrace is very much in the best interest, welfare, and good of every level and form of collective whole.

The term "accept," which lies nearer the Point of Transcendence, infers a willingness and ability to accept regardless of differences. It means the willingness and ability to minimalize the many differences that exist among humanity. It means the willingness and ability to minimalize differences in beliefs, attitudes, opinions, philosophies, and ideologies and accept all Others as members of humanity. In other words, "accept" infers seeing and hearing differences but minimalizing or overlooking the differences seen or heard. It infers an awareness of differences, but overlooking these differences and accepting all Others as a member of the collective whole of humanity. Similar to embracing, accepting Others serves the best interest, welfare, and good of every level and form of the collective whole.

However, it should be recognized that the difference between "tolerant" and "accept", at the Point of Transcendence is, and would be, nearly imperceptible. It would be very difficult to determine which ethic is guiding and motivating acts and behaviors if the ethic lies close to the PoT. As the ethic moves further from the PoT, in either direction, the pattern of acts and behaviors become more distinguishable.

As the ethic moves further away from the PoT in the direction of the Evolved Ethic, acts and behaviors become more accepting and embracing. The pattern of acts and behaviors becomes increasingly more inclusive of Others regardless of differences. The pattern of acts and behaviors reflects the willingness and ability to include Others regardless of differences. This is very consistent with the Transcendent Morality. It is very consistent with the combined, integrated strength of Love and Courage which is the Transcendent Morality. As a result, it is possible to align the term "inclusive" with the Evolved Ethic.

On the contrary, as ethic moves further away from the PoT in the direction of the Unevolved Ethic, acts and behaviors move from tolerant to intolerant. The pattern of acts and behaviors becomes increasingly exclusive of Others. Acts and behaviors reflect the willingness and ability to exclude Others based on differences. These acts and behaviors reflect the willingness and ability to exclude Others based on the differences that categorize and separate humanity. This is consistent with the rational morality and the willingness and ability to minimalize or ignore harm for Others and the collective whole. As a result, it is possible to align the term "exclusive" with the Unevolved Ethic.

Figure 5-5 reflects the proper alignment of the terms "inclusive" and "exclusive" on the Unevolved-Evolved continuum.

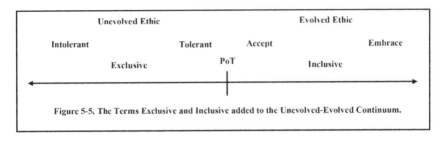

Figure 5-5. The Terms Exclusive and Inclusive added to the Unevolved-Evolved Continuum.

With the addition of "exclusive" and "inclusive" to the Unevolved-Evolved Continuum, it is time to turn to the last subject of this chapter. This is the subject of Happiness and the relationship of Happiness to the Evolved Ethic. In Chapter 2, I drew a deliberate division between Happiness and pleasure. I then associated pleasure with the Unevolved Ethic and Happiness with the Evolved Ethic but deferred the discussion of Happiness.

When I drew that division between Happiness and pleasure, I indicated that this Happiness is not an emotion such as joy or elation. This Happiness is not tied to feelings. Indeed, I indicated that Self senses Happiness. To help clarify this sense of Happiness, I associated Happiness with terms like contentment, satisfaction, and inner peace. I indicated that Self senses contentment, satisfaction, and inner peace. I then indicated that Happiness does not result in feelings or an agitated state. It's quite the opposite. Happiness results in calmness or a calm state. It results in serenity, tranquility, and peacefulness.

In that same discussion, I indicated that Self also senses Unhappiness. I indicated that Self senses Unhappiness and related Unhappiness to a sense of discontentment and dissatisfaction. I further likened this sense of discontentment and dissatisfaction to a sense of void or emptiness. It is a sense that something is missing. It may result in a sense of longing.

Each of these indicators of Unhappiness results in a lack of inner peace, calmness, serenity, and tranquility, which can easily be interpreted as pain for Self. Further, each of these sensed indicators of Unhappiness can and does result in acts and behaviors intended to remove Unhappiness for Self. Unfortunately, Self often manifests acts and behaviors that do not and cannot remove Unhappiness. Self tries to fill the void, the emptiness, the lack of calm, through acts and behaviors that maximize benefit (pleasure) and minimize harm (pain or the privation of pleasure) for Self.

For instance, Self may attempt to remove Unhappiness through the acquisition of material objects: homes, vehicles, clothes, accessories, jewelry, furniture, appliances, electronics and many other objects. Self may eat to the point of obesity, with its accompanying health issues. Self may turn to drugs or alcohol to the point of physical or financial ruin as Self attempts to remove Unhappiness through acts and behaviors that result in pleasure for Self. However, Self cannot remove Unhappiness or find Happiness through these acts and behaviors. Self cannot find Happiness in these acts or behaviors intended to benefit Self because Happiness does not lie in pleasure.

It is said that Happiness cannot be bought. There is great truth in this saying. Try as Self might, Self cannot buy that which is not for sale. Self can buy pleasure, but not Happiness. Neither can Self remove Unhappiness through attempts to buy Happiness. Attempts to buy Happiness can and do result in repeated efforts to make Self feel good. Attempts to buy Happiness can and do result in acts and behaviors intended to fill the sensed void, emptiness, and longing by pursuing that which is pleasing to "I," "Me." Self can buy pleasure for Self, but Self cannot buy Happiness and pleasure is a poor substitute for Happiness.

However, acts and behaviors intended to result in Happiness through pleasure for Self may provide an interesting insight into the historical confusion between Happiness and pleasure. This insight refers back to John Stuart Mills' comment that "by happiness is intended pleasure." While Happiness is not the same as pleasure, there is a very direct link between Unhappiness and pleasure and pain.

Acts and behaviors that maximize pleasure and minimize pain or the privation of pleasure for Self may result in temporary relief from Unhappiness. This is not because pleasure results in Happiness, but rather because it results in pleasure for Self. Pleasure results in good feelings for Self. Self feels good when acting and behaving to maximize benefit and minimize harm for Self. Self feels good when engaged in acts and behaviors that result in pleasure for Self.

But the effect of these acts and behaviors is temporary. It doesn't last. Because the good feelings are temporary, Self must repeat the acts or behaviors that result in pleasure for Self. Self may also add new acts and behaviors that result in pleasure for Self. New acts and behaviors that also offer only temporary relief from Unhappiness but cannot remove Unhappiness long-term. It cannot remove Unhappiness long-term because the path to Happiness is not through Self. Instead, the path to Happiness is through Others and the collective whole.

The path to Happiness is through acts and behaviors that maximize benefit and minimize harm for Others and the collective whole. The path to Happiness lies through acts and behaviors that preserve, protect, and promote the best interest, welfare, and good of Others and the collective whole. It lies through acts and behaviors that manifest nurturing and integrity. It lies through acts and behaviors that manifest the giving and sharing of the resources of Self to benefit Others and the collective whole. The path to Happiness and the removal of Unhappiness lies through these acts and behaviors, but not in them.

On the contrary, only self-satisfaction lies in acts and behaviors intended to maximize pleasure and minimize pain or the privation of pleasure for Self. By definition, self-satisfaction is a selfish, self-centered form of satisfaction. It is a selfish and self-centered illusion of satisfaction associated with the Unevolved Ethic. There may be temporary pleasure for Self in self-satisfaction, but there is not Happiness. There may be temporary removal of Unhappiness in self-satisfaction, but it will return when the short-term effect of pleasure wears off.

These comments concerning Happiness and Unhappiness are not intended to suggest that Self begin acting or behaving in a manner intended to result in Happiness for Self. These comments are not intended to suggest that Self begin acting or behaving to benefit Others and the collective whole in anticipation of finding Happiness for Self. Nor are these comments intended to suggest or infer that Self can even act with the intention of removing Unhappiness for Self. This inference or suggestion would be wrong, incorrect, and inappropriate. It would be incorrect since Self cannot act or behave in a manner intended to result in finding Happiness or removing Unhappiness for Self.

This is because patterns of acts or behaviors intended to benefit Self are guided and motivated by the Unevolved Ethic and the Unevolved Ethic is associated with pleasure and not Happiness. Therefore, acts and behaviors intended to result in Happiness or the removal of Unhappiness for Self could only result in temporary pleasure or the temporary removal of Unhappiness for Self. In fact, to act or behave with the intent to find Happiness or remove Unhappiness would be to confuse temporary pleasure with Happiness. In the longer term, Self will likely only find disappointment (pain) and frustration (more pain) if Self practices acts and behaviors in anticipation of finding Happiness.

The acts and behaviors that can result in Happiness are those performed without consideration or regard for Self. They are those acts and behaviors intended and performed to maximize benefit and minimize harm for Others and the collective whole. They are those acts and behaviors that manifest the willingness and ability to place the best interest, welfare, and good of Others and the collective whole above the interest, welfare, and good of Self. They are those acts and behaviors that require the willingness and ability to minimalize or ignore harm for Self. They are those acts that demonstrate the willingness and ability to transcend or rise above awareness or sentience of only Self. However, it is very important to be crystal clear at this point in the discussion of both Happiness and the Evolved Ethic.

Nothing in this discussion suggests or infers that it is right, correct, or appropriate for Self to give away all possessions and move into a cave. Nothing in this discussion suggests it is right, correct, or appropriate for Self to take a vow of poverty and don sackcloth. For most Selves, these actions would clearly constitute immoderate or extreme acts. Immoderate or extreme acts maximize benefit and minimize harm for Self. For many Selves these acts would more likely indicate the willingness to follow an impulse or urge. For some other Selves, these actions would likely indicate an emotional response. It was long ago established, in this text, that acts or behaviors based on impulses, urges, and emotions all serve only Self. Besides, it simply does not take absolute selflessness to benefit Others and the collective whole.

For instance, it does not take absolute selflessness to tutor, teach, mentor, or coach Others. It does not take absolute selflessness to freely give and share the knowledge, skills, talents, and abilities of Self. It does not take absolute selflessness to share the time and wisdom of Self freely. It does not take absolute selflessness to give respect and dignity to Others. It takes only the willingness and ability to do so without anticipation of reward for Self. It takes only the willingness and ability to do so without concern or regard for Self. It takes only the willingness and ability to consistently act and behave to maximize benefit and minimize harm for Others and the collective whole. It takes only the willingness and ability to consistently minimalize or ignore harm that results for Self when acting for the best interest, welfare, and good of Others and the collective whole.

If and when Self is both willing and able to consistently act and behave to maximize benefit and minimize harm for Others and the collective whole, then Self may experience the sense of satisfaction and contentment that is Happiness. Then Self may experience the sense of calmness, tranquility, and inner peace that is Happiness.

Unfortunately, for so many in today's world, even the very opportunity to act and behave to maximize benefit and minimize harm for Others is hindered or obstructed. This results in the privation of Happiness. The privation of Happiness occurs in situations or circumstances in which the ability of a Self to act or behave for the benefit of Others or the collective whole is hindered or obstructed by the acts or behaviors of a different Self or collective form of Self. As an example, the collective form or level of Self that hinders or obstructs could be a religious group or national government. This privation of Happiness does not result from the acts of Self. However, the privation of Happiness is harm to the Self who cannot act or behave to maximize benefit and minimize harm for Others and the collective whole. Therefore, the privation of Happiness for even one individual Self harms the best interest, welfare, and the good of the collective whole.

For instance, the enslavement of Others is an extreme example of an act or behavior that results in the privation of Happiness. A slave is not free to act or behave for the benefit of Others or the collective whole. A slave cannot act or behave to maximize benefit and minimize harm for Others and the collective whole. A slave is not free to give or share the resources of Self to maximize benefit for Others. They are not free to give or share their knowledge, skills, talents, or abilities for the benefit of Others or the collective whole. A slave is only able to do that which is necessary for the survival of Self.

As a second instance, the systematic denial of opportunity for a quality education also contributes to the privation of Happiness. The denial of opportunity for a quality education results in the privation of Happiness, regardless of the justifications, rationalizations, explanations or excuses for denying the opportunity. It limits the opportunity of those affected by the denial to grow and develop their knowledge, skills, talents, and abilities. It limits the opportunity to gain independence and the potential to contribute to the success of the collective whole. This is true the world over, including in the United States. It is true for every man, woman, and child who has been denied the opportunity for a quality education. The result of this denial is the privation of Happiness.

Yet, in both examples of acts and behaviors that result in the privation of Happiness, there is an individual Self or a collective form or level of Self who benefits from the privation of Happiness for Others. In both examples, there is an individual Self or a collective form or level of Self that is maximizing benefit and minimizing harm for Self. It is the Unevolved Ethic that guides the choices and motivates the acts and behaviors of these Selves or collective forms or levels of Self.

The privation of Happiness will continue, in one form or another, as long as there are those Selves who choose to act and behave in a manner resulting in the privation of Happiness for Others. The privation of Happiness will only end when the Evolved Ethic dominates in the world. Only then will each Self be free to act and behave for the best interest, welfare, and good of Others and the collective whole. Only when all Selves are free to act and behave to maximize benefit and minimize harm for Others will they be able to experience the satisfaction and contentment of Happiness.

At this point, the focus of the overall discussion has been to introduce the components of the two ethics and the overall ethics that result when the components are brought together. The pattern of acts and behaviors of every Self manifest, to some extent or degree, either the Unevolved Ethic or the Evolved Ethic. The same is true of the acts and behaviors of every collective form or level of Self and every form or level of collective whole. Finally, it was the purpose of these first five chapters to provide discussion of a wide range of acts and behaviors that manifest the two ethics. It was the purpose of these first chapters to provide a range of acts that manifest the two ethics at different levels of collective Self and the collective whole. However, there is so much more to come.

Future chapters pick up where these first five chapters leave off. For instance, the next chapter explores the connection between the two ethics and needs, wants, desires, cravings, and obsessions. It also explores the connection between the two ethics and physical, psychological, and spiritual well-being or wellness.

Other chapters explore the development of the two ethics. There is also an examination of both value and principle formation. In addition, that chapter also covers the three states of ethical development. Other future chapters examine the connection between the two ethics and relationships and the connection between the two ethics and leadership.

CHAPTER 6:
ETHICS, NEEDS, AND SPIRITUAL WELL-BEING

The purpose of this chapter is to discuss the connection between the two ethics and the acts and behaviors Self employs to meet or satisfy needs. More specifically, the discussion points to those needs Self can satisfy through acts and behaviors intended to benefit Self and those needs Self can only act or behave to help satisfy for Others. Through this discussion of needs, I will assert that there is a direct link or connection between ethics, needs, and spiritual well-being. I will also assert that there is a direct link or connection between ethics, needs, and spiritual illness. Finally, I will point to the relationship that exists between spiritual well-being and Happiness, as well as the relationship between spiritual illness and Unhappiness.

To frame this discussion, I am going to address six categories of needs. Five of these categories are the categories of needs identified by Abraham Maslow in his 1943 paper, *A Theory of Human Needs*.[5] The categories of needs identified by Maslow are physiological, safety/security, belonging (affiliation), esteem, and self-actualization. These five categories are usually depicted in the form of a pyramid, which is commonly referred to as Maslow's Hierarchy of Needs. However, to these five categories, I am going to add a sixth category of need, self-esteem (dignity).

These six categories of needs provide a means for ordering or aligning many of the acts and behaviors of Self and Others that might otherwise seem random and even chaotic. This alignment or ordering into the six categories of needs then offers insight into the intended beneficiary of acts and behaviors. It gives insight into who (Self) or whom (Others) benefits from acts and behaviors intended to satisfy needs.

Clearly, by adding the self-esteem (dignity) category to this discussion, I am moving away from strict adherence to Maslow's set of five categories of needs. However, I believe the difference between the esteem and self-esteem (dignity) categories is significant enough to warrant separate consideration of each. It is even interesting to note that, in his writings, Maslow also recognized the difference between esteem and dignity.

Maslow wrote,

The difference between the need for esteem (from others) and the need for self-esteem should be made very clear in the final write-up. Make the differentiation sharply, clearly, unmistakably. Reputations or prestige or applause are very nice, and are for children and adolescents even absolutely necessary before real self-esteem can be built up. Or to say it the other way about, one of the necessary foundations for self-esteem is respect and applause from other people, especially in the younger years. Ultimately, real self-esteem rests upon all the things mentioned above, on a feeling of dignity, of controlling one's own life, and of being one's own boss. (Let's call this "dignity.")[6]

By recognizing this significant difference in the need for esteem and the need for self-esteem (dignity), I can now discuss six categories of needs. Two of these categories, physiological and safety/security, relate primarily to the physical well-being of Self. The next two categories, belonging (affiliation) and esteem, relate primarily to the psychological well-being of Self. Through this discussion, I will assert that the final two categories of needs, self-esteem (dignity) and self-actualization, relate to the spiritual well-being of Self. For the sake of clarity, I do need to establish that spiritual well-being, as I am using the term, does not relate to a religious concept of spirit or religious spiritualism. Rather, my use of the term "spiritual well-being" is similar to my earlier use of the term "soul."

In the discussion of the Evolved Ethic, I used the term "soul" to describe the center or seat of the Evolved Ethic. However, I also indicated that I was not tying the term "soul" to the concept of an everlasting soul. The word "soul" simply provides the ability to describe a center or seat of the Evolved Ethic that is neither the heart nor the mind. In this usage, the soul becomes the seat or center of the "sense" of that which is right, correct, and appropriate.

In the same manner, this present discussion of spiritual well-being does not relate to a religious concept of an everlasting spiritual life after death or oneness with a god or gods. It also does not relate to belief in "spirits." Rather, my purpose is to discuss spiritual well-being, which is integral to the overall health and well-being of each Self. It is as integral to the overall health and well-being of Self as both physical and psychological well-being.

As this discussion progresses, I will assert that Self can and does act and behave to satisfy four of these need categories for Self. These are the physiological, safety/security, belonging (affiliation), and esteem needs. Because Self can and does act to satisfy these needs for Self, I will refer to these four needs as the lower-level needs. However, I will also assert that Self cannot act or behave to satisfy the remaining two needs: self-esteem and self-actualization, for Self. Instead, Self can only act or behave to help satisfy these final two needs for Others. Because Self can only help satisfy these two final needs for Others, I will refer to these two needs as higher-level needs. With that said, I can now begin exploring each of the six needs in the context of this discussion of the two ethics. I will start this discussion with the most fundamental category of needs. These are the physiological needs.

The physiological needs are the most fundamental to the survival and preservation of Self. As such, they tie very directly to the physical well-being of Self. Acts or behaviors associated with satisfying physiological needs are some of the very first human beings manifest as infants. For instance, the first behavior every infant manifests is breathing. Even the involuntary act of breathing manifests a physiological need, as breathing is critical to the survival of Self. Breathing is a self-preserving and self-promoting act that serves the interest, welfare, and good of Self. The second behavior infants often manifest is the crying behavior. Infants cry when they are hungry or thirsty. Infants cry when they are sick. Infants cry when they are startled or afraid. Crying is a behavior. It is the behavior available to an infant to attempt to satisfy the physiological need for nourishment. The body's need for nourishment, food, and water is also a physiological need tied very directly to the physical well-being of Self.

The body has a need not just for food and water but also essential nutrients. These include proteins, vitamins, enzymes, and minerals generally obtained through food. Without the right mix of essential nutrients, the body begins to break down; it becomes physically unhealthy. In the most extreme cases, malnutrition, disease, and death result. Therefore, meeting these most fundamental physiological needs at the minimum required level is necessary to maintain a healthy physical Self. Acts and behaviors associated with satisfying these needs at the minimum required level serve the best interest, welfare, and good of Self. There is even pleasure associated with satisfying these needs. It is pleasant to eat when hungry. It is pleasant to drink when thirsty. It is pleasant for Self to feel good physically. Certainly, there is pain or the privation of pleasure associated with the inability to satisfy these needs.

Unsatisfied needs are said to be deficient and emergent. When the physiological needs are deficient and emergent, Self will focus less effort on other categories of needs. This is particularly true if Self is starving or unable to obtain water or other suitable fluids and certainly true if Self cannot breathe. Generally speaking, only when the physiological needs are satisfied is Self likely to focus on deficient and emergent needs at other levels, such as the second category of need, the safety/security needs.

Safety/security refers to the need to be secure from harm or danger, whether predators, the elements (weather, etc.), or even other people represent that harm. This is still a very fundamental, lower-level need focused on the survival and preservation of Self. Like the physiological needs, safety/security needs primarily concern the physical health and well-being of Self. Acts and behaviors intended to satisfy safety/security needs are self-preserving, self-protecting, and self-promoting. Therefore, these acts and behaviors seek to maximize benefit and minimize harm for Self. There is pleasure in meeting the safety/security needs. It is pleasant for Self when these needs are met. It is unpleasant, even painful for Self when they are not. Like acts and behaviors intended to satisfy physiological needs, Self manifests acts and behaviors intended to satisfy safety/security needs very early in life.

For instance, an infant may manifest the crying behavior when frightened and cling to its mother or father for security. As Self grows older, Self will employ other acts and behaviors to meet this need. Self may make or obtain clothing to shield Self from the elements. Self may build a shelter or home. Self may rent or purchase a shelter or home. In the worst examples, Self might simply take the clothing, shelter, or home of Others. There is certainly evidence to suggest that our earliest ancestors fought over shelter, as well as sources of food and water. Even today, there is still competition over water, land, and shelter. Sometimes, these competitions are fought in the legal courts or the court of public opinion, but they are still fought in this country and around the globe.

It should come as no surprise that in each case, these competitions are between the best interest, welfare, and good of one Self or a collective form of Self and the best interest, welfare, and good of another Self or collective form of Self. These competitions involve the survival, preservation, and promotion of Self or a collective Self. As with any competition, "I,"

"Me" wins or "I," "Me" loses. Because these competitions center on the two lowest-level needs, the physical well-being, maybe even the very survival, of Self or a collective form of Self may be at stake. As with any instance of competition, it is pleasant for "I," "Me" to win and unpleasant for "I," "Me" to lose. There is pleasure for Self in winning and pain or the privation of pleasure for Self in losing. Similarly, it is pleasant for Self to satisfy deficient and emergent needs and unpleasant for Self when needs remain unsatisfied. This is true of both the physiological and safety/security needs as well as the next need category, the belonging (affiliation) need.

The belonging (affiliation) need is the first of the two need categories tied to the psychological well-being of Self. This category describes the need for affiliation and association with other human beings. It describes the need to belong, the need for acceptance, and the need for companionship and friendship. It even includes the need for love. However, this is not the higher Love identified as one of the two enabling virtues. Rather, this is the lower form of love or emotional love associated with the acceptance and companionship of another human being or human beings. Self seeks to satisfy the belonging (affiliation) needs through acts and behaviors that result in association and affiliation with other people.

For example, as a small child, Self satisfies this category of need through companionship within the immediate family. In situations where a child has no family, the child may attempt to satisfy the need through companionship and friendship with surrogates. Later, Self may seek to satisfy this need through the more extended family, as well as friends, classmates, colleagues, co-workers, and significant others. Self may seek to satisfy this need through membership in churches, clubs, and civic organizations, as well as neighborhoods and communities. In many instances, Self may seek to satisfy this need through substitutes such as pets.

Satisfying this need to belong and affiliate is essential to the psychological health and well-being of Self. However, it is important to note that while satisfying this need involves association with and acceptance by Others, this is still a very self-interested need. To satisfy deficient and emergent belonging (affiliation) needs, Self can and will demonstrate a wide range of observable acts and behaviors.

The purpose of these acts and behaviors is to satisfy the belonging (affiliation) need for Self. Concern for Self and not concern for Others motivates acts and behaviors intended to satisfy these needs. The intended beneficiary of acts or behaviors demonstrated to satisfy belonging (affiliation) needs is Self. It is the psychological well-being of Self that primarily benefits from acts or behaviors that successfully satisfy these needs. Therefore, acts and behaviors associated with satisfying belonging (affiliation) needs maximize benefit and minimize harm for Self.

Self does not demonstrate behaviors associated with belonging (affiliation) needs to satisfy the belonging (affiliation) needs of Others. Others may benefit from acts intended to satisfy belonging (affiliation) needs for Self, but that benefit is secondary to the intended benefit for Self. It is an incidental by-product of an act or behavior intended to benefit Self, first and foremost. Therefore, acts and behaviors associated with satisfying belonging (affiliation) needs are centered on Self. This is clearly evident through a brief examination of loneliness.

Loneliness is what Self feels when the belonging (affiliation) need is deficient and emergent. Self feels loneliness. Self feels lonely, and feelings are always tied to Self. Loneliness does not feel good. Loneliness is indeed pain or the privation of pleasure for Self. Self will attempt to remove the pain through acts and behaviors intended to satisfy the deficient and emergent belonging (affiliation) need. Satisfying the need is pleasant for Self. There is a "feel good" for Self in removing the feeling of loneliness.

In their extreme forms, loneliness and isolation can and may lead to illogical, extreme, and sometimes even aberrant acts or behaviors intended to remove feelings of loneliness. The deeper the loneliness or isolation, the stronger the emergent need becomes and the more extreme resulting acts and behaviors may become, all with the intent of relieving the pain for Self.

As such, even these extreme acts or behaviors intend to maximize benefit and minimize harm for Self. This is regardless of how illogical or extreme the acts or behaviors may appear. Self then minimalizes or ignores any harm that results for Others or the collective whole in the interest, welfare, and good of Self. This same willingness and ability to maximize benefit and minimize harm for Self and minimalize or ignore harm for Others can be found through examination of the esteem needs.

The esteem needs are the second category of need associated with the psychological well-being of Self. These are the needs Maslow referred to when he wrote, "Reputations or prestige or applause are very nice, and are for children and adolescents even absolutely necessary before real self-esteem can be built up."[7] These esteem needs are tied to the approval of Self by those who comprise a collective whole. As such, these needs concern the standing of Self within a collective whole. This collective whole can be a family, a community, a team, an organization, or any other collective whole. To be in good standing within the collective whole serves the best interest, welfare, and good of Self.

There is a good feeling for Self in the approval of those Selves who comprise various levels of the collective whole. It is psychologically pleasant for Self to be in good standing within the collective whole. Conversely, it is psychologically unpleasant when Self is not in good standing within the collective whole. There is pain for Self in the disapproval or condemnation of the collective whole. Therefore, the esteem needs are tied very closely to the psychological health and well-being of Self. This is especially true if disapproval or condemnation of the collective whole impairs the ability of Self to meet or satisfy the other lower-level needs.

To gain the approval of Others and the collective whole, Self will generally act and behave in a manner that gains the approval and avoids the disapproval of Others and the collective whole. The approval of Others and the collective whole is a reward for Self. It is the sought-after reward for acting and behaving in a manner intended to benefit Self. Therefore, these acts and behaviors also maximize benefit and minimize harm for Self.

Since the esteem category concerns the approval and standing of Self within a collective whole, these needs are easily associated with concern for the position of Self in a group, an organization, or a community. They are associated easily with the need for recognition, praise, admiration, or even adulation from Others who comprise the group, organization, community, or any other example of a collective whole. In addition, these needs associate well with concern for the status, position, power, wealth, and possessions of Self. Further, they associate with concern for reputation, fame, and prestige for Self. Finally, esteem is tied very directly to self-respect and self-worth.

Self-respect and self-worth are both tied to self-image and self-concept. Both self-respect and self-worth are, therefore, tied to regard or concern for Self. The higher the regard or concern Self has for Self, the greater the respect and worth Self will assign to Self. By extension, Self will often assign greater respect and worth to the tangible and intangible resources of Self. These include the time, effort, knowledge, skills, talents, and abilities of Self. Self will also assign greater respect and worth to the beliefs, attitudes, and opinions of Self. At the same time, Self may assign less respect and worth to Others. Self may assign less respect and worth to the tangible and intangible resources of Others. Self will also assign less respect and worth to the beliefs, attitudes, and opinions of Others. Often, the greater the respect and worth Self assigns to Self, the more likely Self is to value Self over Others and the collective whole.

The result is that, to some degree or extent, Self will often manifest acts and behaviors that disrespect or disparage Others or the tangible and intangible resources of Others in some manner or another. When Self acts or behaves in a manner that disrespects or disparages any of these tangible or intangible possessions of Others, Self maximizes benefit and minimizes harm for Self and harms Others and the collective whole. Acts or behaviors that disrespect or disparage Others or the tangible and intangible resources of Others result in harm for both Others and the collective whole. This harm is pain for Others.

Similarly, acts and behaviors that disrespect or disparage the beliefs, attitudes, and opinions of Others also result in pain for Others. However, far worse, acts and behaviors that disrespect and disparage Others or the resources of Others can and do result in the many broader harms for Others and the collective whole. Yet Self often fails to consider these harms to Others and the collective whole. Instead, Self acts to maximize benefit and minimize harm for Self and minimalizes or ignores any resulting pain to Others or the collective whole.

It is also the case that in many of these situations and circumstances, the harm takes the form of hurt pride for Others. This pride is the lower-order or self-pride associated with the esteem need.

Like self-respect and self-worth, lower-order or self-pride is also associated with self-image and self-concept. It is the pride associated with the physical appearance of Self. It is the pride associated with the achievements and accomplishments of Self. Further, it is the pride associated with the tangible and intangible possessions of Self. For instance, it is the pride attached to the material objects of Self, including homes, vehicles, technology, clothes, and other possessions. However, it also the pride attached to the knowledge, skills, abilities, and talents of Self. Finally, it is the pride Self may associate with the race, ethnicity, nationality, and even religion of Self. This lower-order or self-pride is associated with many of the choices of Self and these choices are also related to the esteem need.

For instance, lower-order or self-pride is often associated with the choice of clubs, teams, churches, and community groups Self joins. It is associated with the choice to join a popular clique. Often, the more exclusive the club, clique, team, church, or community group, the more esteem or lower-level pride Self may associate with membership. Cliques, in particular, are always exclusive and always associated with status, position, reputation, and prestige. Membership in a popular, exclusive club, clique, team, church, or community group can and does result in pleasure for Self.

Conversely, there is pain or the privation of pleasure when Self is excluded from a club, clique, team, church, or community group. Indeed, exclusion from clubs, cliques, teams, churches, or community groups, regardless of the basis for exclusion, often results in pain for those excluded. It results in hurt feelings and hurt lower-order or self-pride. However, in each case, the exclusion of Others maximizes benefit and minimizes harm for the Self or collective form of Self that excludes.

However, it is also this self-pride that often manifests itself in prideful or boastful acts or behaviors. Likewise, it may also manifest itself in more extreme acts and behaviors termed self-glorifying and self-aggrandizing. It may manifest in acts and behaviors termed self-important and self-righteous, as well as those that manifest feelings of superiority. Similarly, this self-pride can result in acts or behaviors that suggest Self values material possessions and wealth over people. It can result in acts or behaviors that manifest the willingness and ability to judge Others on the basis of their possessions or lack of possessions. It can result in acts or behaviors that manifest the willingness and ability to judge Others on the basis of their economic standing within a collective whole or on the basis of race, ethnicity, nationality, and religion.

In each instance, these judgments are very subjective. However, there is self-satisfaction that accompanies these subjective judgments concerning Others. There is a "feel good" for Self that accompanies these judgments. Further, there is self-satisfaction and a "feel good" for Self in acts and behaviors that manifest these judgments. Therefore, acts and behaviors that manifest these judgments do maximize benefit and minimize harm for Self. Yet each also results in harm for Others and the collective whole.

These harms clearly include pain for Others in the form of hurt pride. Just as clearly, these harms can and do negatively impact the esteem needs of Others. However, acts and behaviors that manifest these judgments also result in the same broader harms mentioned elsewhere. These are the building of jealousy, envy, greed, and avarice. Further, these harms can and do result in grudges, vendettas, and, unfortunately, even honor killings. In each case, these harms all build discord and disharmony within the collective whole.

However, because lower-order or self-pride is tied to the esteem need, there must be a correspondingly healthy level of self-pride that is essential to the psychological well-being of Self. If a healthy self-image and self-concept are essential to a healthy psychological Self, then there must be a healthy level of self-pride. Yet, even at this psychologically healthy level, lower-level pride is and always will focus on Self. It will always be tied to the esteem needs of Self. Therefore, acts and behaviors that manifest even a healthy level of lower-level or self-pride help satisfy the esteem needs of Self.

On the other hand, I associate higher-order pride with acts and behaviors that maximize benefit and minimize harm for Others and the collective whole. Higher-order pride results from acts or behaviors that benefit the interest, welfare, or good of Others and the collective whole. This higher-order pride is the pride I associate with the higher-level needs of self-esteem (dignity) and self-actualization. However, before discussing these two needs, I first want to recognize a very important point in this discussion of needs and ethics. It is an important point since this discussion of needs has reached the Point of Transcendence.

The discussion has reached the point at which Self cannot act or behave to satisfy the needs of Self. It is the point at which Self can no longer act with the intention of satisfying the needs of Self. Self can and does act and behave to satisfy the four lower-level needs of Self. However, Self can only act to help satisfy the two higher-level needs for Others. To consistently help satisfy these two needs for Others requires that Self be both willing and able to act or behave for the benefit of Others. But the willingness and ability to consistently act and behave for the interest, welfare, and good of Others is only associated with the Evolved Ethic. Therefore, in terms of the theory of two ethics, this discussion of ethics and needs has reached the Point of Transcendence (PoT).

The Unevolved Ethic cannot and will not consistently guide or motivate acts and behaviors that help Others satisfy these two needs. Indeed, it is far more likely that the Unevolved Ethic will guide and motivate Self to attempt to satisfy these two needs for Self. It will guide and motivate acts and behaviors intended to maximize benefit and minimize harm for Self. It will guide and motivate acts that focus on the four needs Self can satisfy for Self. It may even guide and motivate acts and behaviors that result in excess satisfaction of the four lower-level needs. However, guiding and motivating more acts and behaviors that focus on the lower-level needs, including the esteem need, cannot and does not satisfy either the self-esteem (dignity) or self-actualization needs.

The self-esteem (dignity) need is the need to be recognized, respected, and valued as a human being. It is the need to have the resources of Self, such as time and effort, recognized and respected as having worth and value. It is the need to have the knowledge, skills, talents, and abilities of Self recognized and respected as having worth and value. It is the need for dignity, respect, worth, and value that all human beings require, but it can only be satisfied through the acts and behaviors of Others. Self simply cannot satisfy this need for Self. Yet, there are many examples of simple acts or behaviors Self can manifest to help Others satisfy the self-esteem (dignity) need.

For instance, the simple greeting of Others and sharing a smile with Others helps satisfy this need. Similarly, sharing a kind word or exchanging pleasantries with Others helps to satisfy this need for Others. These acts recognize and value Others as human beings. These acts and behaviors give value, worth, and respect to Others. These acts and behaviors speak to the dignity of Others. The same is the case for all forms of courtesy and politeness. By giving value, worth, and respect, Self gives dignity to Others.

Self dignifies the humanity of Others. When Self is consistently willing and able to give value, respect, worth, and dignity to Others, Self is helping to satisfy the need for self-esteem (dignity) for Others.

A further example of a behavior that gives respect, value, and worth to Others is to listen when they speak. Self gives value, worth, and respect to Others when Self listens, not just hears, but listens to them. Listening dignifies Others as human beings. This includes listening to their beliefs, attitudes, and opinions. Hearing, but not listening, serves only the interest, welfare, or good of Self. Hearing but not listening disregards and disrespects Others. It denies respect, value, and worth. It denies dignity. Hearing but not listening is a behavior that maximizes benefit and minimizes harm only for the Self who fails to listen. It demonstrates valuing Self and the beliefs, attitudes, and opinions of Self over Others, and it results in harm for Others.

Another very important set of acts or behaviors that help to satisfy the self-esteem (dignity) need for Others is those acts and behaviors that involve freely giving and sharing the knowledge, skills, talents, and abilities of Self to help Others grow and develop. As growth and development occur, Others learn new methods or approaches to meeting the four lower-level needs. The result is greater independence, self-assurance, self-reliance, and self-sufficiency. When Self helps Others increase their independence, self-assurance, self-reliance, and self-sufficiency, Self helps them meet the need for self-esteem (dignity). There is no dignity in reliance or dependence on Others to meet the lower-level needs.

Similarly, increased confidence, competence, mastery, proficiency, and even freedom are tied to the self-esteem (dignity) need. There is dignity in increased confidence and competence. There is dignity in skill mastery and proficiency. There is dignity in freedom. Therefore, acts and behaviors that increase the confidence, competence, mastery, proficiency, and freedom of Others recognize the inherent value and worth of Others as human beings. These acts and behaviors give respect and dignity to Others as human beings. They enable Others to be their own boss and control their own life. This is the self-esteem (dignity) need as described by Maslow.[8]

It is through acts and behaviors that help Others grow and develop, to become more independent, self-assured, self-reliant, and self-sufficient that Self demonstrates nurturing acts and behaviors. It is through these acts and behaviors that Self manifests caring, helping, sharing, giving, and loving acts and behaviors associated with the Evolved Ethic. It is also through these acts and behaviors that Self may experience higher-order pride.

Higher-order pride is the pride associated with the growth and development of Others. It is associated with the accomplishments and achievements of Others. It is the pride associated with contributing to the interest, welfare, and good of Others and the collective whole. It is associated with an effort or cause that is greater than Self, a cause or effort that transcends the benefit, welfare, and good of only Self. Higher-order pride is associated with an effort or cause that carries primary benefit for Others and the collective whole. Therefore, it is the pride associated with the two highest-level needs of self-esteem (dignity) and Self-actualization.

On the contrary, there is no higher-order pride associated with acts and behaviors intended to maximize benefit and minimize harm for Self. There is only lower-order pride associated with these acts and behaviors. Similarly, there is little or no respect, value, or worth given in these acts or behaviors. These acts and behaviors may carry secondary benefit for Others, but the primary beneficiary is still Self. In many instances, Others simply become the means by which Self is able to satisfy the lower-level needs of Self. However, the use of Others as a means to satisfy the lower-level needs of Self is consistent only with the Unevolved Ethic.

Self recognizes the dignity, value and worth of Others to the extent or degree Self is willing and able to unselfishly help Others grow and develop, to become self-sufficient and independent. Therefore, these acts and behaviors do help Others satisfy the self-esteem (dignity) need. Further, these unselfish acts and behaviors do build community and reduce competition within the collective whole. These are the longer-range benefits that accrue and compound when Self is willing and able to act and behave for the interest, welfare, and good of Others and the collective whole. These same benefits accrue when Self is willing and able to help satisfy the final need for Others, the self-actualization need.

The self-actualization need is often described as the need to reach our highest potential, the need for each Self to reach his or her highest potential as a human being. It is the need to reach fulfillment as an individual, to find purpose and meaning. Words associated with the self-actualization need can include words like compassion, empathy, kindness, accepting, objective, realistic, and creative. For instance, Maslow listed the following characteristics of those he believed to have self-actualized:

> A clearer, more efficient perception of reality.
>
> More openness to experience.
>
> Increased integration, wholeness, and unity of the person.
>
> Increased spontaneity, expressiveness; full functioning; aliveness
>
> A real self; a firm identity; autonomy; uniqueness.
>
> Increased objectivity, detachment, transcendence of self.
>
> Recovery of creativeness.
>
> Ability to fuse concreteness and abstractness, primary and secondary process cognition, etc.
>
> Democratic character structure.
>
> Ability to love, etc.[9]

When the self-actualization need is emergent, Self will experience the same sense of void or emptiness and the same sense that something is missing that I have already associated with Unhappiness. It will result in the same sense of dissatisfaction and discontentment associated with unhappiness. It is characterized by the same lack of inner peace, tranquility, and calmness associated with Unhappiness. In short, Unhappiness is essentially the deficient and emergent self-actualization need. Much as was said earlier concerning Unhappiness, when the self-actualization need is emergent, Self may attempt to satisfy this need for Self. However, Self will be unable to do so. Self can only satisfy the self-actualization need through acts and behaviors that serve the best interest and good of Others and the collective whole.

By helping Others satisfy the self-esteem (dignity) need, Self helps position Others to be better able to satisfy the four lower-level needs by themselves. Through teaching, coaching, and mentoring Others, Self is also teaching, coaching, and mentoring the willingness and ability to act and behave for the benefit of Others and the collective whole. Self is now teaching, coaching, mentoring, and modeling the willingness and ability to maximize benefit and minimize harm for Others and the collective whole. Through this teaching, coaching, mentoring, and modeling, Self may help Others make the evolutionary break with concern and regard for the best interest, welfare, and good of only Self. By modeling concern and regard for the best interest, welfare, and good of Others and the collective whole, Self may help position Others to transcend the selfish, self-centered regard and concern for only Self.

But, as with the discussion of Happiness, Self cannot deliberately set out to satisfy the self-actualization need for Self. Any attempt to do so will likely end in frustration since the path to self-actualization is through Others. It is through those acts and behaviors intended to help Others satisfy the lower-level needs and the self-esteem (dignity) need. Attempts to satisfy the self-actualization need for Self will likely only result in excess at the lower-level needs for Self. But again, just as with the discussion of Unhappiness, excess at the lower-level needs does not satisfy the higher-level need. It may temporarily mask or cover the emergent self-actualization need, but will not satisfy it. Satisfaction can only come through those acts and behavior intended to benefit Others and the collective whole.

It is indeed possible, that through acts and behaviors that help Others satisfy the need for self-esteem (dignity), Self will both self-actualize and find the contentment and satisfaction that is Happiness. Further, by helping position Others to satisfy the self-esteem (dignity) need, Self may start a chain reaction; a chain reaction in which each Self in the chain is better able to satisfy the lower-level needs of Self, along with the self-esteem (dignity) need and is, therefore, better able to help still Others learn to satisfy the lower-level needs and the need for Self-esteem (dignity).

Each Self in the chain is now more capable of minimalizing or ignoring harm for Self in favor of benefit for Others and the collective whole. It is a chain reaction that offers the possibility for exponential growth in the number of Selves both willing and able to act for the benefit of Others and the collective whole. A chain reaction in which each Self is willing and able to transcend Self in favor of the interest, welfare, and good of Others and the collective whole. However, this chain reaction will only occur through those who are willing and able to consistently act and behave to maximize benefit and minimize harm for Others and the collective whole. The chain reaction stops when those Others are unwilling or unable to transcend the interest and good of Self in favor of the interest and good of still Others and the collective whole. It stops when those Others who have benefitted from the teaching, coaching, mentoring, and modeling are unable to do so for the benefit of still Others.

It is through the transcendence of Self in the interest and to the benefit of Others and the collective whole that this chain reaction begins. It is also through this teaching, coaching, mentoring and modeling of Others that Self demonstrates the characteristics Maslow associated with the self-actualization need.

Maslow wrote,

> If the various extent religions may be taken as expressions of human aspiration, i.e., what people would become if only they could, then we can see here too a validation of the affirmation that all people yearn toward self-actualization or tend toward it. This is so because our description of the actual characteristics

of self-actualizing people parallels at many points the ideals urged by the religions, e.g., the transcendence of self, the fusion of the true, the good, and the beautiful, contribution to others, wisdom, honesty and naturalness, the transcendence of selfish and personal motivations, the giving up of "lower" desires in favor of "higher" ones, the easy differentiation between ends (tranquility, serenity, peace) and means (money, power, status), the decrease of hostility, cruelty, and destructiveness and the increase of friendliness, gentleness, and kindness, etc.[10]

Clearly, I have already associated many of the characteristics mentioned by Maslow with both the Evolved Ethic and Happiness. For instance, I associated objectivity, as well as objective reality, with the Evolved Ethic. I associated both detachment and transcendence of Self, as well as the transcendence of selfish and personal motivations, with the Evolved Ethic. I have also associated contribution to the interest, welfare, and good of Others with the Evolved Ethic. Still further, I associated both democratic character and the ability to unconditionally Love Others with the Evolved Ethic. Democratic character structure refers to a greater acceptance of Others, without regard for differences. Finally, I associated tranquility, serenity, and peace with Happiness and Happiness with the Evolved Ethic.

This list of characteristics and Maslow's comments suggest a wholeness or completeness as a human being. It suggests a wholeness or completeness consistent with the highest potential, purpose, or function of a human being. I will assert that the highest potential, purpose, or function of any human being is to serve the best interest, welfare, and good of Others and the collective whole. But meeting this highest potential requires the willingness and ability to maximize benefit and minimize harm for Others and the collective whole. Further, it requires the willingness and ability to minimalize or ignore harm that results for Self.

These last comments infer that a relationship exists between the self-actualization need and the Evolved Ethic. It infers a relationship very similar to the relationship that exists between Happiness and the Evolved Ethic. This is the case.

It is perhaps interesting to note that Maslow himself associated words like happiness, serenity, calmness, and responsibility, to the self-actualization need. In one of his essays, he wrote, "These are the feelings of zest in living, of happiness or euphoria, of serenity, of joy, of calmness, of responsibility, of confidence in one's ability to handle stresses, anxieties, and problems." [11] At another point in the same essay, Maslow wrote, "The subjective signs of self-betrayal, of fixation, of regression, and of living by fear rather than by growth are such feelings as anxiety, despair, boredom, inability to enjoy, intrinsic guilt, intrinsic shame, aimlessness, feelings of emptiness, of lack of identity, etc."[12]

Despite the inclusion of terms associated with emotions, it is easy to suggest an association between the former comments with the previous discussion of Happiness and the latter comments with the previous discussion of Unhappiness. A lack of calmness, serenity, and inner peace characterizes Unhappiness. It is the sense of a void or emptiness that longs to be filled.

Only the Evolved Ethic consistently guides and motivates acts and behaviors that model the willingness and ability to maximize benefit and minimize harm for Others and the collective whole. Only the Evolved Ethic guides and motivates acts and behavior that consistently place the interest, welfare, and good of Others above the interest, welfare, and good of Self. Only the Evolved Ethic enables and encourages the willingness and ability to consistently minimalize or ignore resulting harm for Self. Therefore, it is only the Evolved Ethic that consistently guides and motivates acts and behaviors that help satisfy the two highest-level needs for Others. Only the Evolved Ethic guides and motivates the willingness and ability to consistently transcend the interest, welfare, and good of Self in the interest, welfare, and good of Others.

The Unevolved Ethic may guide and motivate Self to speak the right words or express the right sentiments, but in the end, acts and behaviors will manifest concern or regard for Self and the best interest, welfare, and good of Self. It may guide and motivate Self to extol the right virtues and condemn the right vices, but it can only motivate acts and behaviors that fail to walk the talk and practice what is preached. In the end, the example set will be hypocritical and consistent only with the Unevolved Ethic. In the end, Self will not be willing or able to help satisfy the two higher-level needs for Others. However, Self will likely experience the spiritual illness that accompanies the moral hypocrisy of the Unevolved Ethic and the inability to reach the highest potential as a human being.

By these last comments, I am suggesting a very direct tie between spiritual well-being and satisfaction of the two higher-level needs. However, the tie is not to the satisfaction of the two highest-level needs for Self. Rather, it is tied to acts and behaviors that help satisfy these two needs for Others. Therefore, spiritual well-being is tied to completeness and wholeness as a human being. It is tied to the fulfillment of the highest potential, purpose, or function of each Self. However, it is also tied to the same calmness, serenity, and inner peace associated with Happiness. A spiritually healthy Self is at peace with Self, Others, and the collective whole.

This spiritual well-being is just as integral to the overall health and well-being of Self as are physical and psychological well-being. Indeed, the very notion of completeness or wholeness as a human being infers a physically, psychologically, and spiritually healthy Self.

By contrast, if Self cannot find meaning and purpose that transcends mere Self, then Self will only experience a lack of spiritual well-being or spiritual illness. If Self cannot find meaning and purpose that transcends Self, it follows that only a lack of fulfillment, completeness, or wholeness as a human being result. With this lack of fulfillment, Self will experience the emptiness or void which marks both spiritual illness and Unhappiness. Self will experience the lack of calmness, tranquility, and inner peace that marks both spiritual illness and Unhappiness. To alleviate the spiritual illness and Unhappiness, Self may focus on pleasure associated with the four lower-level needs. However, this focus on pleasure and the four lower-level needs does not result in either spiritual well-being or Happiness.

Indeed, neither spiritual well-being nor Happiness comes through acts and behaviors that focus on the four lower-level needs. Neither spiritual well-being nor Happiness comes through the acquisition of tangible or intangible possessions. It cannot come through bigger or more expensive houses, automobiles, technology, or any other object Self might possess. Attempts to acquire or buy spiritual well-being or Happiness are akin to the search for the mythical Holy Grail. Self can spend a lifetime acquiring possessions in search of the one possession that results in spiritual well-being and Happiness. Self can fill a basement, attic, garage and one or more storage units with possessions, but never find that one possession that truly brings the satisfaction, contentment, inner calm, and peace of spiritual well-being and Happiness, because that one possession does not exist.

Similarly, spiritual well-being or Happiness cannot come through the acquisition of intangible possessions, such as new knowledge or skills, for Self. New knowledge or skills may enhance the ability of Self to meet or exceed the four lower-level needs. New knowledge or skills may enhance the ability of Self to acquire more and greater tangible possessions. However, the acquisition of new knowledge and skills for Self cannot, by themselves, bring satisfaction, contentment, inner calm, and peace of spiritual well-being and Happiness. So long as Self utilizes the new knowledge or skills only to maximize benefit and minimize harm for Self, Self will know only the discontentment, dissatisfaction, and lack of inner peace that is spiritual illness and Unhappiness, the unsatisfied self-actualization need. Likewise, spiritual well-being and Happiness do not come through the tangible or intangible trappings of esteem.

Self cannot find Happiness or spiritual well-being through status, prestige, fame, position, or power. Quite the opposite is true. Self may spend a lifetime in the relentless pursuit of status, prestige, reputation, fame, position, and power. Self may lie, cheat, deceive, and steal in order to gain these trappings for Self. Self may seek every advantage for Self through acts and behaviors intended to gain status, prestige, reputation, fame, position, and power in the belief that Happiness and spiritual well-being lie in these trappings of esteem. They are not and cannot ever be.

At best, acquiring more of the trappings of esteem provides only temporary relief from Unhappiness and spiritual illness. It provides only temporary relief from the emergent self-actualization need. They provide only a distraction from the Unhappiness and spiritual illness that accompanies acts and behaviors that consistently maximize benefit and minimize harm for Self. However, attempts to alleviate Unhappiness and spiritual illness by focusing on pleasure do offer insight into the subject of wants, desires, cravings, and obsessions associated with the four lower-level needs. These wants, desires, cravings, and obsessions are the next subject of this discussion of needs and the two ethics.

Said as simply as possible, that which is excess to adequately satisfy a need is a want. That which is excess to maintaining a healthy physical and psychological Self is a want. A want is not a need. Wants always exceed needs. Wants can grow from the inability of Self to satisfy a deficient and emergent need. However, wants can and do grow even in situations where Self can adequately satisfy needs. This is the case since there is pleasure for Self in exceeding need at the level required to maintain a physically and psychologically healthy Self. There is pleasure for Self in excess. Therefore, acts and behaviors intended to satisfy a want maximize benefit for Self.

On the other hand, unfulfilled or unsatisfied wants may result in pain or the privation of pleasure for Self. As a result of this pain or privation of pleasure, unfulfilled or unsatisfied wants may become desires. Going further, unfulfilled or unsatisfied desires may become cravings. Self may desire and crave that which Self wants but does not need. Self may even desire and crave that which Self cannot or should not have. Completing this progression, an unfulfilled craving may become an obsession.

At each progression from want to obsession, Self is the beneficiary of any act or behavior associated with attempts to satisfy the wants, desires, cravings, or obsessions of Self. Acts and behaviors intended to satisfy a want, desire, craving, or obsession always maximize benefit (pleasure) and minimize harm (pain or the privation of pleasure) for Self. Self will then minimalize or ignore any harm that results for Others or the collective whole.

As an example, when discussing physiological needs, I indicated that each Self needs an appropriate amount of food and nourishment to maintain a healthy physical Self. However, Self often wants more food and nourishment than the amount necessary to maintain a healthy physical Self. Self may want well beyond the amount necessary to adequately satisfy the need. Self may want to the point of gluttony and obesity. If this want is unfulfilled, Self may begin to desire or crave more than the amount of food or nourishment necessary to adequately satisfy the need. If the desire or craving remains unfulfilled, Self may even obsess over the unfulfilled desire or craving for more. This is similar with the safety/security need.

For instance, there is a level of shelter that adequately satisfies the need to feel safe and secure from predators, the elements, and even other people. However, Self may well want, desire, crave, and obsess over far more shelter than is necessary to maintain a healthy physical Self. Self may well want, desire, crave, and obsess over bigger, better, newer, or more extravagant shelter for Self. These wants, desires, cravings, and obsessions are excessive in terms of adequately satisfying safety/security needs. However, the want, desire, craving, or obsession with bigger, better, newer, or more extravagant shelter may also be tied to the lower-level esteem need and self-pride.

There is often status and prestige attached to the shelter of Self. There is status and prestige attached to the location of that shelter. Some locations are more desirable, and some are less desirable. There is status and prestige attached to both the size and construction of that shelter. Status and prestige are tied to both the lower-level esteem need and self-pride. The stronger the want, desire, or craving, regardless of whether this want, desire, or craving is attached to the safety/security need or the esteem need and self-pride, the more likely Self will pursue that excess for Self. This last example suggests that Self can want, desire, crave, and obsess over more than is necessary to satisfy either of the two psychological needs. Similarly, Self can want, desire, crave, and obsess over more belonging (affiliation) or esteem than is required to maintain a healthy psychological Self.

For instance, Self can want more acceptance and approval in the form of more applause, attention, acclaim, fame, reputation, prestige, or even power. More of each of these trappings of esteem does carry a "feel good" for Self. Similarly, more recognition, plaques, and certificates citing the achievements and accomplishments of Self also carry a "feel good" for Self. If a want for more acceptance and approval for Self remains unfulfilled, it can and often does become a desire, craving or obsession. To satisfy these wants, desires, cravings, and obsessions, Self may exhibit a variety of acts and behaviors without regard or concern for harm done to Others or the collective whole. Indeed, these acts and behaviors can result in both physical and/or psychological harm to Others. These harms are pain for Others. They are pain for Others that Self minimalizes or ignores in the pursuit of more pleasure for Self.

However, wants, desires, cravings and obsessions for more than is necessary to maintain a psychologically healthy Self can and do reach the point of being unhealthy for Self. Further, these wants, desires, cravings, and obsessions may and sometimes do lead to unusual, extreme, and aberrant, even deviant acts and behaviors. Each of these acts and behaviors can certainly become very harmful for Self, Others, and the collective whole.

On the contrary, acts and behaviors that satisfy needs and not wants, desires, cravings, or obsessions are in the best interest of the collective whole. Acts and behaviors that satisfy needs within the six needs catego-ries result in physical, psychological, and spiritual well-being. A physically, psychologically, and spiritually healthy Self serves the best interest, welfare, and good of the collective whole at all levels. Fortunately, Self cannot want, desire, crave, or obsess over more of the two higher-level needs than is necessary to satisfy these needs adequately. However, when the two high-er-level needs are deficient and emergent, Self may well try to satisfy these needs through wants, desires, cravings, and obsessions associated with the four lower-level needs.

Unfortunately, the more Self wants, desires, craves, and obsesses, the more Self is likely to accept these wants, desires, cravings, and obsessions as necessary or required to satisfy needs. Self begins to believe and accept that Self must have more for Self. Self begins to rationalize, justify, explain, and excuse the wants, desires, cravings, and obsessions of Self. In time, excess for Self becomes acceptable, even sought after. Wants become accepted as needs, and even the range of acts and behaviors associated with satisfy-ing wants, desires, cravings, and obsessions of Self becomes more accept-able. Acts and behaviors previously viewed as excessive, even gluttonous and avaricious acts become acceptable. Over time, acts and behaviors previously viewed as wrong, incorrect, or inappropriate become accept-able. However, as is always the case, acceptable behaviors reside within the grey area between right and wrong, correct and incorrect, and appro-priate and inappropriate. Black and white becomes grey and the result is moral hypocrisy.

However, no individual Self is alone in the effort to turn wants, desires, cravings, and obsessions into needs. Self receives a great deal of assistance in the form of commercial advertising. Each Self is constantly subjected to enormous amounts of commercial advertising intended to create a felt want for more. Indeed, the vast majority of commercial advertising intends to create a felt want, desire, craving, and obsession for more, bigger, better, newer, or more extravagant than is necessary to adequately satisfy needs at the minimum level necessary to be physically and psychologically healthy.

Virtually the entire spectrum of needs is preyed upon by commercial advertisers. There is advertising which preys on physiological needs and safety/security needs. There is advertising which preys on belonging (affiliation) and the lower-level esteem needs. Indeed, there is an enormous amount of advertising that preys on the lower-level esteem need and lower-order pride. However, there is also advertising which preys on the higher-level needs. Interestingly, this advertising usually suggests the ability to satisfy higher-level needs through material possessions. There is even advertising that suggests Happiness lies in more or excess for Self, including material possessions. Of course, this cannot be the case since Happiness does not lie in more for Self, nor does it lie within material possessions. Only pleasure lies in more or excess for Self. Only pleasure lies within material possessions. However, pleasure is not the same as Happiness and to suggest so is harm in itself.

However, other great harms result from this advertising. These harms include the encouragement of rampant consumerism, selfishness, greed, and avarice within the collective whole. In addition, these harms include the encouragement of jealousy, envy, bitterness, and resentment within the collective whole. Finally, they include the encouragement of competition within the collective whole as each Self acts and behaves to satisfy the wants, desires, cravings, and obsessions of Self. These harms accumulate and compound as each Self acts and behaves to maximize benefit and minimize harm for Self. All of which is contrary to the best interest, welfare, and good of the collective whole.

But much of the same advertising, as well as a great deal of television programming and popular music also fuels the growth of the dreams, wishes, and fantasies of Self. The dreams, wishes, and fantasies of Self may derive from needs; however, far more often, they derive from the wants, desires, cravings, and obsessions of Self.

In this usage, the term "dream" does not refer to the dreams experienced during sleep. In this usage, the term dream refers to visions or imaginings of the future. Both dreams and wishes are an expression of a future end-state. This future end-state usually centers on Self. Both dreams and wishes can derive from and express deficient and emergent needs, both the lower- and higher-level needs. However, dreams and wishes also derive from and express wants, desires, cravings, and obsessions of Self. Dreams and wishes that derive from the wants, desires, cravings, and obsessions of Self result in pleasure for Self in one form or another. Finally, a dream or wish may involve secondary benefit for Others. However, the primary beneficiary of a dream or wish is still Self. Therefore, generally speaking, acts and behaviors intended to make a dream or wish come true maximize benefit and minimize harm for Self.

A dream or wish, once written or spoken, may resonate with Others. Others may even adopt the dream for Self. It then becomes the dream or wish of Others as well as Self. It may become the dream or wish of a collective form of Self. However, because of the subjective nature of both dreams and wishes, a dream adopted by Others or a collective form of Self will mean different things for each Self that adopts the dream. Because of the subjective nature of dreams and wishes, each Self's perception and interpretation of the dream or wish will be guided by the ethic of Self. Dreams and wishes are not objective; they are subjective. Therefore, a dream or wish is tied to subjective Self. Even those dreams or wishes that relate to the higher-level needs are subjective in that they are a vision or imagining of Self. As an example of this assertion, I can offer the famous "I Have a Dream" speech of Reverend Martin Luther King, Jr.

In that speech, Reverend King shared his dream or vision for the future. It was his subjective dream for the future. He even said, "I have a dream." The end-state he expressed was the end-state he desired to see in the future. The dream he expressed indeed carried the potential for great benefit for many Others beyond Reverend King himself. It is also true that the dream he expressed gave substance and form to the dreams of many other people. Still, further, it is also true that many other people adopted Reverend King's dream as their own, and his dream then became the dream of a collective form of Self. However, the dream itself was still Reverend King's dream. And yes, the dream was very much attached to the higher-level need of self-esteem (dignity). Regrettably, after so much time, it is still a dream that has yet to be realized in its entirety.

The strength of the dreams or wishes of Self, much like the strength of the underlying needs, wants, desires, cravings, and obsessions of Self, determines the amount of time, energy, effort, and other resources Self devotes to making a dream or wish become reality for Self. It is the amount of time, energy, effort, and other resources Self commits to making a dream or wish reality that we commonly refer to as drive or ambition. However, upon careful examination it becomes clear that drive or ambition is only the ethic of Self guiding the choices and motivating the acts and behaviors intended to maximize benefit and minimize harm for Self.

Ambition is the ethic of Self guiding the choices and motivating acts and behaviors as Self applies resources toward making dreams and wishes become reality. Any harm that results for Others or the collective whole is minimalized or ignored so long as the benefit serves the interest, welfare, and good of Self. This would be especially true in instances where ambition encourages acts and behaviors that manifest the vices. It would be especially true in each instance in which Self is willing and able to employ any of the vices in order to pursue the dreams and wishes of Self.

The willingness and ability to practice the vices to achieve the dreams and wishes of Self results in harm for Others and the collective whole. This harm may include pain or the privation of pleasure for Others and the collective whole; however, it is often the greater harms of building distrust, doubt, uncertainty, and suspicion within Others and the collective whole. This harm may include the building of competition and disharmony within a collective whole. Many of these same harms result for Others when Self acts and behaves to pursue the fantasies of Self.

Fantasies are similar to dreams and wishes. Like dreams and wishes, fantasies always center on Self. Furthermore, fantasies are always subjective. They are always tied to subjective Self. Therefore, the primary beneficiary of any fantasy is always Self. Fantasies may involve Others, but they still focus on pleasure, in one form or another, for Self. In addition, fantasies may involve acts or behaviors that are excessive to the range of right, correct, and appropriate acts or behaviors. However, Self fantasizes the pleasure contained in the fantasy for Self. Regardless of the specific nature of the fantasy, the outcomes of fantasies are always pleasant for Self. Regardless of how realistic or unrealistic the fantasy is, the outcomes are always pleasant for Self.

Depending on the strength of the fantasy and the underlying want, desire, craving, or obsession, Self may well devote more time, energy, and effort to the fantasy and making the fantasy become a reality. Again, depending on the strength and intensity of the fantasy, Self may manifest the vices in order to enjoy the pleasures that result from a fantasy. Self may even demonstrate acts and behaviors that may seem completely irrational, even harmful to Self. However, Self will overlook this potential harm to Self in order to pursue the pleasure contained in the fantasy. The harm that might result for Others or the collective whole is simply minimalized or ignored so Self can enjoy the pleasure. This is consistent with the Unevolved Ethic, and it is inconsistent with the Evolved Ethic.

It is consistent with the ethic that guides and motivates acts and behaviors that maximize benefit (pleasure) and minimize harm (pain or the privation of pleasure) for Self. It is consistent with the ethic that minimalizes or ignores harm for Others and the collective whole. However, it is inconsistent with the ethic that guides and motivates acts and behaviors that maximize benefit and minimizes harm for Others and the collective whole. It is inconsistent with the ethic that minimalizes or ignores harm for Self.

At various points in future chapters, I will refer back to this discussion of the connection between ethic, needs, and spiritual well-being. In particular, I will revisit this discussion in the next two chapters. These chapters cover the development of the two ethics and the impact of ethic on relationships.

The development of ethic is tied very closely to acts and behaviors intended to satisfy the needs of Self. It is also the case that needs play a very central role in the formation, as well as the duration of relationships. Indeed, Self often enters relationships to facilitate satisfaction of needs. However, before examining relationships, I first want to examine development of the two ethics in the next chapter. In addition, the next chapter also covers the development of values and principles, as well as the three states of ethical development.

CHAPTER 7:
STAGES OF ETHICAL DEVELOPMENT AND RELATED TOPICS

This chapter covers four topics, each of which closely relates to the subject of ethical development. The first topic is the stages of ethical development. Both the Unevolved and Evolved ethics develop in three stages. These three stages align with the development of the three components of each ethic. Stage one of the Unevolved Ethic is the development of the egoistic component and stage one of the Evolved Ethic is the development of the virtue component. Stage two is the development of the utilitarian component, either the hedonistic or pluralistic utilitarian component, of the respective ethics. Finally, stage three is the development of the morality component of the respective ethics, either the rational morality or the Transcendent Morality. From the stages of development, the discussion will move to three further topics related to the development of the ethics.

The first of these related topics is personality development. Personality develops primarily during the same years as the first stage development of ethic. The personality that develops during these years is consistent with and reflective of the developing component of the ethic. If the developing component of the ethic is the egoistic component of the Unevolved Ethic, personality will reflect this component. If the developing component of ethic is the virtue component of the Evolved Ethic, personality will reflect this component. However, the developing ethic also influences the formation of values and principles. Therefore, value and principle formation are the second related topic.

The values and principles that form in conjunction with the developing components of the two ethics are those Self will carry into adulthood. These values and principles reflect both the developing components of the two ethics, as well as the wholly formed ethic. More specifically, the values and principles that form will reflect the focus of the two ethics. In one instance, the values and principles that form reflect a focus on the interest, welfare and good of Self and, in the other instance; they reflect a focus on the interest, welfare, and good of Others and the collective whole. Further, these values and principles then reflect in the beliefs, attitudes, opinions, ideologies, and philosophy of Self and the acts and behaviors of Self.

The final topic of this chapter is the states of ethical development. There are three states of ethical development. These three states reflect the developing and developed ethic. Two of the three states of ethical development align with the Unevolved Ethic and the third aligns with the Evolved Ethic. The characteristics of each of the three states are describable and consistent with the developing and developed ethic of Self. While acts and behaviors are not guided or influenced by the states of ethical development, patterns of acts and behaviors do give insight into the state of ethical development.

It should be clear that the development of ethic is not the same for each Self. Development of ethic varies, sometimes widely, from one Self to another Self because the learning, life experiences, and perceptions of each Self vary. It varies because of the subjective nature of learning, life experiences, and perceptions. It varies because each Self comprehends, interprets, synthesizes, combines, and applies the learning, life experience, and perceptions of Self differently. The result is the development of ethic that can and does vary, to some degree or extent, sometimes even widely, from one Self to the next. Development can vary widely even among siblings. This variation begins in stage one and continues throughout the three stages of ethical development.

Stage one begins at birth and continues through the ages of seven through nine. Stage two begins at approximately age seven through age ten and continues through young adulthood. Finally, stage three begins during young adulthood and can, but does not always, continue throughout adulthood. Indeed, for many, ethic reaches full development in early adulthood and does not change after that point in life. This does not mean it cannot continue developing, it simply does not. While these timeframes for the stages of development are certainly not exact and will vary from one Self to another, the ethic of each Self develops through these three stages.

Stage One Development

Stage one development follows the learning, experiences, and perceptions of a child during the years that comprise infancy through early childhood. Many, if not most of the learning, experiences, and perceptions during this stage derive from efforts to satisfy the four lower-level needs of Self. During these earliest years, acts and behaviors tend to focus on the survival and preservation of Self, as well as the acceptance and approval of Self within the context of the family. Acts and behaviors focus on the physical as well as the psychological health and well-being of Self. As a child seeks to satisfy the lower-level needs of Self, the child learns the concepts of benefit and harm. The child learns what feels good to Self and what feels bad to Self. The good or bad feelings learned, experienced, and perceived may be either physical or psychological depending upon the situation and circumstance.

As an example, in these earliest years, a child may learn that the taste or texture of some foods is much more pleasurable than others. A child will gravitate toward those foods that carry more pleasure and avoid those that do not carry pleasure. Similarly, a child may learn that acceptance and approval are given more readily by one parent or grandparent and given less readily by another. A child will gravitate toward the parent or grandparents who more readily demonstrate acceptance and approval. For a child, this extends to the acceptance and approval of the acts and behaviors of the child and not just to the child. After all, there is pleasure in acceptance and approval of Self, as well as the acts and behaviors of Self. On the other hand, a child may avoid a parent or grandparent who is more likely to demonstrate disapproval of the acts or behaviors of the child. There is no "feel good" for a child in disapproval. There is only a "feel bad" in disapproval. Unfortunately, it is also during these early, formative years that a child may learn to want more than is necessary to satisfy a need.

The appearance and growth of wants, as well as desires, cravings, and even obsessions during these early years, are not surprising. A child learns that satisfying needs is pleasant; it results in pleasure for Self. A child learns to want more since more results in more pleasure for the child. During these early years, many children are exposed to commercial advertising. As with most commercial advertising, the intent is to create a felt want, desire, and craving for the products advertised. It teaches to want, desire, crave, and obsess over more than is necessary to satisfy needs.

In addition, it is also during these years that a child may begin to learn to use manipulative acts and behaviors as a means to satisfy the wants, desires, cravings, and obsessions of Self. An example of this last assertion is use of a crying behavior to satisfy wants, desires, cravings, and obsessions of Self. Crying is the primary behavior available to an infant to signal deficient and emergent lower-level needs. However, a young child may also learn crying can result in pleasure for Self. Certainly, not all crying behavior is tied to satisfying deficient and emergent needs.

Take the example of a child who has a crying fit in a store when told they cannot have a toy or candy. It is still a crying behavior; however, the intent is no longer to satisfy a deficient and emergent lower-level need. The goal is now to satisfy a want, desire, craving, or obsession, and the child is manifesting crying behavior as a means to gain benefit (pleasure) for Self.

This is not to suggest the child is consciously employing a manipulative behavior, however; if the crying behavior is successful, the child gains pleasure for Self. The lesson is learned, and the child will likely repeat the crying behavior in the same or similar situations. Self does tend to repeat the same or similar behaviors that result in benefit for Self. If repetition of the behavior is successful in the same or similar situations or circumstances throughout childhood, Self may well carry this lesson and the behavior into adulthood. For instance, if throwing a fit results in pleasure as a child, Self may, to some extent or degree, continue to throw fits even as an adult. Therefore, the importance of what and how the child learns during these early years, from birth through approximately age seven to nine, cannot be overstated.

This is because what a child learns and how they learn during these years greatly impacts the developing component of ethic. If a child learns to focus on pleasure for Self, it will be the egoistic component that develops. Similarly, if a child learns to focus on avoiding pain or the privation of pleasure for Self, it will be the egoistic component that develops. If a child learns to consider consequences, pleasure and pain or the privation of pleasure, benefit and harm, only as these concepts apply to Self, the egoistic component of the Unevolved Ethic will develop. These last comments point to the developmental emphasis of the egoistic component first noted in Chapter 2.

In that chapter, I indicated that the emphasis of the egoistic component would be either maximizing pleasure _or_ minimizing pain and the privation of pleasure for Self. In situations and circumstances in which the lower-level needs, wants, desires, cravings, or obsessions of Self are routinely met, it is more likely that the emphasis of the egoistic component will be maximizing pleasure for Self. On the other hand, in situations and circumstances in which one or more of the lower-level needs of Self are not routinely met and are routinely deficient and emergent, the emphasis of the egoistic component will likely be avoiding pain or the privation of pleasure for Self. The inability to satisfy those needs tied to physical or psychological well-being will likely result in an emphasis on avoiding pain or the privation of pleasure for Self. This would certainly be the case in situations and circumstances where the very survival of Self is routinely at issue. The result is a component that emphasizes either maximizing benefit _or_ minimizing harm for Self.

On the other hand, if during these years, a child learns to act for the benefit of Others, then the virtue component may develop. For instance, if a child learns to act and behave to maximize benefit for Others, the virtue component of the Evolved Ethic will likely develop. This is similar if a child learns to act and behave to minimize harm for Others. By learning to act and behave to either maximize benefit _or_ minimize harm for Others, the first developmental component will likely be the virtue component. Whether the emphasis of the component is maximizing benefit _or_ minimizing harm for Others will largely depend on the teaching and modeling of the significant adults in a child's life.

For instance, if significant adults emphasize acting and behaving to benefit Others, that teaching and modeling will influence the emphasis of this component. If, on the other hand, significant adults emphasize minimizing harm for Others, that teaching and modeling will influence the emphasis of this component. Whether the emphasis is maximizing benefit _or_ minimizing harm, Others are still the beneficiaries of the acts and behaviors of the child. Regardless of emphasis, the child is still learning to act and behave for the benefit of Others and, likely, to accept pain or the privation of pleasure for Self. In either case, the acts and behaviors are still consistent with the virtues and virtuous behaviors. However, for the virtue component to fully develop, the significant adults in the child's life must teach and model the full range of lesser masculine and feminine virtues.

Here, it is important to note that much of the experience and learning in this stage occurs within the context of the immediate family. Similarly, the vast majority of a child's perceptions during these years also occur within the context of the immediate family. This suggests that parents heavily influence the child's early learning and perceptions of benefit and harm. If there is extensive exposure to extended family members, such as grandparents or aunts and uncles, these family members will also influence the child's learning and perceptions of benefit and harm. Finally, if the child attends daycare or is raised, at least in part, by a nanny or babysitter, this person or these persons will also likely influence the learning and perceptions of benefit and harm.

This influence lies, at least partially, in the significant adult's ability to reward or punish the acts and behaviors of a child. In this context, reward equals approval and punishment equals disapproval. Therefore, it is these significant adults who teach consequences, benefit and harm. If these significant adults do not teach consequences for acts and behaviors, the child will simply gravitate toward benefit for Self. The child will gravitate toward that which feels good to Self. The child's learning or lack of learning and understanding of consequences will then influence the developing component of ethic. As the foundational component of ethic develops, the developing component will become evident in the acts and behaviors of the child.

For instance, it will become evident to the extent or degree the child is willing and able or unwilling and unable to control or restrain the acts and behaviors of Self. The developing component will become evident to the extent or degree the child is willing and able or unwilling and unable to control or restrain the wants, desires, cravings, and obsessions of Self. It will be evident to the extent or degree the child is willing and able or unwilling and unable to control or restrain the urges, impulses, and emotions of Self.

The more a child learns to focus on pleasure for Self, the less the child will demonstrate the willingness or ability to control the wants, desires, and cravings of Self. The more a child learns to focus on pleasure for Self, the less the child will demonstrate a willingness or ability to control the urges, impulses, and emotions of Self. The more a child learns to focus on pleasure for Self, the less the child will demonstrate control or restraint over Self.

Conversely, the more a child learns to avoid pain or the privation of pleasure for Self, the more the child will demonstrate a willingness and ability to control the wants, desires, and cravings of Self to the extent or degree necessary to avoid pain or the privation of pleasure for Self. The more a child learns to avoid pain or the privation of pleasure, the more the child will demonstrate a willingness and ability to control the urges, impulses, and emotions of Self to the degree necessary to avoid pain or the privation of pleasure for Self. However, this level of control generally follows the setting of limits or parameters by significant adults. Under each of these circumstances, at best, the child is learning to control acts and behaviors only within the limits or parameters set by those adults with the power to reward or punish.

As the child learns these limits or parameters of acts and behaviors, the child may conform to these limits or parameters to gain pleasure for Self in the form of acceptance and approval *or* to avoid harm in the form of disapproval. If parents or other significant adults do not teach limits or parameters of acts or behaviors, the child will simply learn to act for the benefit of Self. The focus of the child will become benefit (pleasure) for Self. However, it is important to note that if, during this stage of ethical development, the child learns to act only for pleasure *or* the avoidance of pain or the privation of pleasure for Self, the child may also learn to avoid taking responsibility and accountability for Self. This is consistent with learning to seek pleasure *or* avoid pain or the privation of pleasure for Self.

Taking responsibility and accountability for the acts and behaviors of Self carries with it the risk of harm in the form of disapproval from significant adults. Instead, a child learning to focus on pleasure *or* avoid pain or the privation of pleasure for Self may attempt to deflect or avoid responsibility and accountability through the use of rationalizations, justifications, explanations, and excuses. In these early years, these may be very childish sounding, even silly and ridiculous. Still with each success and each failure, the child learns. I can illustrate this with the example of a small child caught with their hand in the cookie jar without permission.

The cookie represents pleasure for Self. Reaching into the cookie jar without permission is acting to maximize benefit (pleasure) for Self. It demonstrates the inability or unwillingness to control the wants, impulses, and urges of Self. Self wants a cookie, so the child takes the cookie without permission. If the child is caught and attempts to deflect or avoid responsibility and accountability for the act, no matter how clever, clumsy, or cute the attempt, the child is attempting to minimize pain or the privation of pleasure for Self. This suggests that the developing ethical component is the egoistic component of the Unevolved Ethic.

If a significant adult gives approval to the act or withholds disapproval, the adult reinforces the learning on the part of the child. It reinforces learning to act or behave for the benefit of Self. It reinforces avoiding harm for Self. Finally, it reinforces avoiding responsibility and accountability for the acts and behaviors of Self. Learning to avoid responsibility and accountability for the acts of Self is also consistent with the egoistic component of the Unevolved Ethic. On the contrary, learning to accept responsibility and accountability for the acts and behaviors of Self is consistent with the virtue component of the Evolved Ethic.

Through learning the full range of lesser virtues, a child learns to consider consequences in terms of maximizing benefit *or* minimizing harm for Others. A child learns to consider the impact of acts and behaviors of Self on Others. By learning to consider benefit in terms of Others, a child begins to learn self-control or self-restraint. The child learns to control acts and behaviors associated with the wants, desires, cravings, emotions, impulses, and urges of Self. This self-control derives from acting or behaving with regard or consideration for Others and not consideration only of Self.

This form of control is different from the level of control practiced only as a means of avoiding pain or the privation of pleasure for Self. It is different from the control or restraint that requires limits or parameters set by parents or other significant adults. It is different from the external control or discipline that comes from parents or significant adults. Later in life, it is different from the control or restraint that requires rules, standards, codes, and laws to limit and restrain acts and behaviors of Self. However, this self-control or self-restraint requires that a child learn to practice the virtues. If a child is learning to practice the virtues, then it is more likely that the virtue component of the Evolved Ethic will develop.

Which of the two foundational components develops in stage one impacts development of the second component in stage two of ethical development. If the foundational component is the egoistic component of the Unevolved Ethic, it will likely be the hedonistic utilitarian component that develops in stage two. If, on the other hand, the foundational component is the virtue component of the Evolved Ethic, it may be the pluralistic utilitarian component that develops in stage two.

Stage Two Development

This stage begins at approximately seven to ten years of age and continues into young adulthood. As in stage one, the acts and behaviors of a child or young adult focus on efforts to satisfy the four lower-level needs during these years. However, five points are significant to formation of the utilitarian component of ethic. First, stage two development of ethic is essentially a continuation of stage one. Second, it is in stage two that the second or complimentary emphasis of the utilitarian component adds to the emphasis learned in stage one. In other words, it is in this stage that *or* becomes *and*. Third, much of the experience, learning, and perceptions of this stage take place in an expanded range of situations and circumstances. Fourth, the teaching and modeling of significant adults continues to influence the developing utilitarian component significantly. Finally, it is during stage two of ethical development that a child or young adult may learn to comprehend and apply concepts such as right and wrong, correct and incorrect, appropriate and inappropriate, as well as acceptable and unacceptable, to the acts and behaviors of Self and Others. The developing component will impact how a child or young adult learns to apply these concepts. This will, in turn, impact how the adult Self will apply the concepts in stage three.

Development in stage two reflects what a child learned or did not learn in terms of consequences for Self and Others. If a child learns to consider primarily benefit for Self in stage one, it is likely the hedonistic utilitarian component will develop in stage two. Similarly, if a child learns to avoid harm for Self, it will still be the hedonistic utilitarian component that develops in stage two. If, on the other hand, a child learns to consider benefit or harm as they relate to Others or the collective whole, then it is possible the pluralistic utilitarian component will develop in stage two. It is during stage two that the second or complimentary emphasis of the developing utilitarian component is added to the emphasis that developed during stage one.

For instance, if the emphasis of the egoistic component is maximizing pleasure for Self, then to some extent or degree, an emphasis on minimizing harm develops in stage two. On the other hand, if the emphasis of the egoistic component is minimizing harm for Self, then to some extent or degree, an emphasis on maximizing benefit for Self will develop during stage two. While the emphasis of the egoistic component is either maximizing benefit *or* minimizing harm for Self, the emphasis of the hedonistic utilitarian component becomes maximizing benefit *and* minimizing harm for Self. However, the hedonistic utilitarian component will often continue to favor the emphasis of the egoistic component.

The same is similar if the virtue component developed in stage one. If the emphasis of the virtue component was maximizing benefit for Others, then to some extent or degree, an emphasis on minimizing harm develops in stage two. If the emphasis of the virtue component was minimizing harm for Others, then to some extent or degree, an emphasis on maximizing benefit for Others develops in stage two. Therefore, the emphasis of the pluralistic utilitarian component becomes maximizing benefit *and* minimizing harm for Others and the collective whole. However, much as the hedonistic utilitarian component will continue to favor the emphasis of the egoistic component, the pluralistic utilitarian component will continue to favor the emphasis of the virtue component. It is important to note that much of the development of stage two occurs outside the immediate family.

In this stage, many, if not most, of the new experiences, learning, and perceptions are typically gained in settings or contexts outside the immediate or even extended family. During these years, many, if not most, children attend school. In addition, a child may participate in sports or other activities outside the family. For example, a child may participate in scouting or similar clubs or activities. A teen or young adult may hold a job. This means exposure to an even broader range of situations, circumstances, environments, and experiences. It is in and through experiences, learning, and perceptions gained in these broader settings or contexts that the complimentary emphasis of the utilitarian component develops. It is in and through the experiences, learning, and perception gained in these broader setting or contexts that *or* becomes *and* which completes the formation of the utilitarian component.

If the egoistic component developed during stage one, the formation of the hedonistic utilitarian component occurs as a child learns the limits and parameters of acts and behaviors within the new situations, circumstances, and environments. As a child or young adult learns the limits and parameters of acts and behavior within the new situations, circumstances, and environments, the child often learns to control or restrain Self to avoid disapproval (pain or the privation of pleasure) for Self.

Similarly, a child may learn to seek the approval that often accompanies learning to control or restrain acts and behaviors within the set limits or parameters. Therefore, by demonstrating acts or behaviors within the set limits or parameters, a child or young adult learns to avoid harm but also learns that acting or behaving within the limits or parameters is a pathway to benefit (pleasure) for Self in the form of acceptance and approval. Development of the pluralistic utilitarian component is similar.

It is within the expanded number of situations, circumstances, environments, and experiences that the pluralistic utilitarian component forms. It is within the expanded situations, circumstances, environments, and experiences that a child learns to practice acts and behaviors that maximize benefit *and* minimize harm for Others and, by extension, the collective whole. Some of these new situations, circumstances, environments, and experiences offer the opportunity to act and behave to maximize benefit for Others and the collective whole. Others offer the opportunity to act and behave to minimize harm for Others and the collective whole. Therefore, it is in and through the expanded range of situations, circumstances, environments, and experiences that the emphasis of this component becomes maximizing benefit *and* minimizing harm for Others and the collective whole.

However, each new situation, circumstance, environment, and experience exposes a child or young adult to an expanding number of additional significant adults. These include teachers, coaches, scouting leaders, and other adult authority figures. These additional significant adults may include managers, supervisors, and co-workers. Many of these additional significant adults are in a position to reward (approve) or punish (disapprove) the acts and behaviors of a child. As such, they are in a position to significantly influence the developing utilitarian component of ethic. As with parents and other significant adults in the child's early years, these adults also influence through what they teach and how they teach, as well as through the example they set or model.

During these years, a child or young adult learns much from what they see practiced by the significant adults in their life. They learn much from their perceptions of the acts and behaviors of the significant adults in their lives. If the teaching and example of the adult suggest it is right, correct, appropriate, or even acceptable, to act and behave for the benefit of only Self, this will likely influence the developing utilitarian component. If the teaching and example of the adults suggest it is right, correct, appropriate or acceptable to want, desire, crave, and obsess over more for Self, this will likely influence the developing utilitarian component. Similarly, if the teaching and example of adults suggest it is right, correct, appropriate, or acceptable to act on the impulses, urges, and emotions of Self, this may well influence the developing utilitarian component.

Additionally, if the teaching and example of the adults suggest that avoidance of responsibility or accountability is right, correct, appropriate, or acceptable, this will carry influence. Finally, if the teaching and example of significant adults suggest moral hypocrisy is right, correct, appropriate or acceptable, this may also influence the developing utilitarian component of a child or young adult. If the teaching and example suggests "Do as I say and not as I do," this will likely influence the developing utilitarian component.

However, it is not just other significant adults who exert significant influence during these years. There are also friends, each of whom has a developing ethic and each of whom can influence the developing utilitarian component of a child or young adult. This influence of friends is often termed "peer pressure". If the developing utilitarian component of a friend or friends is the hedonistic utilitarian component, the acts and behaviors of the friend or friends will manifest this component. The influence or pressure exerted by these friends will also reflect the egoistic component.

The acts and behaviors of the friend or friends will encourage maximizing benefit and minimizing harm for Self. They will encourage acting and behaving to satisfy the wants, desires, cravings, and obsessions of Self. They will encourage failing to control the urges, impulses, and emotions of Self. They may encourage failing to demonstrate regard for the feelings and emotions of Others. They may also encourage the exclusion of Others through participation in cliques. Finally, they may encourage demonstrating a lack of willingness and ability to accept responsibility or accountability for the acts and behaviors of Self. In whatever form or forms peer pressure takes during stage two, it is entirely possible that the influence of friends can encourage the hedonistic utilitarian component and even reverse stage one ethical development.

This last comment suggests that despite learning to act for the benefit of Others and the collective whole during stage one, the influence of both friends and significant adults in stage two can result in the development of the hedonistic utilitarian component. Essentially, and as a result of the influence of friends or significant adults, a child or young adult can learn to focus on benefit for Self during the stage two years. A child or young adult can learn to consider consequences, benefit and harm, only as they apply to Self. A child or young adult can learn to focus on maximizing benefit and minimizing harm for Self.

Unfortunately, the development of the hedonistic utilitarian component in stage two may significantly impact how a child or young adult learns and applies the concepts of right and wrong, correct and incorrect, and appropriate and inappropriate to the acts and behaviors of Self. A child or young adult can learn to view right and wrong, correct and incorrect, appropriate and inappropriate only as these terms result in benefit or harm for Self. This view suggests acts or behaviors are right, correct, and appropriate as they result in benefit for Self and wrong, incorrect, and inappropriate only as they result in harm for Self. The impact or harm for Others and the collective whole becomes obscured or lost in this view of benefit or harm for Self. It may also become lost in acts and behaviors termed "acceptable."

It is during these years that many children and young adults begin to learn and adopt those acts and behaviors that fall within the grey area between right and wrong, correct and incorrect, and appropriate and inappropriate. These are acts and behaviors that are not right, correct, or appropriate but are still considered "acceptable" within society.

As a child or young adult learns the acts and behaviors that are "acceptable" within society, they also learn those considered "unacceptable." Unlike "acceptable" acts and behaviors, which society permits, "unacceptable" acts and behaviors are often considered wrong, incorrect, or inappropriate and are not encouraged. Indeed, the learning of acts and behaviors considered "acceptable" and "unacceptable" is an integral part of learning to function within society. This learning begins in the earliest years of this stage and continues throughout the stage.

For instance, it is often within and through the new situations, circumstances, environments, and experiences associated with this stage that a child learns to raise their hand to be heard and to take one's place in line. It may be where a child learns to take turns and sit quietly. It may be where a child learns not to throw temper tantrums. It may be where a child learns not to hit, kick, or bite. These are all examples of acts and behaviors that are right, correct, appropriate, and acceptable or wrong, incorrect, inappropriate, or unacceptable. Each of these is also a very fundamental rule or standard of behavior necessary to function well within society.

The extent or degree to which a child or young adult demonstrates the willingness and ability to practice acts and behaviors considered right, correct, appropriate, or even acceptable within society is a reflection of the developing component of ethic. Generally, those acts and behaviors considered right, correct, and appropriate are those acts and behaviors that maximize benefit and minimize harm for Others and the collective whole. However, the extent or degree to which a child or young adult demonstrates the willingness and ability to practice acts and behaviors considered "acceptable," as well as wrong, incorrect, inappropriate, or even "unacceptable," is also a reflection of the developing ethic.

If the developing stage two component is the pluralistic utilitarian component, it is likely the Transcendent Morality will develop in stage three. If, however, the developing component is the hedonistic utilitarian component, it is likely the rational morality will develop in stage three.

Stage Three Development

This stage begins in early adulthood and can continue throughout the remainder of a lifetime. As with stage two development, this stage is generally a logical progression of stage two. If the hedonistic utilitarian component developed in stage two, then the logical progression is the rational morality that completes development of the Unevolved Ethic. If the pluralistic utilitarian component developed in stage two, then the logical, but not necessarily given, progression is the Transcendent Morality that completes the development of the Evolved Ethic.

As with stage one and stage two, Self must and will continue to seek to satisfy the four lower-level needs of Self. The physical and psychological health of Self requires that Self continue to act and behave to satisfy these needs. However, in stage three, the focus for many Selves also becomes satisfying the wants, desires, cravings, and obsessions of Self. The exception will be those in whom the components of the Evolved Ethic are developing. These Selves will continue to demonstrate the willingness and ability to control the wants, desires, cravings, and obsessions of Self.

It is important to note that, during this stage, the ability of other adults to influence the development of the final component lessens. This does not mean there is no influence by other adults. It simply means the number of adults in a position to reward (approval) or punish (disapproval) the acts and behaviors of Self is greatly reduced. In addition, the number of adults viewed as authority figures is greatly reduced. However, adults can and often do continue to experience and learn as they mature. Adults are often exposed to new beliefs, attitudes, opinions, philosophies, and ideologies. Further, adults are often exposed to the teaching and example of new friends and adults. The difference is the extent or degree of influence exerted by these adults.

With the lessening of influence by significant adults, development of the morality component is heavily influenced by the components that developed in stages one and two. The degree or extent to which the virtue or egoistic components, as well as the hedonistic or pluralistic utilitarian components developed has the greatest influence in determining the morality that develops during stage three.

Assuming the egoistic and hedonistic utilitarian components developed, the rational morality will develop in stage three. The rational morality provides the rationalizations, justifications, excuses, and explanations that necessarily accompany a focus on benefit for Self. It is the rational morality that provides the rationalizations, justifications, excuses, and explanations that necessarily accompany efforts to satisfy the wants, desires, cravings, and obsessions of Self. The rational morality encourages the rationalizations, justifications, explanations, excuses, and self-deception strategies that result in moral hypocrisy. It is the rational morality that is the willingness and ability to minimalize or ignore harm that results for Others and the collective whole when Self consistently acts to maximize benefit and minimize harm for Self.

The plausible and reasonable-sounding rationalizations, justifications, explanations, excuses, and self-deception strategies that often manifest the rational morality are simply not available in the early stages of ethical development. A small child is not capable of creating the often elaborate and credible sounding rationalizations, justifications, explanations, and excuses intended to minimalize or avoid harm for Self. A small child is not capable of creating and employing believable-sounding self-deception strategies. A small child may attempt a lie to cover a self-serving act, but the lie is often clumsy and transparent. Likewise, a small child may attempt to blame someone or something else for the acts and behaviors of Self, however these attempts are also often clumsy and transparent. The ability of a child to reason is simply not well developed. However, as a child develops through stage two, the ability of the child to create more elaborate and plausible rationalizations, justifications, explanations, and excuses increases.

This ability is often aided and assisted through the teaching and example of significant adults and authority figures in a child's life. Through this teaching and example, a child, teenager, or young adult may well begin to learn that it is acceptable to act and behave for the benefit of Self so long as the acts and behaviors of Self fall within the accepted standards of society. Further, a teenager or young adult may well learn that it is possible to avoid or at least minimize harm for wrong, incorrect, inappropriate, and unacceptable acts and behaviors by adopting rationalizations, justifications, explanations, excuses, and self-deception strategies considered acceptable within society. This encourages the teen or young adult to learn that avoiding responsibility and accountability for the acts and behaviors of Self is also acceptable. This learning begins during stage two, but the rational morality does not reach full development until stage three.

During the early years of stage three, the young adult will begin to hone, sharpen, and perfect the rationalizations, justifications, explanations, excuses, and self-deception strategies they may well repeat throughout the remainder of life. During the early years of stage three, the young adult may also adopt rationalizations, justifications, explanations, excuses, and self-deception strategies learned from other adults, especially friends and co-workers. These are no longer the simple or clumsy attempts of a young child. These are now the oft-repeated and oft-accepted rationalizations, justifications, explanations, excuses, and self-deception strategies of adulthood. They are the self-deception strategies that result in moral hypocrisy. They are the strategies that enable Self to believe that Self is ethical and moral despite sometimes obvious evidence to the contrary.

The rationalizations, justifications, explanations, excuses, and self-deception strategies adopted, created, and honed in stage three will generally include only those strategies acceptable for adults. This will certainly not always be the case. However, an adult Self will often discard the rationalizations, justifications, explanations, and excuses of childhood and young adulthood in favor of the more elaborate rationalizations, justifications, explanations, excuses, and strategies of adulthood. In other instances, an adult may simply adapt an earlier rationalization, justification, explanation, or excuse to adulthood. For instance, if a child or young adult was taught and learned to blame everyone and everything else for the acts and behaviors of Self, this may continue into adulthood. The adult may learn to blame a spouse, children, and co-workers for the acts and behaviors of Self. If successful, an adult may adopt this strategy for the remainder of their life.

Because stage three continues throughout adulthood, an adult may well continue to collect information and knowledge that supports and encourages maximizing benefit and minimizing harm for Self. As the adult adds new learning and experiences, they may well continue developing new and creative rationalizations, justifications, explanations, excuses, and strategies that enable minimalizing or ignoring harm to Others and the collective whole. This would be very consistent with the rational morality and the completely formed Unevolved Ethic.

On the other hand, if the two ethical components that develop during stages one and two are the virtue and pluralistic utilitarian components, it is more likely that the Transcendent Morality will develop during stage three. If, during stages one and two, it is the two components that focus emphasis on the interest, welfare, and good of Others and the collective whole, it may well be the Transcendent Morality that develops in stage three. Just as the rational morality is a logical progression of the egoistic and hedonistic utilitarian components, the Transcendent Morality is the logical progression of the virtue and pluralistic utilitarian components.

This is the logical progression if the young adult continues to practice the lesser virtues and if the continued practice of the lesser virtues continues to strengthen the Enabling Virtues of Love and Courage. It is the logical progression if a child and young adult learns and practices acts and behaviors that forego Self in the interest of Others. It is the logical progression if, to some extent or degree, a child and young adult learns to deny Self in the interest of Others and the collective whole, to control pleasure for Self, and to accept the privation of pleasure for Self in the best interest, welfare, and good of Others and the collective whole. It is the logical progression if a child and young adult learns to minimize harm for Others and the collective whole. Finally, it is the logical progression if the young adult continues to practice and hone the ability to minimalize or ignore harm to Self that results when Self consistently acts and behaves for the benefit of Others and the collective whole. Under these circumstances, the Transcendent Morality will likely develop and solidify.

If, on the other hand, a young adult or adult is unwilling or unable to continue practicing acts and behaviors that serve the interest, welfare, and good of Others and the collective whole, ethical development will likely reverse. If reversal occurs, the young adult or adult will go through the stages of ethical development as an adult. The young adult or adult will begin to demonstrate behaviors in line with the egoistic and hedonistic utilitarian components. The young adult or adult will learn to act and behave for the benefit of Self. The adult will learn to both maximize benefit and minimize harm for Self. The adult will learn to minimalize or ignore harm to Others and the collective whole through the creation and use of rationalizations, justifications, explanations, excuses, and self-deception strategies. In short, the Unevolved Ethic will develop. But this potential reversal of ethical development is in line with the belief that ethic does not necessarily remain the same throughout a lifetime. Ethic can change. It can move along the Unevolved-Evolved Continuum.

If the ethic that develops is the Unevolved Ethic, and the perceptions, experiences, and learning of adult life further encourage the Unevolved Ethic, ethic can actually devolve. It can move further away from the Point of Transcendence. An adult may become more self-interested, self-absorbed, self-centered, self-promoting, and self-aggrandizing throughout their lifetime. An adult can become more selfish, conceited, vain, and narcissistic. However, ethic can also evolve. It can move toward the Point of Transcendence. It can become less self-interested, less self-absorbed, less self-centered, less self-promoting, and less self-aggrandizing. In addition, ethic can cross the Point of Transcendence and become the Evolved Ethic.

This change in ethic, this movement along the continuum, may result from a single powerful influence or powerful event, an influence or event powerful enough to move ethic and the resultant pattern of acts and behaviors in either direction along the continuum. For instance, a young adult or adult may encounter a teacher or mentor whose teaching and example are powerful enough to influence the movement of ethic, and powerful enough to influence the movement of ethic along the continuum. The young adult or adult may encounter a teacher or mentor whose teaching and example are powerful enough to influence change in the long-term pattern of acts and behaviors.

For ethic to move along the continuum in either direction, the influence of the teacher or mentor would necessarily need to result in a long-term, permanent change in the pattern of acts and behaviors. A short-term, temporary change in the pattern of acts or behaviors would not indicate movement of ethic along the continuum. A short-term, temporary change in the pattern of acts or behaviors is more likely driven by emotion, and change driven by emotion is generally only short-lived.

But there is also the possibility that a single yet powerful experience or event can influence a change in ethic. This is an event that is significant enough to cause a movement of ethic along the continuum. It is an event or experience significant enough to change the long-term pattern of acts and behaviors. Such an event is termed a significant ethical event. This is not the same as a significant emotional event or experience.

The field of psychology has long recognized the behavior-changing influence of a significant emotional event or significant emotional experience. These phrases refer to an emotional event or experience powerful enough to influence the acts and behaviors of Self. However, consistent with this discussion of ethics, an emotional event or experience, by itself, cannot cause a shift or movement of ethic along the continuum. It cannot because the impact of emotions tends to be erratic, inconsistent, and only short-term in duration.

Patterns of acts and behaviors may change temporarily as a result of an emotional event; nevertheless, as emotions fade, the impact on acts and behaviors also fades. While a specific behavior or behaviors may change, as emotion fades, acts and behaviors generally settle back into the long-term pattern motivated by the underlying ethic. This does not result in a long-term or permanent change to the overall pattern of acts and behaviors; therefore, it does not indicate the movement of ethic in either direction along the continuum.

However, a significant emotional event or experience can trigger a significant ethical event and a significant ethical event can change or alter long-term patterns of behavior and move ethic along the continuum. This movement or shift of ethic along the continuum causes a corresponding long-term, permanent shift in the pattern of acts and behaviors. It causes a shift in acts and behaviors that is not inconsistent, erratic, or random. However, this movement of ethic along the continuum may be in either direction.

If the significant emotional event triggers acts and behaviors that serve primarily the interest, welfare, or good of Self, these acts and behaviors may lead to a significant ethical event that moves ethic further away from the Point of Transcendence. If the movement of ethic is further away from the PoT, the long-term pattern of acts and behaviors will follow. The pattern of acts and behaviors will become more self-interested, more self-serving, and more self-absorbed. If, on the other hand, the movement is toward the PoT, the long-term pattern of acts and behaviors will follow this movement. The pattern of acts and behaviors will become less self-interested, self-serving, and self-absorbed. However, even a significant ethical event cannot, by itself, change ethic from the Unevolved Ethic to the

Evolved Ethic. It cannot because changing ethic from the Unevolved to the Evolved ethic requires developing the components of the Evolved Ethic.

Instead, a significant ethical event can set in motion the practice and adoption of acts and behaviors consistent with the virtue component of the Evolved Ethic. As Self practices acts and behaviors consistent with the virtue component, the pluralistic utilitarian component begins to develop. In addition, the enabling virtues of Love and Courage begin to develop. If Self continues to practice acts and behaviors consistent with the virtue and pluralistic utilitarian components, Love and Courage will continue to strengthen. As Love and Courage strengthen, the Transcendent Morality strengthens.

However, it takes time and practice for the Evolved Ethic to fully develop since evolution of ethic from the Unevolved Ethic to the Evolved Ethic requires development through all three stages. It takes time, effort, and practice to learn to consistently maximize benefit and minimize harm for Others and the collective whole while minimalizing or ignoring harm for Self. This just does not occur quickly or as a result of a single event or experience.

It is a much longer journey to move ethic above the Point of Transcendence. A significant ethical event may trigger the first step of that journey. It may trigger awareness or sentience that transcends Self, but that awareness alone is not the Evolved Ethic. Awareness is only the first step of a journey that takes both time and effort on the part of Self. It is the journey that can result in the development of the Evolved Ethic. It is also a journey that can and often does result in significant changes to the personality of Self, and personality is the next topic related to the stages of ethical development.

Personality Development

Throughout this discussion of ethics, I have always maintained that it is the long-term pattern that sheds light on the ethic motivating the acts and behaviors of any Self. However, it is also the long-term pattern of acts and behaviors that is commonly referred to as personality. Therefore, regardless of which ethic develops, the personality of each Self will reflect the developing or developed ethic of Self.

Personality is defined, in part, as, "the sum total of the physical, mental, emotional, and social characteristics of an individual. The organized pattern of behavioral characteristics of the individual." Further, it is "the visible aspect of one's character as it impresses others." If personality is the organized pattern of behaviors of Self, then personality is a window to the developing or developed ethic of Self. It is a window to ethic since ethic motivates the organized pattern of acts and behaviors that are the visible aspect of one's character. Interestingly, it is generally believed that personality largely develops during the first seven or so years of life. This timeframe coincides closely with the estimate of stage one of ethical development.

Whether personality reflects the egoistic or virtue component of ethic is very dependent on the learning, experiences, and perceptions of a child during those early years. If a child is learning to act for the benefit of Self, their developing personality will reflect the egoistic component of the Unevolved Ethic. If a child is learning to act for the benefit of Others, their developing personality will reflect the virtue component of the Evolved Ethic. However, one's ethic is not completely developed during these years. Therefore, neither is personality completely developed during these years.

Consistent with the discussion of the stages of development of ethic, the developing, and even developed ethic can move as Self moves through the stages of ethical development. Most of this opportunity for change occurs after age seven. Experiences, learning, and perceptions in the years following age seven influence the developing components of ethic. The developing ethic can move along the continuum. It can evolve or devolve.

It can improve or get worse. As a result, personality can also change. It can also evolve or devolve. This is because the long-term pattern of observable, manifest acts and behaviors interpreted as personality characteristics or traits will reflect change or movement of ethic along the continuum. In short, personality characteristics or traits align with the location of ethic along the Unevolved-Evolved Continuum.

Personality traits and qualities associated with the Evolved Ethic are those traits and qualities consistent with the description of the Ethic. They will include traits and qualities termed nurturing. They will include traits and qualities termed giving, helping, caring, and sharing. Likewise, the personality traits and qualities will include traits and qualities consistent with integrity. These personality characteristics and traits might be termed genuine and authentic. Further, they might be termed accepting, self-sacrificing, and selfless. Finally, these traits and characteristics might be described as good character or even a good soul. These are not the personality qualities or traits associated with the Unevolved Ethic.

The personality traits associated with the Unevolved Ethic are very much different. These are characteristics and traits more consistent with terms like egotistical, self-centered, and self-regarding. They are traits and qualities described as self-important, self-interested, self-absorbed, and self-righteous. They will include traits and qualities termed selfish, conceited, vain, proud, arrogant, self-aggrandizing, and perhaps even narcissistic. Few would describe this personality as nurturing, and few would suggest this personality exemplifies integrity. Few would describe this personality as giving, helping, sharing, caring, genuine, or authentic. Similarly, few would suggest this personality demonstrates good character or a good soul. They would not because this personality is consistent with the Unevolved Ethic.

Ultimately, personality will mirror the developed ethic, be it the Evolved or Unevolved Ethic. If, as a result of new experiences, learning, and perceptions, the developing or developed ethic shifts or moves along the continuum, the characteristics and traits of personality will follow this shift or movement. However, the developing ethical components influence more than just personality development. The developing ethical components also play a very significant role in the development of the values and principles of Self.

Formation of Values and Principles

Unlike personality, which develops predominately during the years that comprise stage one ethical development, values and principles may begin developing during the years that comprise stage one, but continue developing during the years that comprise stage two, and, generally speaking, solidify during the stage three years. The developing and developed values and principles will reflect the developing ethical components and the fully developed ethic. These values and principles then influence the beliefs, attitudes, and opinions formed and adopted by Self. Going a step further, beliefs, attitudes, and opinions then influence the ideologies and philosophies formed and adopted by Self. By taking this progression one step further still, ideologies and philosophies formed and adopted, then influence and guide many of the choices, acts and behaviors of Self. But this influence is always consistent with the underlying developing ethical components or the fully developed ethic of Self. Figure 7-1 illustrates the progression from ethic to acts and behaviors as a nested diagram.

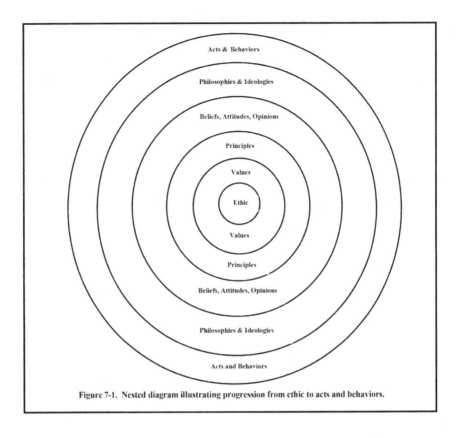

Figure 7-1. Nested diagram illustrating progression from ethic to acts and behaviors.

The diagram indicates that ethic is the starting point or center of this progression. Each successive, outward progression includes, but transcends the previous progression. Values are the first progression and are inclusive of and influenced by ethic. Values encompass, but transcend ethic. This holds throughout the progression to acts and behaviors. However, the heart of the nested diagram is always the developing or developed ethic. It is the developing or developed ethic that ultimately influences the formation of the values and principles of Self. As such, it is the developing or developed ethic that ultimately influences the beliefs, attitudes, opinions, philosophies and ideologies of Self. Therefore, it is still the developing or developed ethic that ultimately influences and guides the choices, acts and behaviors of Self. Understanding how ethic influences the development of values requires a very short look back to Chapter 5.

In Chapter 5, I discussed the values associated with the virtues and their opposite, the vices. In that chapter, I indicated that a value is a quality or characteristic desirable both as an end in itself and as a means to an end. I then demonstrated that the values that derive from the virtues are desirable both as ends and means to ends. I asserted that acts and behaviors that manifest these values serve the best interest, welfare, and good of Others and the collective whole at all levels of the collective whole. Acts and behaviors that manifest these values maximize benefit and minimize harm for Others and the collective whole.

I also demonstrated that the values derived from the vices are desirable both as ends and means to ends. However, these values are desirable only as ends and means that serve the best interest, welfare, and good of Self. Acts and behaviors that manifest these values serve only to maximize benefit and minimize harm for Self. Therefore, acts and behaviors that manifest values that derive from the vices are always contrary to the best interest, welfare, and good of the collective whole. But, in that earlier chapter, I did not discuss how these values form. To understand how these values form, one needs to look again at the learning that occurs during stage one of the development of ethic.

As a child learns and practices the lesser masculine and feminine virtues, the child becomes habituated to the acts and behaviors that manifest the virtues. As the child becomes habituated to these acts and behaviors, the child learns to value the various manifestations of the virtues in the acts and behaviors of both Self and Others. As a child learns to practice the manifestations of virtue in an expanding variety of situations, circumstances, and environments, the child also learns to value the manifestations of virtue in Self and Others in these new situations, circumstances, and environments. These manifestations are the values. They are the desirable qualities and characteristics that derive from the virtues.

As an example, as a child learns, practices, and becomes habituated to practicing the lesser masculine virtue of honesty, the child learns to value the various manifestations of honesty as practiced by both Self and Others. These manifestations include truthfulness, forthrightness, straightforwardness, and fairness. With habituation to honesty and the various manifestations of honesty, the child learns to be truthful, forthright, straightforward, and fair. Similarly, the child learns to value these qualities and characteristics in Others. It is through the habitual practice of the virtue of honesty that these qualities and characteristics derive. The same is similar for the other lesser masculine and feminine virtues. In each case, as a child learns and becomes habituated to practicing the virtues, the child learns to value the manifestations of the various virtues in Self and Others. A child learns to value the qualities and characteristics that derive from the various virtues in Self and Others. This is value formation consistent with the developing Evolved Ethic.

However, it is also through habituation to practicing the virtues that a child may become aware that not every Self practices the virtues and values associated with virtues. A child may become aware that the acts and behaviors of some Selves often fail to manifest virtue and values associated with virtue. A child or young adult may well learn disappointment in the acts and behaviors of those Selves who do not practice virtue. Further, depending on the age of a child or young adult, they will become aware of the moral hypocrisy of Selves who profess virtue and the values that derive from virtue, but fail to practice them. Indeed, a child or young adult will become aware that many Selves learn and practice the opposite of virtue. They become aware that many Selves learn and practice the vices and the values that derive from the vices.

An examination of the complete list of vices yields the same result. For each vice there are various manifestations of the vice. The various manifestations of the vices become the values that derive from and are associated with the vice. These values develop as a young child and young adult learn and practice them. They develop as a child and, later, as a young adult and adult, become habituated to the practice of the vices and the various manifestations of the vices. However, it should be noted that very few

Selves openly claim habituation to the vices. They do not claim habituation to the vices or claim values associated with the vices because of the belonging (affiliation) and esteem needs.

A child and young adult generally learn that the practice of the vices and the values that derive from the vices results in disapproval. Disapproval is pain or the privation of pleasure for Self. So, the child (and later the young adult and adult) learns to voice the virtues and values that derive from the virtues. This learning occurs in school, through clubs and other activities, and possibly through participation in religious instruction. They learn voicing the virtues and values derived from the virtues leads to approval of Self. There is a benefit (pleasure) in approval for Self. Approval for Self satisfies the belonging (affiliation) and esteem needs. But learning to voice the virtues and values derived from virtue while practicing the vices and values that derive from the vices is moral hypocrisy. It is the moral hypocrisy associated with the Unevolved Ethic.

But this is not the only reason Self learns to voice the virtues and values that derive from virtue. There is a second reason Self learns to voice the virtues and values associated with virtue. This second reason is tied to the way in which Self wants to be treated by Others.

Self wants the benefits for Self that result when Others practice virtue and the values that derive from the virtues. Further, and perhaps more importantly, Self does not want the harm for Self that results when Others practice the vices or the values derived from the vices. However, neither does Self always want the harm that results for Self when the acts and behaviors of Self manifest virtue or the values that derive from virtue. So, Self wants and expects Others to act virtuously, but often exempts Self from doing so. To want and expect Others to act virtuously while exempting Self is another manifestation of moral hypocrisy that Self will attempt to rationalize, justify, explain, and excuse in the best interest, welfare, and good of Self.

But value formation is just the beginning of the nested progression. Regardless of which ethic and its accompanying set of values develop and form, those values become the basis for the next progression. This next progression is the formation of the principles of Self.

If the developing components of ethic are the components of the Evolved Ethic and the forming values derived from the virtues, then it follows that the principles that form will also be consistent with the Evolved Ethic. These principles will favor the interest, welfare, and good of Others and the collective whole. These principles will be inclusive, and, in that sense, they will be universal. However, if the developing components are the components of the Unevolved Ethic and the forming values derive from the vices, it follows that the principles that form will be consistent with the Unevolved Ethic. These principles will favor the best interest, welfare, and good of Self. Further, these principles will be exclusive. They will favor Self over Others and the collective whole.

Just as it is possible to name the values that derive from the virtues or the vices, it is possible to name the principles that form from these values. For examples, if the components of the Evolved Ethic and the values derived from this ethic form and develop, principles that form will include truth, justice, equality, fidelity, equity, impartiality, and fraternity. These principles are simply a progression of values such as truthfulness, trustworthiness, faithfulness, fairness, righteousness, goodness, and the many other values that derive from the practice of and habituation to the lesser virtues associated with the Evolved Ethic.

As a child becomes habituated to the acts and behaviors that manifest the virtues and values that derive from virtues, these principles begin to form. Assuming the pluralistic component of the Evolved Ethic develops during the years of stage two ethical development, these principles will continue to form. Finally, these are the principles that solidify in stage three. In each case, these principles serve the best interest, welfare, and good of Others and the collective whole.

For instance, equality is one of the principles mentioned above. Equality recognizes each human being as an equal among other human beings. As such, it recognizes the importance of the Self-esteem (dignity) need. It recognizes that all human beings, regardless of differences, need respect and dignity. It recognizes that all human beings want to be free and self-determinant. All want to live free of pain and fear. All want to be self-sufficient and independent. In application, it recognizes the value and worth of each human being as a member of the collective whole of humanity.

However, the principle of equality does not suggest, for instance, that every Self should receive equal pay regardless of the level of effort, contribution, responsibility, knowledge, skill, talent, or ability. The notion that every Self should receive equal pay without consideration of these factors results in inequality and inequity. It reflects the value of unfairness. Similarly, giving greater or lesser consideration to the contribution, responsibility, knowledge, skill, talent, or ability of members of one race, gender, ethnic group, or any of the other differences that exists among human beings reflects the values of unfairness and unscrupulousness.

Much as interrelationships exist within and among the values that derive from the virtues, interrelationships also exist among the principles that derive from these values. For instance, as Self practices the principle of equality, Self often also practices other principles, such as justice and impartiality. Similarly, Self also practices truth, equanimity, and fraternity. Indeed, it is unlikely Self can actually practice one principle to the total exclusion of all other principles. This is because of the web of interrelationships that exists within and among the principles. Figure 7-2 illustrates this web of interrelationships.

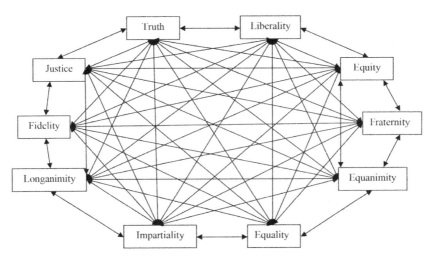

Figure 7-2, The Web of Interrelationships of Principles Associated with the Evolved Ethic.

These principles are objective. As such, these principles do not and cannot, by themselves, distinguish one Self from another Self. They are, therefore, universal in and of themselves. They cannot be otherwise. Further, these principles are desirable both as ends and as means to ends. In each case, these objective principles serve the best interest, welfare, and good of all Others and the collective whole at all levels.

Furthermore, the objective application of these principles necessarily includes all Others. For instance, the objective application of the principle of justice results in justice for all. If the principle of justice is not objectively applied to all Others, then it is a subjective application of the principle of injustice being practiced. As a second example, the objective application of the principle of impartiality results in impartiality for all. If this principle is not objectively applied to all Others, it is a subjective application of the principle of partiality being practiced. The more objective the application of a principle becomes, the more universal this application becomes. The same is the case with each of the principles that derive from values associated with virtues and the Evolved Ethic.

The objective, universal application of each of these objective principles gives respect and worth to all human beings. The universal application of these objective principles can result in all people living free from pain and fear. Without the objective, universal application of these principles, human beings will always live in pain and fear. Unfortunately, more often, it is the subjective principles associated with the Unevolved Ethic that are more readily visible.

This list of subjective principles would include untruth, injustice, inequity, inequality, infidelity, partiality, illiberality, unequanimity, illonganimity, and individuality. If the principle of fraternity is understood to mean fellowship or community and community is inclusive, then the opposing principle would necessarily be exclusive. Therefore, the subjective principle that is the opposite of fraternity is individuality. Individuality, in this usage, is consistent with the view of primacy of the individual.

This view holds that the interest, welfare, and good of the individual trump the interest, welfare, and good of the collective whole. It suggests the needs, wants, desires, cravings, and obsessions of Self trump the interest, welfare, and good of the collective whole. It suggests Self can and should act and behave for the benefit of Self so long as Self does no harm to Others or the collective whole. Unfortunately, but consistent with this view, harm is most often limited to consideration of only quantifiable, measurable harm. This view tends to minimalize or ignore the less quantifiable or measurable harms. Therefore, this view of "individuality" is very consistent with the Unevolved Ethic.

By their very meaning, the subjective principles that form from values derived from vices favor Self and exclude Others. Each favors the interest, welfare, and good of Self or a collective form of Self over the interest, welfare, and good of Others and the collective whole. As such, each is desirable only as an end or means to an end that favors Self or a collective form of Self. Further, the subjective application of these principles also favors the interest, welfare, and good of Self or a collective form of Self. The subjective application of these principles always results in harm for Others and the collective whole. It denies dignity and respect to Others. It denies value and worth to Others. It ensures that people will continue to live in pain and fear.

But just as was the case with values that derive from vices, most Selves would not claim to hold the subjective principles that form from these values. Despite evidence to the contrary, most Selves would not suggest they hold untruth, inequality, or infidelity as principles. Similarly, most would not claim to hold partiality, illiberality, unequanimity, or illonganimity as principles. Most Selves recognize holding these principles may well lead to disapproval, perhaps even condemnation, by Others and the collective whole. It may well lead to harm for Self. So again, most Selves learn to voice the set of objective principles more likely to gain the approval of Others and the collective whole. Most learn to voice the principles consistent with the Evolved Ethic, but practice the principles consistent with the Unevolved Ethic.

Much as with values, most people learn to voice the principles consistent with the Evolved Ethic when attending school or through other sources, but practice and become habituated to the subjective principles consistent with the Unevolved Ethic. They claim to hold the objective principles that trace to the Evolved Ethic because they want to be treated in a manner consistent with these principles. They want justice, equality, impartiality, and the other principles that trace to the Evolved Ethic for Self. There is benefit for Self when Self is treated according to these principles. There is potential and even realized harm when Self is treated according to the subjective principles that trace to the Unevolved Ethic. Self wants the benefit for Self and will try to avoid the harm for Self. So, Self learns to voice the objective principles that trace to the Evolved Ethic and practice the subjective principles that trace to the Unevolved Ethic.

Consistent with the developing components of the Unevolved Ethic, the rational morality will encourage and enable the creation, adoption, and practice of the rationalizations, justifications, explanations, and excuses that accompany the application of these subjective principles. Since harm for Others and the collective whole necessarily results from the application of these principles, Self requires these rationalizations, justifications, explanations, and excuses to minimalize or ignore that harm. As a result, Self will practice moral hypocrisy. This hypocrisy often becomes apparent in the acts and behaviors influenced by these principles. But it will also become apparent in the beliefs, attitudes, and opinions held and espoused by Self.

Beliefs, attitudes, and opinions held and expressed by Self often give insight into the ethic, values and principles of Self. As an extreme example, there are those Selves who staunchly adhere to the belief of "Aryan or white supremacy." This is a belief indicative of subjective principles such as injustice, inequality, inequity, and partiality. It is indicative of values that derive from the vices and the Unevolved Ethic. Acts and behaviors that manifest these or similar beliefs, attitudes, and opinions manifest the willingness and ability to exclude Others. Acts and behaviors that manifest these or similar beliefs, attitudes, and opinions manifest the willingness and ability to deny value, worth, and dignity to Others. These acts result in harm for Others and the collective whole, harm that is minimalized or ignored by those Selves who hold these beliefs, attitudes, and opinions. However, this is only one extreme example of beliefs, attitudes, and opinions that trace back to principles and values consistent with the Unevolved Ethic.

Many other less extreme, but equally harmful examples exist. Many of these beliefs, attitudes, and opinions also center on issues of race, creed, ethnicity, gender identity, nationality, language, religion, disability, and sexual preference. Other beliefs, attitudes, or opinions center on education level or political affiliation. Still, other beliefs, attitudes, and opinions center on social or economic standing.

In each instance, acts and behaviors that manifest these beliefs, attitudes, and opinions give insight into the principles and values of those

Selves who hold them. In each instance, these beliefs, attitudes, and opinions give insight into the developing or fully developed Unevolved Ethic. Acts and behaviors that trace to these beliefs, attitudes, and opinions result in harm for Others and the collective whole that is minimalized or ignored. Just the opposite is the case when beliefs, attitudes, and opinions form from principles and values consistent with the developing or developed Evolved Ethic.

Beliefs, attitudes, and opinions that form as the Evolved Ethic develops are not exclusive. These beliefs, attitudes, and opinions will be consistent with the objective principles that derive from values based on the virtues. These beliefs, attitudes, and opinions will reflect the willingness and ability to include all Others. They will reflect the willingness and ability to accept and embrace all people and maximize benefit for Others and the collective whole. They will reflect the willingness and ability to minimize harm for Others and the collective whole. These beliefs, attitudes, and opinions build trust, security, certainty, and confidence. They build harmony and community.

The beliefs, attitudes, and opinions of Self then form the basis for the next progression of the nested diagram. This progression is the ideologies and philosophies of Self. Ideologies and philosophies are essentially beliefs, attitudes, and opinions that combine to form an aggregate. This aggregate is the ideology or philosophy of Self.

Since ideologies and philosophies form from the beliefs, attitudes, and opinions of Self, they reflect the principles and values that underlie the beliefs, attitudes, and opinions. They reflect the developing or developed ethic of Self. More moderate beliefs, attitudes, and opinions, influence more moderate ideologies and philosophies. More extreme beliefs, attitudes, and opinions, influence more extreme ideologies and philosophies. These more extreme beliefs, attitudes, and opinions often indicate less tolerance and no acceptance of Others.

If the developing or developed ethic is the Unevolved Ethic, the developing ideology and philosophy of Self will reflect this ethic. The ideology and philosophy of Self will favor Self and the interest, welfare, and good of Self. The ideology and philosophy of Self will favor maximizing benefit and minimizing harm for Self. At worst, it will be exclusive of Others and reflect intolerance of Others. At best, it may reflect tolerance of Others. Finally, it will minimalize or ignore the harm that results for Others and the collective whole.

Conversely, if the developing or developed ethic is the Evolved Ethic, the developing ideology and philosophy of Self will reflect this ethic. The ideology and philosophy of Self will, to some extent or degree, favor the interest, welfare, and good of Others and the collective whole. It will favor maximizing benefit and minimizing harm for Others and the collective whole. The ideology and philosophy of Self will be inclusive of Others. It will reflect the acceptance and embrace of Others. It will minimalize or ignore harm that results for Self in the interest of Others and the collective whole.

In the last progression, regardless of which ethic develops, the long-term pattern of acts and behaviors of Self trace through the ideology and philosophy of Self to provide insight into the beliefs, attitudes, opinions, principles, and values of Self. This pattern of acts and behaviors provides insight into the very ethic of Self. The pattern provides insight into the ethic that guides the choices and motivates the acts and behaviors of Self.

However, the same long-term pattern of acts and behaviors also give insight into the state of ethical development of Self. It provides the characteristic clues to the state of ethical development of Self. These states of ethical development are the final topic related to ethical development.

States of Ethical Development

There are three states of ethical development, the irrational, the rational, and the transrational. The long-term pattern of acts and behaviors of each Self corresponds to one of these three states. For the sake of brevity, throughout this discussion, I will often refer to the states of ethical development using the shorthand titles "irrational," "rational," and "transrational" and simply leave off the extension "state" or "state of ethical development." However, I do want to establish that these terms do conform to the definition of "state."

The term "state" is defined in part as, "The condition of a person or thing with respect to circumstances, qualities, etc." Consistent with this definition, each of the three states of ethical development is easily described in terms of general qualities or characteristics. These general qualities or characteristics describe the condition of Self with respect to those qualities or characteristics. In this usage, the terms describe the condition of being irrational, rational, or transrational. In each case, the terms are a direct tie back to the ethic of Self.

For instance, the irrational state of ethical development is generally associated with feelings and the heart. Characteristic acts and behaviors associated with the irrational state reflect a basis in feelings and emotions, both positive and negative. These acts and behaviors may well reflect the unwillingness or inability to control the emotions of Self. Indeed, acts and behaviors associated with the irrational often seem inconsistent and erratic. These acts and behaviors may often swing from one emotion to another, from high to low and back again. Similarly, the irrational may seemingly move from one emotional crisis to the next emotional crisis.

Further, acts and behaviors associated with the irrational state will often, to some extent or degree, reflect a lack of control over the wants, desires, cravings, obsessions, impulses and urges of Self. This results in acts and behaviors that also appear inconsistent and erratic. These acts or behaviors may appear unconscious or without purpose. They may even appear insensible or senseless. They may appear immature or childish.

As a result, control over the acts and behaviors characteristic of the irrational must often come from external sources. Similarly, conformance to the rules and standards of society must often come from external sources. Conformance must come through the various standards, codes, and laws that constrain or restrain the acts and behaviors of Self.

Acts and behaviors characteristic of the irrational state of ethical development often seem contrary to the best interest, welfare, and good of Self. They often seem to fail even to consider possible harm for Self and completely fail to consider harm for Others and the collective whole. As a result, they often manifest a lack of common sense. This is the case since common sense dictates that Self act and behave in a manner that does not result in harm to Self or the best interest, welfare, and good of Self. Yet, acting or behaving from feelings and emotions, as well as wants, needs, cravings, obsession, impulses, and urges is tied very directly to pleasure for Self.

Acting or behaving from feelings or emotions carries benefit (pleasure) for Self. This is the case whether Self is acting from positive or negative feelings or emotions. The intensity of the pleasure will vary with the intensity of the feelings or emotions. Likewise, acting on the wants, desires, cravings, obsessions, impulses, and urges of Self also carries benefit (pleasure) for Self. This is regardless of how unhealthy the pleasure may be for Self. This is also regardless of the harm that may ultimately result for Self and the interest, welfare, or good of Self. Finally, this is regardless of the harm that results for Others and the collective whole.

As a result, it is easy to associate the irrational state of ethical development with acts and behaviors that are focused on a selfish, self-centered, self-promoting pursuit of pleasure for Self. Often, this is immediate or instant pleasure for Self. It is also easy to associate the irrational state of ethical development with acts and behaviors that focus on regard or concern for Self to the exclusion of Others. Further, it is also easy to associate the willingness and ability to minimize or avoid responsibility and accountability for Self with the irrational state. Therefore, it is easy to associate the irrational state of ethical development with the willingness and ability to employ rationalizations, justifications, explanations, excuses and self-deception strategies. Finally, it is easy to associate the irrational state of ethical development with the developing and developed Unevolved Ethic.

Historically speaking, there has been a certain disdain for those Selves whose state of ethical development is the irrational. This disdain is generally tied to the attitude or belief that the state of ethical development is directly associated with knowledge level and the pursuit of knowledge. Unfortunately, this attitude or belief ignores the relationship between the states of ethical development and ethic itself. Neither the pursuit of knowledge nor education level solely determines the state of ethical development. However, the failure to pursue educational (learning) opportunities can be an indicator of the irrational state.

The pursuit of education and knowledge is generally in the best interest of Self. Certainly, education and knowledge enhance the ability of Self to satisfy the lower-level needs. Similarly, the development of skills, abilities and talents, all improve the ability of Self to meet lower-level needs. As knowledge, skills, abilities, and talents of Self increase and improve, a wider array of options for meeting the lower-level needs within the range of right, correct, and appropriate acts and behaviors becomes available. It is also the case that education and knowledge reduce fear of the unknown. Often, through the pursuit of knowledge, the unknown becomes known. This is also in the best interest, welfare, and good of Self.

Therefore, it is easy to suggest that failure to pursue education and knowledge, as well as failure to develop skills, talents, and abilities, is characteristic of the irrational. However, it is only one characteristic. It is one characteristic set of acts or behaviors within a larger pattern of acts and behaviors. It is one set of acts or behaviors within a larger pattern of acts and behaviors that focuses on the pursuit of more immediate pleasure for Self. Finally, it is only one set of acts or behaviors within a pattern that indicates a lack of control or restraint over the acts and behaviors of Self. This seeming lack of control or restraint differs considerably with the rational state of ethical development.

Generally speaking, acts and behaviors associated with the rational state of ethical development are based on reasoning and the center of reasoning is the mind. Therefore, characteristic acts and behaviors of the rational state reflect a basis in reasoning and not feelings or emotions. As such, acts and behaviors associated with the rational state are generally thought to be opposite of those associated with the irrational state. This does not mean a rational Self can never manifest emotion or emotional outbursts or never act from an urge or impulse. It simply means those manifestations are outside the characteristic pattern of acts and behaviors associated with the rational state.

Acts and behaviors characteristic of the rational state are much more likely to be calculated, measured, and deliberate. These acts and behaviors follow a pattern that is much more conscious, purposeful, and premeditated. These acts and behaviors are often termed mature, settled, or adult. They are, generally speaking, the opposite of the inconsistent, erratic, impulsive, or unconscious acts and behaviors characteristic of the irrational state. As such, the acts and behaviors characteristic of the rational state are far more consistent with common sense. They do generally reflect consideration of potential harm for Self. For instance, acts and behaviors consistent with the rational state may be termed emotionless. This characteristic is consistent with efforts to minimize harm for Self. It is consistent with acts and behaviors that guard and protect Self from emotional harm as well as physical harm.

In a more general sense, the characteristic pattern of acts and behaviors of the rational state will reflect control over the emotions, wants, desires, cravings, obsessions, impulses, and urges of Self. This control stems from consideration of the best interest, welfare, and good of Self. It reflects a level of control or restraint necessary to minimize harm for Self. As such, acts and behaviors associated with the rational generally reflect a more deliberate and measured control over the pursuit of pleasure for Self. They reflect a more deliberate, measured consideration of pain or the privation of pleasure for Self. Where the emphasis of the irrational is most often pleasure for Self, the emphasis of the rational is most often the avoidance of harm for Self. This emphasis of the rational and irrational provides a link back to comments concerning the development of the egoistic and hedonistic utilitarian components of the Unevolved Ethic.

In Chapter 2, I indicated the emphasis of the developing egoistic component will be either maximizing benefit (pleasure) for Self *or* minimizing harm (pain or the privation of pleasure) for Self. I then indicated the emphasis of the egoistic component remains the stronger emphasis of the hedonistic utilitarian component. This means that as the hedonistic utilitarian component develops, the emphasis of the egoistic component will, to some extent or degree, remain the more dominant emphasis. Conversely, the complimentary emphasis will remain, to some extent or degree, the weaker emphasis of the utilitarian component.

It follows then, that the emphasis of the egoistic component figures prominently in determining the state of ethical development. It follows that if the emphasis of the egoistic component is benefit (pleasure) for Self, the state of ethical development will be the irrational. Acts and behaviors will manifest the characteristic willingness and ability to focus on pleasure for Self. It follows also that if the emphasis of the egoistic component is minimizing harm (pain or the privation of pleasure) for Self, the state of ethical development will be the rational. Acts and behaviors will manifest the characteristic willingness and ability to consider consequences for Self.

This rational consideration of consequences for Self is a form of risk assessment. It is an assessment of potential harm for Self. Self will not act if Self determines potential harm for Self outweighs the benefit. Self will act if Self believes the benefit of an act or behavior outweighs the potential harm for Self. The rational will act if the risk of harm to Self is reasonable or manageable. Said a little more simply, the rational are more likely to think first and then act (if at all) while the irrational are more likely to act first and think later (if at all). This consideration of harm for Self also results in a characteristic adoption and conformance to the rules, codes, standards, and laws of society by the rational.

The rational recognize that the rules, codes, standards, and laws of society assist Self in minimizing harm for Self. Further, they facilitate the efforts of Self to meet the lower-level needs of Self. As such, they facilitate the preservation and promotion of Self. As a result, they serve the best interest, welfare, and good of Self. Therefore, it is very reasonable for Self to adopt and conform to these rules, codes, standards and laws. It is also very reasonable for Self to engage in reciprocity within the collective whole.

The concept of reciprocity is easily associated with and characteristic of the rational state of ethical development. The treatment of Others as Self wants to be treated is very rational. Reciprocity infers consideration of the impact an act or behavior of Self may have on Others and a refrain from those acts and behaviors that would result in harm to Others. However, this consideration stems primarily from consideration or regard for the best interest, welfare, and good of Self. It stems from the desire to minimize harm for Self. Self will control acts and behaviors that result in harm to Others because Self wants Others to do the same. Reciprocity is, therefore, consistent with a more deliberate, conscious, reasoned approach to maximizing benefit and minimizing harm to Self. Similarly, the willingness to engage in compromise is also characteristic of the rational state of ethical development.

Compromise is often useful for resolving contention or conflict between two or more interests. It is, therefore, associated with some level of competition between the interests of two or more Selves. These may be the interests of two or more individual Selves or the interests of two or more collective forms of Self, such as companies, corporations, cities, states, or even nation-states. Compromise is also useful to establish or reestablish a balance or status quo between two or more competing interests. However, compromise does not always result in a fair or equitable balance.

Compromise will generally favor the stronger or more powerful interest. As a result, Self or a collective form of Self will generally only engage in compromise when it becomes clear that compromise is in the best interest, welfare, and good of Self. Self or a collective form of Self will generally only agree to compromise to minimize a loss or further loss to Self or the interest, welfare, or good of Self. But compromise often requires accepting some level of loss to the interest, welfare, or good of the Self initiating compromise since it is often the weaker Self or the Self in the weaker position that initiates compromise. To gain compromise, the weaker Self will often sacrifice some level of self-interest to lessen the possibility of even greater loss to Self, perhaps even the very survival of Self.

It is very rational to seek compromise, especially in situations or circumstances that threaten the preservation or survival of Self or a collective form of Self. Seeking compromise becomes a very rational approach to minimizing harm or further harm for Self. Unfortunately, compromise is and can only be successful to the extent or degree the stronger Self or the Self in the stronger position also believes it is in the best interest, welfare, and good of Self to compromise. If the stronger Self does not believe compromise serves the interest, welfare, or good of Self, attempts at compromise will likely fail.

Interestingly enough, throughout history, many philosophers championed the rational state of ethical development as the highest state of ethical development for humankind. They celebrated humankind's ability to reason and to act and behave rationally. They championed that it is right, correct, and appropriate for Self to act and behave for the interest, welfare, and good of Self. Some even argued that each Self, acting and behaving for the interest, welfare, and good of Self, serves the best interest, welfare, and good of the collective whole.

Unfortunately, this suggestion overlooks or ignores that reasoning is the ability employed to create and employ the rationalizations, justifications, explanations, and excuses that minimalize or ignore harm for Others and the collective whole in the interest of Self. It seems to overlook or ignore that reasoning is the ability by which Self creates and employs the self-deception strategies that minimalize or ignore harm to Others and the collective whole in the interest of Self. Indeed, at this point in the discussion, this seems to be a very subjective argument. A subjective argument used to justify and excuse acts and behaviors that maximize benefit and minimize harm for Self at the expense of harm to Others and the collective whole.

The more objective argument suggests acting and behaving to maximize benefit and minimize harm for Self necessarily carries harm for the collective whole and the best interest, welfare, and good of Others and the collective whole. These acts and behaviors result in competition, contention and conflict, between Selves and collective forms of Self. They build distrust, doubt, uncertainty, and suspicion. They build pessimism, skepticism, and cynicism. They build dissonance and disharmony within the collective whole. But, the ability to reason always stands ready to minimalize these harms to Others and the collective whole. It always stands ready to rationalize, justify, explain, and excuse these harms in the interest of Self. This is not the case with the third state of ethical development, the transrational state.

The prefix "trans", in conjunction with another word suggests meanings such as "across", "through", or "beyond". Combining the prefix "trans" with the word "rational" suggests beyond rational. It suggests a state of ethical development that transcends the rational state of ethical development. It suggests a state of ethical development that transcends focus on the best interest, welfare, and good of Self. It suggests a state of ethical development that transcends focus on consideration of harm only for Self. The characteristics associated with the transrational state satisfy this suggestion of transcendence.

It is characteristic of the transrational state to focus on the interest, welfare, and good of Others and the collective whole. It is characteristic of the transrational state to focus on the preservation and promotion of Others and the collective whole. It is characteristic of the transrational state to focus on benefit (trust, security, certainty, etc.) for Others and the collective whole. But it is also characteristic of the transrational state to minimalize or ignore harm for Self when acting or behaving to benefit Others and the collective whole. Additionally, it is characteristic of the transrational to control and restrain the emotions, impulses, and urges of Self. Finally, it is characteristic of the transrational to control and restrain the wants, desires, cravings, and obsessions of Self.

This control is not the control that comes from external sources. This control is not the control that comes from the rules, codes, standards, and laws of society. It is not the control based on concern for the interest, welfare, and good of Self. Nor is it the control based on efforts to minimize or avoid pain or the privation of pleasure for Self. This is the self-control and self-restraint that develops in conjunction with the components of the Evolved Ethic.

Clearly, from this list of characteristics, it is easy to equate the transrational state of ethical development with the Evolved Ethic. Characteristic acts and behaviors associated with the transrational are consistent with the developing and developed Evolved Ethic. These acts and behaviors demonstrate the willingness and ability to act for the benefit of Others and the collective whole without consideration or regard for the best interest, welfare, or good of Self. They are acts and behaviors that require the willingness and ability to minimalize or ignore harm for Self in the interest of benefit for Others and the collective whole. However, these characteristic acts and behaviors also reflect the emphasis of both the virtue and pluralistic components of the Evolved Ethic.

In Chapter 5, I indicated the virtue ethic will develop with an emphasis of either maximizing benefit *or* minimizing harm for Others. I also indicated the pluralistic utilitarian component will also reflect this emphasis. In other words, the pluralistic utilitarian component will, to some extent or degree, reflect the emphasis of the virtue component. However, since an emphasis on either maximizing benefit *or* minimizing harm for Others manifests the Evolved Ethic, both are transrational. Unfortunately, the willingness and ability to manifest acts and behaviors consistent with the transrational state can be misunderstood.

The willingness and ability to manifest acts and behaviors consistent with the transrational state are misunderstood since acts and behaviors that serve the interest, welfare, or good of Others and the collective whole do not directly serve the interest, welfare, or good of Self. Quite the opposite is the case. Acts and behaviors that serve the interest, welfare, or good of Others and the collective whole often result in harm (pain or the privation of pleasure) for Self. Therefore, these acts and behaviors appear inconsistent with the best interest, welfare, or good of Self. As such, they give the appearance of being irrational since acts or behaviors that are not in the best interest, welfare, or good of Self are generally labeled irrational. However, this is not the case. These acts and behaviors simply reflect the state of ethical development that transcends the rational. They reflect the state of ethical development consistent with the developing or developed Evolved Ethic. Of course, this last statement infers that both the irrational and rational states of ethical development are consistent with the Unevolved Ethic.

Figure 7-3 illustrates the placement of the three ethical states of development on the Unevolved-Evolved Continuum. The dotted line, placed between the irrational and rational states, indicates the developmental shift point between these two states of development. The developmental shift point between the rational and transrational states is the same location as the Point of Transcendence.

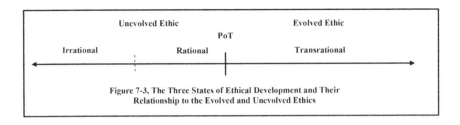

Figure 7-3, The Three States of Ethical Development and Their
Relationship to the Evolved and Unevolved Ethics

Both the irrational and rational states of ethical development lie under the Unevolved Ethic since characteristic acts and behaviors of these states are characteristic of the ethic. On the other hand, the transrational state of ethical development lies under the Evolved Ethic since characteristic acts and behaviors of this state are characteristic of this ethic. The long-term pattern of acts and behaviors of Self will reflect both the state of ethical development and the guiding and motivating ethic of Self. Conversely, acts and behaviors that appear inconsistent with both the state of ethical development and ethic of Self will also be inconsistent with the long-term pattern of acts and behaviors. They will most likely be only arbitrary, transitory, or random acts or behaviors.

Finally, as it is possible, with sufficient observation of manifest acts and behaviors, to use the Unevolved-Evolved Continuum to estimate ethic, it is also possible to estimate the location of states of ethical development. However, it is important to acknowledge a critical point concerning estimating the state of ethical development on the continuum. Earlier in this discussion of ethics, I recognized that it is difficult to estimate the location of an ethic on the Unevolved-Evolved Continuum if that ethic resides at or near the Point of Transcendence. It is difficult because observable, manifest acts and behaviors are very similar in appearance at or near the PoT. It becomes easier to distinguish as ethic moves away from the PoT.

Estimating states of ethical development is much the same. It is difficult to estimate states of ethical development at or near the developmental shift points between the irrational and rational states and again between the rational and transrational states. This difficulty arises because acts and behaviors are very similar at or near those shift points. It becomes easier to distinguish states of ethical development as acts and behaviors tend to demonstrate more characteristics of one or the other state. However, even then it would be imprudent, perhaps even rash, to attempt to estimate the state of ethical development based on a small number of observable acts or behaviors. As I have said from the beginning of this discussion of the two ethics, it is always patterns of behavior that give insight into the ethic of Self. This is also true of states of ethical development.

One situation in which the pattern may be most apparent is through the acts and behaviors demonstrated within the relationships in which an individual Self participates. The characteristics associated with the three states of ethical development may become most evident within the context of relationships. They become evident within the relationships Self enters or leaves. Therefore, both the ethical state of development and the underlying ethic have a profound effect on relationships. This impact on relationships is the subject of the next chapter.

CHAPTER 8:
ETHIC AND RELATIONSHIPS

The purpose of this chapter is to discuss the impact of ethic on relationships. I believe it is within the context of relationships that human beings often manifest the most complex acts and behaviors. These acts and behaviors manifest themselves in each of the many relationships in which human beings engage. They manifest themselves in the interactions that take place within relationships. The chapter begins with the introduction and discussion of the two types of relationships. Much of the remainder of the chapter focuses on the impact of ethic and the states of ethical development on relationships.

In the context of this theory of ethics, there are two types of relationships. These are alliances and unions. All relationships, regardless of form and duration, are either an alliance or a union. The difference between the two types centers on who or what is served by the existence of the relationship. In other words, the type depends on who or what benefits from the existence of the relationship. Alliances always exist to serve the interest, welfare, or good of Self. To some extent or degree, alliances serve the interest, welfare, and good of each Self participating in the relationship. On the contrary, unions exist to serve the interest, welfare, and good of the collective whole that is the relationship. Each Self participating in a union seeks to maximize benefit and minimize harm for the union.

Alliances are often short-term or temporary. This does not mean an alliance cannot last a considerable amount of time. It simply means alliances tend to be shorter-term. Some last only very briefly. They last only so long as each Self participating in the alliance determines Self benefits from the relationship. They last only so long as each Self determines continued participation in the relationship sufficiently serves the interest, welfare, or good of Self. Therefore, subjective consideration of benefit for Self is paramount within alliances. The consideration of benefit for Others or the alliance itself is secondary, if at all. Because of this subjective focus on the interest, welfare, and good of Self, alliances exist at the level of "I," "Me." There is always consideration of that which is good or best for "I," "Me" within an alliance.

Self will often abandon an alliance when Self determines the alliance no longer sufficiently serves the best interest, welfare, or good of Self. Self will also abandon an alliance if Self determines a different alliance would better serve the interest, welfare, or good of Self. This is also a subjective assessment. For instance, the alliance formed when an individual enters a store to make a purchase will often last only long enough to conclude a purchase. This interaction is still an alliance. An alliance of a very short duration, but an alliance all the same.

The duration of the alliance depends largely on how each Self perceives the interaction that occurs within the alliance. If both Selves perceive the interaction as pleasant, the alliance may continue in the form of repeat visits and repeat purchases. If one or both Selves perceive the interaction as unpleasant, that Self or Selves will withdraw, to the degree possible, from the alliance. Many, many very brief alliances form and dissolve in this same manner. On the other hand, unions have the potential to be longer-lasting.

Unions have the potential to be longer lasting because they do not exist for the benefit of each Self participating in the relationship. Unions do not exist to serve the best interest, welfare, or good of Self. Therefore, their duration is not driven by a subjective assessment of benefit or harm for Self. Within a union, a participating Self does not seek to maximize benefit and minimize harm for Self. Therefore, unions do not end based on a subjective assessment of benefit or harm for Self or the best interest, welfare, or good of Self. Rather, Self minimalizes or ignores harm to Self that derives from participation in the union. The consideration of benefit to the relationship, the union, is paramount. This is the consideration of benefit at the level of "We," "Us." Therefore, unions exist at the level of "We," "Us" and not at the level of "I," "Me." It is consideration of benefit at the level of "We," "Us" that sustains the union. Figure 8-1 illustrates the level of both alliances and unions.

Relationship	Level
Unions	"We", "Us"
Alliances	"I", "Me"

Figure 8-1, The Level of Alliances and Unions

While there is always subjective consideration of benefit for Self within an alliance, there is also subjective consideration of harm for Self that results from participation in an alliance. If harm for Self begins to outweigh benefit, Self will often abandon an alliance. This harm for Self can take many forms, but can be thought of as the cost or loss to Self for participating in a particular alliance. This harm might be stated in terms of tangible or intangible resources of Self. It might also be stated in terms of the emotional cost of participating in an alliance. Finally, it can be thought of as the physical, psychological, or even spiritual cost of participating in an alliance.

If the real or perceived cost or harm to Self for participating in an alliance outweighs the reward or benefit, then Self will likely abandon the alliance and may seek a different alliance. However, even in situations in which the cost or harm outweighs the benefit for Self, Self may choose to continue in an alliance. This is because alliances often facilitate the efforts of Self to satisfy the four lower-level needs of Self.

Participating in alliances facilitates the ability of Self to satisfy both the physical and psychological needs of Self. Indeed, Self often participates in an alliance to satisfy the belonging (affiliation) and esteem needs through the interactions that occur within an alliance. The belonging (affiliation) needs concern the acceptance of Self by other Selves. Satisfying this need relies on the acceptance of Self through the friendship, companionship, and comraderie found in alliances. The esteem need concerns the approval of Self within a collective whole. Esteem needs pertain to the good standing of Self within the collective whole, that is, the alliance.

Entering and participating in alliances to meet the belonging (affiliation) and esteem needs contributes to the psychological well-being of Self. On the other hand, failing to enter alliances to meet these needs is psychologically unhealthy. Isolation from alliances, in the form of friendships and other forms of relationships, can lead to psychological illness. In many cases, this can take the form of depression or other related psychological illnesses. It is therefore, in the best interest, welfare, and good of Self to seek out and participate in alliances. But Self will often find that the lower two needs, physiological and safety/security, are also easier to satisfy through participation in alliances.

For instance, entering an alliance with an employer often provides the funds necessary for Self to feed and nourish Self. Similarly, entering an alliance with an employer often provides the funds necessary to clothe and shelter Self. In a somewhat larger sense, it is through alliances with Others that often enables Self to feel safe and secure. These alliances are often called neighborhoods, villages, towns, cities, states, and provinces, as well as nation-states. Each of these various examples of a collective whole is also an example of an alliance in which Self participates.

Generally speaking, each of these examples of an alliance enables and facilitates the efforts of Self to satisfy all four of the lower-level needs. Each enables and facilitates the ability of Self to remain physically and psychologically healthy. Without alliances, each Self would likely find it much more difficult, if not impossible, to meet even the most fundamental physiological needs.

It is also the case that Self will often find that alliances enable Self to satisfy the wants, desires, cravings, and obsessions of Self. To support this assertion requires only the recognition that alliances with employers often provide the funds that enable Self to satisfy many of the wants, desires, cravings, and obsessions of Self. However, the ability to satisfy the needs, as well as the wants, desires, cravings, and obsessions of Self, even within alliances, is sometimes hindered or impaired by the level of competition that exists within an alliance.

In fact, generally speaking, there is always the potential for competition within alliances and there is often competition between alliances. The competition that occurs within an alliance is internal competition and the competition that occurs between alliances is external. In both cases, the level of competition can and often does range from contention to conflict. It can and does extend even to the level of conflict termed war. In the case of internal competition, the contention or conflict is between the Selves participating in an alliance. It arises as each Self seeks to maximize benefit and minimize harm for Self within the context of the alliance. It occurs as each Self acts and behaves for the best interest, welfare, and good of Self, often at the expense of harm to Others participating in the alliance.

However, the intensity of competition within an alliance is lessened or tempered to the extent or degree there is concern for mutual benefit and reciprocity within the alliance. It may also be tempered or lessened if those Selves participating in the alliance are willing to engage in compromise within the alliance.

Mutual benefit infers benefit for Self as well as for all other Selves participating in an alliance. The term mutual benefit infers the interest, welfare, and good of each Self in the alliance benefits from participation in the alliance. Self is often more likely to remain in an alliance in which benefit favors Self or is, at least, mutual. Similarly, Self may remain in an alliance in which reciprocity, among and between members of the alliance, ensures a reasonable level of balance of benefit for all Selves participating in the alliance.

By definition, reciprocity means "a reciprocal state or relation. Reciprocation: mutual exchange." Reciprocation is then defined as, "an act or instance of reciprocating. A returning, usually for something given. A mutual giving and receiving." In the context of this discussion of alliances, reciprocity infers benefit for Others in exchange for benefit to Self. This emphasis on benefit for Self is suggested by the comment, "Do for others as you would have them do for you." While this comment suggests benefit for Others in exchange for benefit to Self, the benefit maximized for Self includes the lessening or tempering of internal competition within an alliance. On the other hand, the harm minimized for Self includes the escalation or intensification of competition within an alliance.

Ultimately, each Self in an alliance is the beneficiary of acts and behaviors that manifest reciprocity. Therefore, reciprocity maximizes benefit and minimizes harm for Self. The lessening or tempering of internal competition is in the best interest, welfare and good of each Self participating in an alliance. Likewise, minimizing the escalation or intensification of competition within an alliance is also in the best interest, welfare, and good of each Self participating in the alliance. However, reciprocity will only occur to the extent or degree to which each Self gives secondary consideration to the interest, welfare, and good of Others.

If each Self fails to give this secondary consideration reciprocity cannot and will not exist within the alliance. Similarly, if each Self fails to give secondary consideration to harm for Others, reciprocity cannot and will not exist within the alliance. In either event, the intensity of competition will increase within the alliance. At some point, if allowed to persist, internal competition will cause the alliance to become dysfunctional and possibly dissolve. As the intensity of competition increases, each Self in the alliance essentially becomes a "free agent" focusing greater attention on the best interest, welfare, and good of only Self. Self may exercise this free agency by choosing to abandon the alliance.

As more and more Selves exercise free agency, the alliance may completely dissolve. This is evident in the number of friendships that dissolve every day. It is evident in the number of marriages that dissolve every day. It is often evident in the number of teams, clubs, organizations, and even companies that dissolve every day. However, dissolution of the alliance may be avoided or at least delayed if the Selves participating in the alliance are willing to engage in compromise within the alliance. As stated in Chapter 7, compromise is often useful for establishing or restoring balance between the interests of two or more competing Selves.

In the context of this discussion of internal competition within alliances, compromise offers the possibility of establishing or restoring balance between the interest, welfare, and good of two or more Selves participating in an alliance. However, as stated earlier, Self will generally only compromise when it is in the best interest of Self to compromise. In addition, Self will only compromise to the extent necessary to serve the best interest, welfare, and good of Self. The willingness to compromise within an alliance reflects the extent or degree to which Self believes Self benefits from the alliance. If Self no longer believes Self benefits sufficiently from the alliance, Self will not compromise and may instead abandon the alliance. Likewise, if Self believes the harm to Self outweighs the benefit of continued participation in the alliance, Self will fail to compromise and may abandon the alliance.

Much of this discussion of internal competition within alliances also applies to external competition. The intensity level of external competition may also be lessened or tempered through mutual benefit, reciprocity, and compromise.

External competition is the competition that occurs between and among two or more alliances. This competition occurs as competing alliances act and behave for the best interest, welfare, and good of Self at the expense of other alliances. This competition is evident in the competition between the alliances known as corporations. It is evident in the competition between the alliances called cities, states, and even nation-states. It is evident in the competition that arises between dissimilar alliances such as corporations and cities or states. Each of these is an example of competition between and among like or differing forms of alliances. This competition can range from contention to conflict. But whatever the intensity level, the competition always centers on the best interest, welfare, and good of Self as opposed to the best interest, welfare, and good of other alliances. Therefore, this competition is also always at the level of "I," "Me" even if "I," "Me" refers to a collective form of "I," "Me."

But much like internal competition, external competition can and will be tempered to the extent to which competing alliances are willing to engage in mutual benefit, reciprocity, and compromise. That willingness to engage in mutual benefit, reciprocity, and compromise is very dependent on the organizational ethic of the competing alliances. The concept of organizational ethic was first introduced in chapter 3. I indicated that the organizational ethic reflects the cumulative, collective ethic of all those Selves who are members of an organization. It will especially reflect the ethic of those Selves occupying the senior positions within the organization.

I will now assert that any ongoing alliance, even the alliances termed friendships and marriages also has a cumulative, collective ethic. Much the same as the previously identified organizational ethic, the collective ethic of an alliance will reflect the cumulative ethic of those Selves participating in the alliance. This collective ethic will then guide and influence the choices and motivate the acts and behaviors of the alliance.

For instance, if the collective ethic of an alliance resides nearer to the PoT on the Unevolved-Evolved Continuum, the alliance will likely manifest greater secondary concern for other similar and dissimilar alliances. It will do so to minimize harm to Self. As the collective ethic of an alliance moves further away from the PoT, the collective ethic will manifest less or no secondary concern for other similar or dissimilar alliances. It will do so to maximize benefit for Self. Therefore, as the collective ethic moves further away from the PoT, the acts and behaviors of these alliances will manifest an increasing unwillingness to engage in mutual benefit, reciprocity, and compromise. As the collective ethic moves further from the PoT, the acts and behaviors of an alliance will place greater emphasis solely on the best interest, welfare, and good of Self. In many instances, the acts and behaviors of alliances may reflect only the best interest, welfare, and good of those Selves in the strongest position to influence the collective ethic.

Often, the level of contention and conflict, within and among alliances results in standards, codes, policies, and even laws intended to lessen or temper competition. For instance, laws that govern fair trade and commerce exist to lessen or temper the level of contention and conflict between and among those alliances engaged in trade and commerce. These laws exist to restrain the collective ethic of those alliances that act and behave with little or no consideration of harm for other alliances. These laws exist to restrain the acts and behaviors of alliances that act only to maximize benefit and minimize harm for Self.

As is always the case, Others and the collective whole bear the harm that results when an alliance or alliances choose to act only to maximize benefit and minimize harm for Self. These harms may take the form of economic harm to the Selves included in the collective whole but also include all the harms listed elsewhere in this discussion of ethics. They certainly include encouraging the growth and intensity of competition, contention and conflict, within and among the various forms of alliances. They further include the building of distrust, uncertainty, insecurity, skepticism and pessimism. They build enmity and bitterness within the collective whole. This is, of course, contrary to the best interest, welfare, and good of the collective whole. The relationships termed unions are much different.

The level of a union, the level of "We," "Us," always resides one level above the level of "I," "Me." As a result, the emphasis or focus of those Selves participating in a union is benefit to the union and not benefit to Self. The emphasis or focus is that which serves the best interest, welfare, and good of the union and not that which serves the interest, welfare, and good of Self. Therefore, the acts and behaviors of those Selves in a union maximize benefit and minimize harm for the collective whole that is the union and minimalize or ignore harm for Self. As a result, unions are potentially more enduring than alliances.

They are potentially more enduring so long as the acts and behaviors of each Self maximize benefit and minimize harm for the collective whole that is the union. The benefits maximized are those benefits mentioned previously in this discussion of ethics. They include the building of trust, certainty, assurance, and security. They include the building of optimism. They include the building of concord, harmony, unity, and community. At the same time, these acts and behaviors minimize harm to the union. Therefore, unions last so long as the acts and behaviors of each participating Self serves the interest, welfare, and good of the relationship, of the union, and not the interest, welfare, and good of Self.

These last comments should make it clear that the formation of a union pre-supposes the ethic of each Self participating in the union is the Evolved Ethic. A true union will not form, nor will a relationship remain a union, if the ethic of a participating Self or Selves is the Unevolved Ethic. A union cannot form or continue as a union if the ethic of one or more Selves guides choices and motivates acts and behaviors that maximize benefit and minimize harm for Self. This is the case whether Self refers to an individual Self or a collective form of Self. The union will end or devolve into an alliance if the focus shifts from the level of "We," "Us," "Our," and "Ours" to the level of "I," "Me," "My," and "Mine." The result may be an alliance, but it will no longer be a union.

This should not be a surprise since acts and behaviors that focus on maximizing benefit and minimizing harm for Self are contrary to the good of the collective whole that is the union. Therefore, these acts and behaviors are not and cannot be in the best interest of the union. Self simply cannot act for the best interest, welfare, and good of Self and the best interest, welfare, and good of the union at the same time. Either the best interest of Self or the best interest of the union will prevail. If the focus becomes Self and the best interest, welfare, and good of Self, it will be to the detriment of the union.

Self may try to minimalize or ignore this harm for the union, but that is only consistent with the Unevolved Ethic. The more Self attempts to minimalize or ignore this harm to the relationship, the more likely the union will end or devolve into an alliance. The same dissolution of a union will occur if a Self or Selves participating in a union begin to utilize the union solely as a means for satisfying the four lower-level needs of Self. While an alliance or alliances provide the means for Self to satisfy one or more of the four lower-level needs, unions do not form or exist to provide this means. Neither does a union provide a means for satisfying the wants, desires, cravings, or obsessions of participating Selves.

As indicated above and elsewhere, acts and behaviors intended to satisfy needs, as well as wants, desires, cravings, and obsessions maximize benefit and minimize harm for Self. At best, these acts and behaviors may result in secondary benefit for Others and the collective whole. As such, attempts by one or more Selves to use a union as a means to satisfy the lower-level needs, as well as wants, desires, cravings, and obsessions associated with these needs, will harm the union. However, this does not mean that unions are not associated with any of the six needs discussed in Chapter 6. Unions are certainly associated with the two higher-level needs of self-esteem (dignity) and self-actualization.

In Chapter 6, I indicated that Self cannot act or behave to satisfy the two highest-level needs of Self. Self can only act or behave to help satisfy these needs for Others. I indicated the willingness and ability to consistently act and behave to help satisfy these needs for Others maximize benefit and minimize harm for Others and the collective whole. In the case of self-esteem (dignity), it maximizes benefit and minimizes harm by giving worth, value, and dignity to Others. Many of the example acts and behaviors provided in Chapter 6 help Others to learn and develop knowledge, skills, talents, and abilities that enable them to satisfy the four lower-level needs better. These acts and behaviors also give worth, value, and dignity to Others by enabling them to become more independent and self-determinant. I indicated these example acts and behaviors that manifest the willingness to give, share, love, and nurture. They manifest integrity. Finally, I indicated that Self must be both willing and able to minimalize or ignore harm for Self that results when Self acts to help Others satisfy these two needs. To translate that conversation to the present conversation of unions is not difficult.

A union will only form and continue to exist if each Self is acting and behaving to maximize benefit and minimize harm for the relationship and, by extension, those Others in the relationship. A union will only continue to exist if each Self is nurturing both the relationship and, by extension, those Others in the relationship. It will form and continue to exist so long as each Self treats the union and those Others in the union with integrity. In other words, it will form and continue only so long as each Self in the union gives respect, worth, and dignity to the union and those Others participating in the union. In this sense, the union becomes a means through which Self helps satisfy the higher-level needs of self-esteem (dignity) for Others. So long as acts and behaviors remain focused on the best interest, welfare, and good of the union itself and, by extension, Others in the union, the union is likely to grow and develop.

As the union grows and develops, the teaching and example set by those Selves participating in the union then help to satisfy the self-actualization need of Others participating in the union. As the union continues to grow and develop, still others practice acting and behaving for the benefit of Others and the union. In this sense, the union becomes a pathway to spiritual wellness since spiritual wellness is tied directly to the willingness and ability to act and behave for the benefit of Others. It is tied directly to the highest function or purpose of each human being which is to serve the best interest, welfare, and good of Others and the collective whole.

Unfortunately, because unions only form and exist when each participating Self is willing and able to act and behave to maximize benefit and minimize harm for the union and Others in the union, it is difficult to point to a true example of a union. The vast majority of relationships that exist are, in fact, alliances. Even those existing relationships that include the word "union" in their title are, upon examination, only examples of alliances. For instance, it is clear that although marriages are often referred to as unions, the vast majority are actually alliances. As a second example, labor unions, while perhaps theoretically conceived as unions, are alliances that exist to serve the best interest, welfare, and good of the individual Selves that comprise the union. Ultimately, it is the ethic of individual Selves or collective forms of Self that determine whether or not a relationship is an alliance or a union.

It is also the ethic of the Selves or collective forms of Self that determine how an alliance will interact with other similar or dissimilar alliances and how a union will interact with other similar or dissimilar unions. Finally, ethic impacts the tone and duration of both alliances and unions. The tone is the level of contention and conflict or cooperation and collaboration within the relationship. The duration is the stability and length of the relationship. However, the states of ethical development also play a significant role in determining the tone and duration of an alliance or union.

In the last chapter, I covered the three states of ethical development. These are the irrational, the rational, and the transrational states of ethical development. When introducing and discussing these states, I provided the characteristics of each. I also aligned both the irrational and rational states of ethical development under the Unevolved Ethic and the transrational state under the Evolved Ethic. These states can have a significant, even profound, impact on the tone and duration of relationships. To appreciate the impact states of ethical development have on relationships requires an examination of the various pairings of states of ethical development that are possible.

With each pairing of the states of ethical development, the result is either a matched pairing or a mismatched pairing. A match occurs in each instance in which two Selves with the same state of ethical development enter into a relationship. There are three possible match pairings. These are irrational to irrational, rational to rational, and transrational to transrational. However, if the state of ethical development of one Self is the irrational and the other Self is the rational, this is a mismatch. The possible mismatches of states of ethical development are depicted in Figure 8-2.

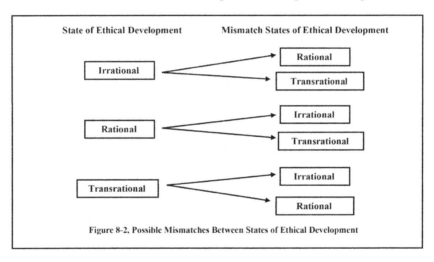

Figure 8-2, Possible Mismatches Between States of Ethical Development

Before progressing too far with this discussion of matches and mismatches, it is appropriate to note that unless the state of ethical development for both Selves participating in a relationship is the transrational, the relationship can only be an alliance. Consistent with the discussion of unions above, a relationship can only be a union if the ethical state of development for both Selves in a relationship is the transrational. It is now possible to examine the impact of mismatches between the states of ethical development and then address the three possible matches.

Two very significant impacts arise when the state of ethical development between two Selves in a relationship mismatch. The greatest impact of mismatched states is the potential for misunderstanding and miscommunication within these relationships. It is the potential for misunderstanding the choices, as well as the acts and behaviors, of those Selves in the relationship. These misunderstandings rest in the differing characteristics of the states of ethical development. As misunderstandings occur, communication can and often does become more difficult and stressed within the relationship. As misunderstandings occur and communication becomes more stressed, the tone of the relationship becomes increasingly contentious and conflicted. The tone of the relationship then impacts the duration, stability, and longevity of the relationship.

The second significant impact is the inability of one or both Selves in the relationship to satisfy the two psychological needs of belonging (affiliation) and esteem within the relationship.

Self is often able to satisfy both of these needs through relationships with another Self or other Selves. However, the misunderstandings and miscommunications that arise from the mismatch of states of ethical development can interfere with or block the ability to satisfy one or both of the two critical psychological needs. The inability to satisfy these needs then impacts the tone and duration of the relationship. It raises the level of contention and conflict within the relationship. It also increases instability within the relationship.

The inability of one or both Selves to satisfy the two psychological needs within the relationship does not necessarily cause the relationship to dissolve. The relationship may continue because each Self is still able to satisfy the two lowest-level physical needs despite the inability to satisfy the psychological needs. In this instance, the relationship is psychologically unhealthy for one or both Selves, but it may well continue. This is perhaps most evident in a mismatch between a Self whose state of ethical development is the irrational and a Self whose state is the rational.

In this mismatch, the guiding and motivating ethic of both Selves is the Unevolved Ethic. Therefore, both Selves are, to some extent acting and behaving to maximize benefit and minimize harm for Self. Yet, as discussed previously, the emphasis for each Self is different. The emphasis for the irrational Self is maximizing pleasure for Self, while the emphasis for the rational Self is minimizing harm for Self. However, within this mismatch of states of ethical development, each Self will often expect the same emphasis from the other. In other words, the irrational Self is likely to expect the rational Self to display acts and behaviors consistent with the irrational, and the rational Self is likely to expect the irrational Self to display acts and behaviors consistent with the rational. Misunderstandings and miscommunication result when the expectation of each Self is unmet by the other Self.

For instance, the irrational Self is unlikely to understand the lack of feelings and emotions displayed by the rational Self. Similarly, the irrational Self is unlikely to understand the reluctance of the rational Self to act on the urges and impulses of Self. The irrational Self is unlikely to understand the more deliberate and measured approach of the rational Self. Correspondingly, the irrational Self is unlikely to appreciate the purposeful level of control and restraint of acts and behaviors demonstrated by the rational Self. The irrational Self is not likely to understand that this level of control and restraint is intended to minimize harm for the rational Self. As a result, the irrational Self will likely be somewhat, if not entirely, intolerant of this control and restraint.

Further, the irrational Self will likely resent expectations on the part of the rational Self that suggest the irrational Self display greater control or restraint. The irrational Self will likely resent attempts by the rational Self to impose control or restraint over the acts and behaviors of the irrational Self. Indeed, the irrational Self may begin to view these expectations or attempts to impose control or restraint as both judgmental and parental.

Clearly, these attempts to impose control or restraint can lead to hurt feelings and emotions. They can also impact the ability of the irrational Self to satisfy the belonging (affiliation) and esteem needs of Self within the relationship. It is difficult to satisfy these needs when the acts and behaviors of Self are questioned or criticized by the rational Self within the relationship. The hurt feelings and emotions, as well as the inability to satisfy the two psychological needs can lead to increased contention and conflict within the relationship. However, much of the reverse is also the case in this mismatch.

The rational Self will likely not understand the willingness of the irrational to act from feelings and emotions. Similarly, the rational Self will likely not understand the willingness of the irrational Self to act on urges and impulses of Self. The rational Self will likely not understand the inconsistent and erratic acts and behaviors of the irrational Self. The rational Self is unlikely to understand that acting on feelings, emotions, urges, and impulses maximizes benefit for the irrational Self.

Further, the rational Self is unlikely to understand the lack of control and restraint of the irrational Self over the acts and behaviors of Self. The rational Self is unlikely to understand the unwillingness on the part of the irrational to act and behave in a more deliberate, measured, and purposeful manner. The rational Self may tolerate the lack of control and restraint, but is likely to view acts and behaviors of the irrational Self as juvenile or childlike.

However, in this mismatched relationship, the rational Self will likely resent expectations on the part of the irrational Self which suggests the rational Self should display less control or restraint. The rational Self is also likely to resent attempts by the irrational Self to impose a lack of control or restraint on the part of the rational Self. These attempts will clash with reasoning and they can result in hurt feelings and emotions for the rational. This then impacts the ability of the rational Self to satisfy the belonging (affiliation) and esteem needs within the relationship. This can raise the level of contention and conflict in the relationship as each Self acts and behaves to satisfy the needs of Self within the relationship. However, so long as the level of this contention and conflict remains minimal, the relationship or alliance may continue.

The relationship may continue as both Selves will likely still find it easier to meet the two lowest-level needs within the alliance which may be sufficient to give the alliance duration. Further, both Selves are likely to find it easier to satisfy the wants, desires, cravings, and obsessions of Self within the relationship. The ability to satisfy the physical needs, as well as the wants, desires, cravings, and obsessions of Self can give the relationship, the alliance, some stability and longevity. Although the relationship is psychologically unhealthy for one or both Selves, the relationship may well continue. On the other hand, it may hasten the dissolution of the alliance. Whether the alliance has some duration or dissolves will depend to some extent on how irrational or rational the state of ethical development is or is not.

If the proximity of both the irrational and rational states of development is near the developmental shift point, the choices, acts, and behaviors of the two Selves will be more similar. There will be less misunderstanding and miscommunication in this mismatch. There will still be contention between the interest, welfare, and good of the two Selves. However, the level of contention may remain relatively minor as each is able to satisfy the lower-level needs, as well as the wants, desires, cravings, and obsessions of Self.

As the proximity of either or both the irrational or rational state of ethical development moves further away from the developmental shift point, the possibility for misunderstanding and miscommunication becomes far greater. Indeed, as the state of ethical development moves further from the shift point, the differences in characteristics of the highly irrational and highly rational are so pronounced that it is likely that continued interaction will result in little more than an ongoing string of misunderstandings and miscommunications. This will lead to much higher levels of contention and conflict intensifies, additional characteristics of the two mismatch states may well come into play.

For instance, the irrational Self may become less willing to engage in mutual benefit and reciprocity within the relationship. This stems from the emphasis on maximizing pleasure for Self. On the other hand, the rational Self may become more willing to engage in mutual benefit and reciprocity to give the relationship stability and longevity. This stems from the emphasis on minimizing harm for Self.

As the level of contention and conflict within the relationship intensifies, the irrational may view mutual benefit and reciprocity as contrary to the best interest, welfare, or good of Self. However, the rational Self may view mutual benefit and reciprocity as still in the best interest, welfare, and good of Self. This characteristic movement of the irrational Self away from mutual benefit and reciprocity coupled with the movement of the rational toward mutual benefit and reciprocity can lead to even greater misunderstanding and miscommunication.

The same is the case when discussing compromise within the mismatch between the irrational and rational states of ethical development. The irrational may be less willing to engage in compromise to manage conflict within the relationship, while the rational may be more willing to engage in compromise. Indeed, the irrational may accept the terms of a compromise only grudgingly. The unwillingness of the irrational to compromise is consistent with the focus on maximizing pleasure for Self and the unwillingness to accept a real or perceived loss for Self, which arises from the compromise. The willingness of the rational to compromise is consistent with the focus on minimizing harm for Self and the willingness to accept some real or perceived loss to Self that arises from compromise in order to avert an even greater loss to Self. The greater loss would, of course be the potential increased inability to satisfy the four lower-level needs, as well as the wants, desires, cravings, and obsessions of Self.

However, the characteristic tendency to act on urges and impulses suggests that the irrational Self is more likely to break compromises (promises) within the relationship which will, of course, increase the level of contention and conflict within the relationship. But this comment suggests that the rational Self will not break a compromise (promise) within the relationship. The rational Self may well break a compromise (promise) if doing so minimizes the possibility of greater harm for Self. It simply points to the characteristic tendency on the part of the irrational to act from the feelings, emotions, urges, and impulses of Self which can result in broken compromises (promises).

It is also the case that characteristics of the irrational and rational states of ethical development will manifest in negotiating a compromise. For example, the irrational are more likely to negotiate a compromise from the feelings and emotions of Self. The strength of the irrational is in the feelings and emotions of Self. As a result, the irrational will seek advantage for Self through negotiating from the feelings and emotions of Self. These attempts to gain advantage through feelings and emotions can appear manipulative and likely will be viewed as manipulative by the rational Self. That notwithstanding, the irrational Self may negotiate from very strong feelings and emotions. Negotiating from strong emotions and feelings may well result in a more aggressive and confrontational style of negotiation on the part of the irrational.

On the contrary, the rational will negotiate compromise through reasoning. Reasoning is the strength of the rational and the rational will seek advantage for Self through reasoning. These attempts to gain an advantage through reasoning can also appear manipulative and likely will be viewed as manipulative by the irrational Self. However, the calmer, more deliberate, measured approach to compromise is only characteristic of the rational Self's emphasis on minimizing harm for Self. This more deliberate and measured approach will likely be much less aggressive and confrontational. This would, of course, be different if the emotions of the rational enter into the negotiation process.

Consistent with the Unevolved Ethic, both the irrational and rational Selves are likely to employ rationalizations, justifications, explanations, and excuses to support their respective positions. Both will employ rationalizations, justifications, explanations, and excuses to maximize benefit and minimize harm for Self within the compromise. In the negotiation process, both are likely to minimalize or ignore harm to the Other and harm to the relationship itself. This is completely consistent with the ethic that guides the choices and motivates the acts and behaviors of both the irrational and rational.

Ultimately, the duration of this relationship depends on the subjective consideration of benefit and harm for Self. Both the stability and longevity of this relationship are tied to this subjective assessment of benefit and harm for Self. The relationship will continue so long as both the irrational and rational Selves believe staying in the relationship serves the interest, welfare, and good of Self. This includes the ability of Self to satisfy at least the two lowest-level needs. Indeed, Self may stay in an extremely contentious and conflicted relationship so long as one or both of the two lowest-level needs are met, regardless of how healthy or unhealthy the relationship is. The relationship may also find some stability and longevity to the extent or degree each Self is able to satisfy the wants, desires, cravings, and obsessions of Self through the relationship.

However, both the rational and irrational are more likely to leave a relationship if they believe the interest, welfare, and good of Self would be better served in a different relationship. Either or both will leave an existing relationship if they believe a new relationship will improve the ability of Self to maximize benefit for Self or minimize harm for Self. This includes the ability to satisfy all four lower-level needs, as well as the wants, desires, cravings, and obsessions of Self. If Self determines Self would be better served in a different relationship, Self will depart, and the relationship will dissolve.

This is not so dissimilar in a mismatch between both the irrational or rational states of ethical development and the transrational state of ethical development. Even in a relationship in which the ethical state of development of one of the Selves is the transrational, misunderstandings and miscommunication can and will occur. They occur since the characteristics of the states of ethical development are still different.

For instance, the rational Self is likely to appreciate the willingness and ability of the transrational to control and restrain the feelings and emotions of Self, as well as the willingness and ability to give, share, care, and love within the immediate relationship. This benefits the rational Self by minimizing harm within the relationship. While the irrational is likely to misunderstand the control and restraint demonstrated by the transrational Self, they are likely to appreciate the willingness to give, share, care, and love within the relationship since these maximize benefit for the irrational Self. Both the rational and irrational Selves are likely to appreciate the willingness and ability of the transrational Self to act and behave for the best interest, welfare, and good of the immediate relationship. However, neither the rational nor the irrational are likely to understand or appreciate these characteristics when applied to Others or relationships outside the immediate relationship.

The focus of both the irrational and rational is maximizing benefit and minimizing harm for Self within the context of the immediate relationship. The focus is satisfying the needs, as well as the wants, desires, cravings, and obsessions of Self within the context of the relationship. Acts and behaviors that manifest a focus on Others or a different or larger collective whole are contrary to this focus. As a result, both the irrational or rational Self will likely view acts and behaviors that manifest a focus on Others or a different or larger collective whole as contrary to the best interest, welfare, and good of Self.

Therefore, both the rational and irrational Selves are unlikely to understand or appreciate the willingness and ability of the transrational to give and share the resources of Self outside the bounds of the immediate relationship. This is regardless of whether the resource given or shared is intangible, such as time or effort, or tangible, such as property or even money. An irrational Self will be, to some extent or degree, intolerant of acts and behaviors that benefit Others or a collective whole outside the immediate relationship. This intolerance may well fuel increased contention and conflict within the immediate relationship.

As an exception to this last comment, both an irrational or rational Self may tolerate acts and behaviors that benefit Others or a collective whole outside the immediate relationship, but only to the extent or degree there is corresponding benefit to Self or the immediate relationship. This benefit can take many forms but would certainly include praise or recognition of Self or the immediate relationship. It would also include greater status or position for Self or the immediate relationship.

If the real or perceived reward equals the real or perceived loss to Self or the immediate relationship, an irrational or rational Self will likely tolerate the sacrifice. However, both the irrational and rational Self will be less tolerant, perhaps even intolerant, if the real or perceived reward does not equal the real or perceived loss. In this instance, resentment will grow on the part of the irrational or rational Self which will likely increase the level of contention and conflict within the relationship.

Another source of contention in this mismatch is the difference in the values and principles of the two Selves. Regardless of whether the state of ethical development is the irrational or rational, the values and principles of this Self will differ from those of the Self whose state of ethical development is the transrational. This is because the values and principles of the irrational or rational Self will derive from the Unevolved Ethic and the vices. In contrast, the values and principles of the transrational Self will derive from the Evolved Ethic and the virtues. Near the PoT, this difference will be very minimal, however, as the ethic and state of ethical development move further from the PoT, the difference will become more pronounced. As the difference becomes more pronounced, it will add to the level of contention and conflict within the relationship.

Conflict management in a mismatch involving a Self whose state of ethical development is the transrational will largely depend on the acts and behaviors of the Self whose state is not the transrational. This statement stems from the characteristic willingness and ability of the transrational to manifest acts and behaviors that are cooperative and collaborative. The acts and behaviors of the transrational are consistent with harmony and community and not competition. Generally speaking, the transrational will not compete for the interest, welfare, or good of Self within the context of a relationship. This even applies to acts and behaviors intended to satisfy the four lower-level needs of Self. However, they will seek cooperation and collaboration, or harmony within the relationship. Therefore, it is really the acts and behaviors of the other Self in the relationship that determine both the tone and duration of the relationship.

Tone will largely depend on the willingness and ability of the irrational or rational Self to engage in mutual benefit and reciprocity within the relationship. However, the willingness to compromise will also affect the tone, as well as the duration of the relationship. If the irrational or rational Self fails to act or behave in a manner that manifests mutual benefit and reciprocity, the level of contention and conflict will increase. The tone of the relationship will become increasingly contentious and conflicted, and the duration is likely to shorten accordingly. On the other hand, if the irrational or rational Self demonstrates the willingness and ability to act and behave in a manner that results in mutual benefit and reciprocity, the level of contention and conflict may remain relatively low.

Unfortunately, the characteristic inclination of the transrational Self to cooperate and collaborate within a relationship may actually have the effect of encouraging the Unevolved Ethic of the Self whose ethic is not the Evolved Ethic. The Self whose ethic is the Unevolved Ethic may well perceive the cooperative and collaborative acts and behaviors of the transrational as a win for Self. If Self perceives "I," "Me" is winning a competition in which Self benefits, this may encourage the Unevolved Ethic to grow and strengthen which will then lead to further contention and conflict within the relationship. Eventually, the transrational Self may choose to leave the relationship.

Choosing to leave the relationship does not indicate an unwillingness or inability to accept the irrational or rational Self, or even the acts and behaviors of the irrational or rational; it simply indicates an unwillingness to continue in the relationship. Even the transrational Self satisfies the four lower-level needs through the relationship. As misunderstandings, miscommunications, and resentment grow within the relationship, even the transrational will find it more difficult to satisfy the psychological needs of Self within the relationship. While mutual benefit, reciprocity, and even compromise within the relationship may delay departure, the transrational Self may eventually make the subjective decision to depart and seek a different or new relationship.

Unfortunately, so long as a relationship involves one or more Selves whose ethic is the Unevolved Ethic, there will always be some level of competition within the relationship. The level may be minimal, but it will be there. So long as it is present, there will always be the possibility that one or more Selves will determine it is in the best interest, welfare, and good of Self to depart the relationship. This is even evident in two of the three possible match pairings of states of ethical development. It is evident in the match of irrational-to-irrational and in the match of rational-to-rational states of ethical development.

The match between two or more Selves whose state is the irrational is a match between two or more Selves whose acts and behaviors will, to some extent or degree, manifest emphasis on maximizing benefit for Self. It is the match between two Selves whose acts and behaviors will manifest the feelings, emotions, urges, and impulses of Self. It is a match between two or more Selves whose acts and behaviors will be inconsistent and erratic.

It is a match between two or more Selves whose acts and behaviors will demonstrate a lack of control or restraint of Self. It is a match between two or more Selves whose acts and behaviors will manifest the willingness and ability to focus on the needs, wants, cravings, desires, and obsessions of Self, often without regard for harm to Self, Others, or the relationship itself.

As such, the tone of a match between two or more Selves whose state of ethical development is the irrational is often marked by a high degree of contention and conflict. This match will generally be contentious and conflicted as each Self seeks to maximize benefit for Self through the relationship. It may even be marked by outright conflict. Indeed, this match of irrational states may resemble a series of ongoing battles marked by brief periods of calm. The level of conflict may become extreme, even physical.

The extent or degree of competition will mirror both the ethic and state of ethical development for both or all Selves in the relationship. As the location of ethic on the Unevolved-Evolved Continuum moves further away from the PoT, acts and behaviors will reflect this location. The ethic will become more selfish and self-centered. Similarly, as the state of ethical development moves further away from the developmental shift point that separates the irrational from the rational state of ethical development, it will also reflect a higher degree of selfishness and a lower degree of concern for harm for Self, Others, and the relationship itself. Acts and behaviors become more erratic, inconsistent, and extreme.

On the contrary, less distance from the PoT and developmental shift point suggests somewhat less erratic, inconsistent, and extreme acts and behaviors. The pattern of acts and behaviors still manifests the characteristics of the irrational state of ethical development, but less extreme. Less distance from the PoT and developmental shift point also suggests somewhat greater concern for harm to Self, while further from the shift point suggests less concern for harm to Self. This applies to both Selves in a match of irrational to irrational. The question of nearness or distance from the PoT and developmental shift point also impacts the willingness of both Selves to engage in mutual benefit, reciprocity, and compromise within the relationship.

As the location of the state of ethical development moves further away from the PoT and the developmental shift point, the ethic of Self becomes more focused on benefit (pleasure) for Self. It becomes more selfish and self-centered. Therefore, as the location of the state of ethical development moves further from the PoT and developmental shift point, Self is less likely to manifest concern for balance in a relationship. This is similar to reciprocity.

Reciprocity requires the willingness to demonstrate at least secondary concern for harm to Others to limit harm for Self. As the ethic and state of ethical development moves further away from the PoT and the developmental shift point, Self will likely demonstrate less concern for harm to Self and correspondingly less, if any, concern for harm for the other Self or the relationship itself. Therefore, as the location of the irrational state of ethical development moves farther from the PoT and the developmental shift point, acts and behaviors are more likely to fail to manifest reciprocity.

Without mutual benefit or reciprocity, there will be little or no balance in the relationship. There will be little or no balance between the competing interests of the two Selves participating in the relationship, and the level of internal competition will rise. As the level of internal competition rises, there will be little or no balance in terms of satisfying the needs, wants, cravings, desires, and obsessions of those Selves participating in the relationship. This will, of course, lead to even greater levels of contention and conflict within the relationship. Unfortunately, the highly irrational are unlikely to engage in compromise to extend the duration of the relationship.

Compromise always involves the giving up of some measure of the interest of Self in order to minimize even greater harm to Self and the interest, welfare, and good of Self. As a result of the unwillingness to give up a measure of self-interest, the highly irrational may be unwilling to compromise. In those instances where the irrational Selves do engage in compromise, they may accept the terms of a compromise only grudgingly. It is also highly likely they will break the terms of the compromise if doing so maximizes benefit for Self. The likely result will be a string of broken compromises (promises) and, very likely, an ongoing string of broken relationships.

However, the match between two or more Selves whose state of ethical development is the irrational does not always result in a seemingly endless battle between the Selves participating in the relationship. Indeed, the match between two individuals with the irrational state of ethical development can result in the two Selves finding what might be termed a playmate.

In a relationship that might be described as a playmate relationship, the playmate may actually encourage the irrational acts and behaviors of Self in the relationship. The playmate will encourage the lack of control over feelings and emotions. The playmate will encourage and may even participate in the emotional highs and lows of the other Self in the relationship. In addition, the playmate may encourage acting from the urges and impulses of Self. The playmate will encourage the lack of control or restraint in the pursuit of pleasure for Self.

Still further, in this relationship, the needs, wants, cravings, and desires of Self may find a friend in the needs, wants, cravings, and desires of the playmate. Indeed, the wants, desires, cravings, and obsessions of each Self may feed off of the wants, desires, cravings, and obsessions of the other Self in the relationship. Finally, there is encouragement to satisfy these wants, cravings, and desires despite the harm to Self or Others that may result and to do so without consideration of harm or consequences before acting.

These relationships may have some duration because each Self is satisfying one or more needs, wants, desires, cravings, or obsessions within the relationship. It may have duration since each Self is encouraged to act out the feelings, emotions, urges, and impulses of Self within the relationship.

It may prove to have some duration since each Self is able to pursue pleasure for Self within the relationship. Each Self is encouraged to pursue the "feel good" that results from the pursuit of pleasure for Self. Within the relationship, the pursuit of that which feels good for Self may override even consideration of the harm that results for Self, Others, and the relationship itself. In this sense, the relationship may have duration.

In these playmate relationships or alliances, the level of contention and conflict may be fairly negligible since the focus of both participants is benefit (pleasure) for Self. The level of competition may be fairly negligible since the playmate becomes an ally in the pursuit of pleasure for Self. There is usually mutual benefit and reciprocity within these relationships. Likewise, there is some willingness to engage in compromise within these relationships.

The mutual benefit, reciprocity, and willingness to compromise stem from the nature of the relationship. So long as both Selves in this relationship are able to focus on the benefit for Self within the relationship, the level of contention remains somewhat low. The level of contention and conflict will increase if the pursuit of pleasure for one Self is blocked by the other Self. Similarly, the level of contention and conflict will increase if one Self determines there is insufficient balance of interests or reciprocity within the relationship. This determination results in a greater need for compromise within the relationship. A greater need for compromise results in more opportunities for broken compromises (promises) as each Self places benefit for Self ahead of the interest, welfare, and good of the relationship. If the Selves in the relationship cannot reestablish balance within the relationship, internal competition will increase, and the relationship will likely dissolve.

The importance of mutual benefit, reciprocity, and compromise is also prominent in the second match to consider. This is the match between two or more Selves whose state of ethical development is the rational. This match is characterized by reasoning. It is characterized by a measured, deliberate, conscious consistency of acts and behaviors that maximize benefit and minimize harm for Self. In this match, the Selves in the relationship are not inclined to act or behave from the feelings or emotions of Self. Similarly, the Selves in this relationship are less inclined to act or behave from the impulses and urges of Self. However, if the location of the state of ethical development is close to the developmental shift point, acts and behaviors will likely demonstrate a higher degree of willingness to act from feelings, emotions, urges, and impulses.

Mutual benefit and reciprocity play an important role in this match. Both rational Selves are likely to recognize that mutual benefit and reciprocity hold the potential for greater satisfaction of needs, wants, cravings, desires, and obsessions for Self. Both rational Selves will likely recognize mutual benefit and reciprocity lessen or temper competition within the relationship. Further, the rational Selves will likely reason that contention and conflict are contrary to the best interest of the relationship and, therefore, also contrary to the best interest, welfare, and good of Self. As a result, the overall tone of this match may be less competitive. It will be less contentious and conflicted. In those instances, in which competition does escalate, the Selves in this match will likely compromise to re-establish balance within the relationship. However, even in this match, the willingness to compromise is based on the subjective assessment of harm to Self on the part of each rational Self.

In the end, both Selves may reason that compromise is superior to elevated levels of competition, as well as dissolution of the relationship. Both are likely to reason that the continuation of the alliance serves the best interest, welfare, and good of Self. Assuming balance is restored and the level of competition reduced, both Selves in the relationship will likely accept the real or perceived level of harm to Self that results from the compromise. This can have a profound impact on the duration of the alliance. But this does not necessarily result in a healthy relationship. Indeed, it may result in a relationship that is devoid of the feelings and emotions associated with the irrational state. However, it will also be devoid of the caring, sharing, giving, and loving characteristics associated with the transrational state.

In the absence of some measure of acts and behaviors that manifest feelings and emotions associated with the irrational or the giving, sharing, caring, and loving characteristic of the transrational, the match between two or more rational Selves can result in the inability of both Selves to satisfy the belonging (affiliation) and esteem needs within the relationship. It is often through acts and behaviors that manifest feelings and emotions that acceptance and approval of Self is affirmed within a relationship. Likewise, acts and behaviors that manifest giving, sharing, caring, and loving also affirm acceptance and approval within the relationship.

Without these acts and behavioral clues to acceptance and approval, the Selves in this relationship may find it difficult to satisfy the two psychological needs. This can result in contention and conflict within the relationship. It results in an unhealthy relationship. It is healthier, perhaps even far healthier, than the match between two highly irrational Selves, but still unhealthy. It is still at the level of "I," "Me," "My," and "Mine". And the level of "I," "Me" always contains some level of competition between the best interest, welfare, and good of the two Selves in the relationship.

It is not until the match of two Selves, both functioning from the transrational state of ethical development, that a relationship becomes truly healthy. It is through this match that the two highest-level needs of the Selves are satisfied through the acts and behaviors of the other Self in the relationship. It is the match through which the Selves in the relationship are better able to satisfy the four lower-level needs of Self, as well as the higher-level need of self-esteem (dignity). Therefore, it is the match in which both or all Selves in the relationship are physically, psychologically, and spiritually healthy.

Further, this match reflects the characteristics associated with the transrational state. It is characterized by caring, sharing, giving, and loving acts and behaviors. The match reflects the willingness and ability of the

Selves to nurture the relationship and treat the relationship with integrity. Each Self places the best interest, welfare, and good of the union above the best interest, welfare, and good of Self. Each Self maximizes benefit and minimizes harm for the relationship and minimalizes or ignores harm for Self. It is the match in which the focus of each Self is at the level of "We", "Us," "Our," and "Ours," and not "I," "Me," "My," and "Mine."

Because the focus of both Selves is the best interest, welfare, and good of the relationship, these matches are not characterized by competition. They are not characterized by contention and conflict between the competing interests of those Selves in the relationship. The tone of this match is one of cooperation and collaboration. The tone is characterized by the ability and willingness of both or all Selves to place the best interest, welfare, and good of the relationship above the interest of Self. It is characterized by the ability and willingness of both or all participants to maximize benefit and minimize harm for the relationship. This suggests the potential for greater duration, stability, and longevity for the relationship.

The greatest threat to this potential for greater duration is the possibility that one or both Selves in the relationship will begin manifesting the willingness and ability to place the best interest, welfare, and good of Self above the interest, welfare, and good of the relationship and Others in the relationship. It is the possibility that one or both Selves will begin acting and behaving to maximize benefit and minimize harm for Self within the relationship. This would, of course, change the relationship. No longer would this be a match of the transrational state of ethical development.

Unfortunately, the match between two or more Selves with the Evolved Ethic is the rarest simply because the Unevolved Ethic is so overwhelmingly dominant in the world. There are simply far fewer opportunities for a match between those with the transrational state of ethical development to occur. Since there are fewer opportunities for this match to occur, unions become far less likely to form, develop, and flourish, to grow and multiply. It is unfortunate since unions characterized by cooperation and collaboration have the potential to unite all humankind in harmony and community. This cannot and will never happen so long as the only relationships that form are alliances. Alliances simply do not have the potential to unite all of humankind.   By using a series of figures, it is possible to demonstrate that the potential to unite all of humankind can never be met through alliances. It is also possible to demonstrate that this potential can be met through unions.

I will start with a single circle, representing a single Self whose ethic is the Unevolved Ethic. For this illustration, it does not matter if the ethical state of development is the irrational or rational. In Figure 8-3, "S1" represents one Self.

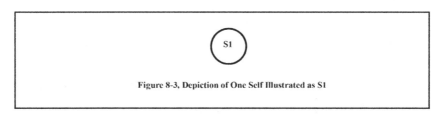

Figure 8-3, Depiction of One Self Illustrated as S1

I will now add a second circle, representing a second Self, also with the Unevolved Ethic. I will identify this second Self as "S2". I will also add a line linking these two circles. This line represents the link between two Selves in an alliance. The link between the two Selves represents the self-interest of each Self. It represents the best interest, welfare, and good of Self. As such, the level of this relationship is the level of "I," "Me," "My," and "Mine."

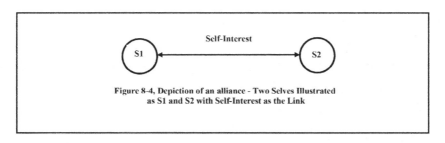

Figure 8-4, Depiction of an alliance - Two Selves Illustrated as S1 and S2 with Self-Interest as the Link

Any decision to include another Self or Selves into the alliance will reflect concern for the best interest, welfare, and good of those Selves already in the relationship. This concern for Self will necessarily result in exclusivity. An alliance remains exclusive to the extent or degree to which those Selves in the relationship believe the exclusion of another Self or Selves serves the best interest, welfare, or good of Self. It will only demonstrate inclusivity in the event those Selves in the alliance believe the inclusion of an additional Self or Selves serves the best interest, welfare, and good of Self. I illustrate this by simply adding another circle to the previous illustration and linking the new circle (labeled S3) with a line representing the self-interest of the new Self in the alliance. Inclusion will stop when it no longer serves the best interest, welfare, and good of those Selves in the alliance.

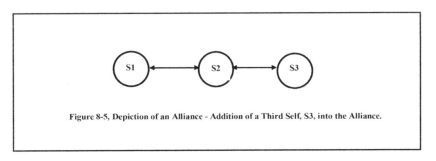

Figure 8-5, Depiction of an Alliance - Addition of a Third Self, S3, into the Alliance.

However, the inclusion of an additional Self or Selves will raise the level of internal competition within the alliance as the new Self or Selves begin using the alliance to maximize benefit and minimize harm for Self. The intensity of contention and conflict within the alliance will vary based on the ethic and the state of ethical development of those Selves in the alliance. It will depend on the ability of each Self to serve the interest of Self through the alliance.

The intensity of contention and conflict will increase if still another Self or Selves is included in the alliance. This is predictable as each included Self also acts and behaves to benefit Self and the interest, welfare, and good of Self through the alliance. Consistent with the previous discussion of matches and mismatches between the states of ethical development, the duration of the alliance will depend in large part on the tone within the alliance. However, this is the same or at least similar when discussing the tone and duration of an alliance of alliances.

Alliances between alliances can and do occur. But they only occur if each alliance believes it is in the best interest of Self to enter an alliance with another alliance. In the case of an alliance of alliances, the focus of each alliance will still be the best interest, welfare, and good of Self. This will and usually does result in contention and conflict between the two alliances, as well as those Selves who comprise each alliance. The level of contention and conflict will reflect the collective ethic of each of the alliances that comprise the alliance of alliances.

In some instances, the level of competition between the two or more alliances that comprise the alliance of alliances will cause the alliance of alliances to fail. In other instances, the pressures of external competition from still other similar or dissimilar alliances may result in an uneasy calm, but only because that uneasy calm serves the best interest, welfare, and good of the alliances that comprise the alliance of alliances. In other instances, efforts to establish and maintain mutual benefit and reciprocity between the two or more alliances that comprise the alliance of alliances will reduce or temper the level of internal competition. Compromise may also temper the level of competition internal to the alliance of alliances.

In diagraming an alliance of alliances, the depiction is identical to the diagram used to illustrate an alliance involving two or more individual Selves, which recognizes that each alliance represents a collective form of Self. The focus of an alliance within an alliance of alliances is still the best interest, welfare, and good of Self. As such, the arrow that connects the alliances still represents the self-interest of the individual Self of the alliances. Further, an alliance will only join another alliance when there is benefit to Self for doing so. An alliance will only join another alliance if doing so maximizes benefit and minimizes harm for Self. Any concern for the interest, welfare, and good of the alliance itself is secondary, if at all. Therefore, the focus of an alliance of alliances is still at the level of "I," "Me," "My," and "Mine."

Further, an alliance of alliances will still manifest exclusivity. Each alliance will emphasize the best interest, welfare, and good of Self when considering adding additional alliances. It is this exclusivity that limits the ability of an alliance of alliances to continue growing. At some point exclusivity will prevent further growth.

Much of this is different when examining the ability of a union to continue to grow. To illustrate this difference, I again begin with a single circle representing one Self. It is assumed that the ethic of this Self is the Evolved Ethic since a union can and will only form and continue if the ethic of each participating Self is the Evolved Ethic.

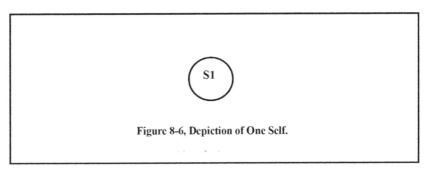

Figure 8-6, Depiction of One Self.

I now add a second Self, but because this is a union, I must also include a third, larger circle. This third circle represents the union and is shown at the level of "We," "Us," "Our," and "Ours." I then link each of the two Selves to the larger circle.

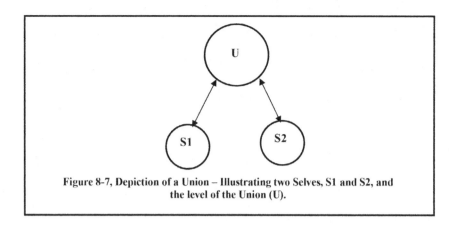

Figure 8-7, Depiction of a Union – Illustrating two Selves, S1 and S2, and the level of the Union (U).

Unlike the diagram illustrating an alliance, the link is not shown connecting the two Selves. Now, the link is between the two Selves and the union itself. In addition, this link no longer represents self-interest. The link now represents the interest of the whole, that is, the union. Which is a significant change in orientation.

This change emphasizes that each Self in the union is acting and behaving to maximize benefit and minimize harm for the union. They are acting and behaving for the best interest, welfare, and good of the collective whole that is the union. Further, they are minimalizing or ignoring the harm that results for Self when acting and behaving for the union. Therefore, there is no direct line that links the interest of one Self to subsequent Selves in the union.

Unlike alliances, the decision to include additional Selves into a union is not based on an assessment of benefit to Self on the part of the Selves in the union. There is no assessment of benefit or harm to Self since each Self is acting and behaving for the best interest, welfare, and good of the union. Further, it is characteristic of those Selves within the union to accept and embrace Others. Therefore, unions are inclusive. It is possible to illustrate this inclusiveness in two ways. First, it is possible to illustrate the inclusion of still other Selves into the union. Second, it is possible to illustrate the inclusion of other unions into unions of unions. I'll begin with a figure illustrating the inclusion of an additional Self into the union.

I illustrate the inclusion of an additional Self into the union by adding a new circle to the previous depiction of the union of two Selves. I then link this Self to the union, but not to either of the two Selves already depicted. Again, this represents the focus of the now three Selves in the union. It represents the focus on the best interest, welfare, and good of the relationship, the union itself.

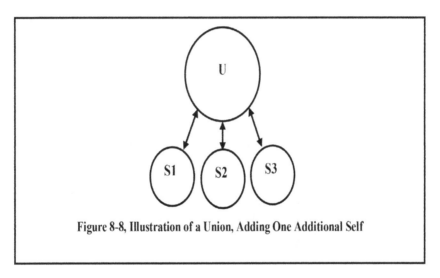

Figure 8-8, Illustration of a Union, Adding One Additional Self

Now, I can illustrate the effect when unions join other unions in a union of unions. In this illustration, "U1" represents the initial union, and "U2" represents the second union.

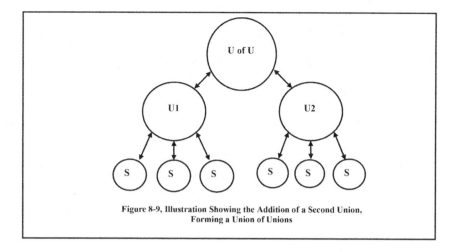

Figure 8-9, Illustration Showing the Addition of a Second Union, Forming a Union of Unions

Since the focus of those Selves who make up the union is the best interest, welfare, and good of the union, this focus continues to manifest in a union of unions where the focus of each union is the best interest, welfare, and good of the union of unions. In addition, since unions are inclusive, this characteristic inclusion can lead to an even larger union of unions. It might begin to look like Figure 8-10.

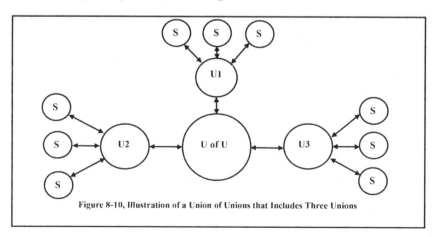

Figure 8-10, Illustration of a Union of Unions that Includes Three Unions

Because unions are not constrained by the interest, welfare, or good of Self, they not constrained in their ability to continue to expand and to form still larger unions of unions, larger collective wholes. Because unions are not characterized by competition, contention and conflict, their growth and development are not hindered by the competing interests of those who comprise each level of the union. Because unions are characterized by harmony, cooperation and collaboration, they are not constrained in their ability to continue to grow and develop, to continue to include and to form still greater unions, still greater collective wholes at a higher level of "We," "Us," "Our," and "Ours."

The ability to continue illustrating even larger unions of unions is confined only by the dimensions of the paper on which the illustration rests. However, it is interesting to note that the illustration begins to somewhat resemble the illustration of a chemical element. Hence, I term this final depiction the Unity Element. Figure 8-11 illustrates the Unity Element.

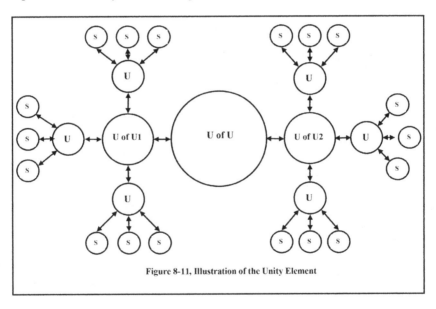

Figure 8-11, Illustration of the Unity Element

Just as sub-atomic particles combine to form atoms and atoms combine to form elements, individual Selves come together to form unions, and unions come together to form unions of unions. In this sense, unions become the elements that, when further joined together, form a whole. As I am using the term whole, I am suggesting that the coming together of unions to form unions of unions holds the potential for uniting the whole of humankind in community.

The covalent bond or glue that holds unions together and gives them duration is the Evolved Ethic. It is the Evolved Ethic of those Selves participating in the union and unions of unions. It is the ability and willingness to act and behave for the benefit of the union at the expense of Self and self-interest that is the covalent bond of the union. It is the ability and willingness to act without regard for the best interest, welfare, and good of Self that is the covalent bond of the union. It is the ability and willingness to give, to care, to share, and to love without regard for benefit or harm for Self that is the bond of the union. It is the ability and willingness to transcend Self that is the bond of the union. As unions combine to form unions of unions, this covalent bond extends to the union of unions. This is not the case with an alliance.

In an alliance, the only bond or glue that holds the alliance together is concern for the best interest, welfare, and good of Self or collective Self. This is a very weak bond. It is weak since it ties together two or more Selves willing and able to act and behave to maximize benefit and minimize harm for Self. It is weak because it binds together two or more Selves, both willing and able to minimalize or ignore harm for the alliance. It binds together two or more Selves that will place the interest, welfare, and good of Self ahead of the interest, welfare, and good of the alliance.

While the employment of reciprocity and the willingness to compromise may extend the life of an alliance, it cannot eliminate competition within the alliance. While the alliance may continue, its only hope for expansion lies in the self-interest of those Selves participating in the alliance. However, in the face of external competition, the bond of self-interest may dissolve quickly and completely. As a result, alliances do not hold the potential to unite all of humankind into a community of humankind. By their nature, alliances contain the seed of their own destruction; they contain the seed of disunity. That seed is the competition that exists between the best interest, welfare, and good of those Selves participating in the union. Whether discussing individual Selves or collective forms of Self participating in an alliance or even an alliance of alliances.

In the next chapter, I will build from this discussion of ethics and relationships as I turn my attention to the subject of leadership. The reader may remember that it was the quote that suggested, "Leaders do the right thing," that is responsible for this quest to understand how leaders or anyone else knows the right thing to do and then consistently does it. However, it is also appropriate to transition from relationships to leadership for another, more practical reason. The ability to build and maintain relationships is generally recognized as a critical ability for leaders. As seen in the next chapter, this critical ability is very directly impacted by the ethic of Self.

CHAPTER 9:
EVOLVED LEADERSHIP

I present this short examination of leadership and the impact of ethics on leadership as a means of closing the loop I opened back in the first chapter. To some extent, this entire discussion of ethics has been a discussion of leadership. It has been a discussion of the characteristics and traits of good leaders, true leaders, as well as not so good leaders. I begin by separating leadership from management. Leadership and management are not the same, and separating the two subjects from each other facilitates the ability to focus the remaining discussion on leadership. I then present and discuss characteristics of Evolved leaders, as well as characteristics of what I term Unevolved leaders. In each case, the characteristics are consistent with the guiding and motivating ethic.

Following the discussion of Evolved and Unevolved Leadership, I will briefly address the subject of follower ethic. While it is the case that ethic guides and motivates the acts and behaviors of leaders, it is also the case that ethic guides and motivates the acts and behaviors of followers. I will then conclude the chapter with a discussion of several short subjects very related to leadership. With that said, I will start by separating leading from managing.

The term "manage" is defined in part as, "to bring about; to succeed in accomplishing. To have charge of or responsibility for. To dominate or influence (a person) by tact or artifice. To handle, direct, govern, or control in action or use." The term "management" is defined as, "the act or manner of managing; handling, direction, or control. Skill in managing; executive ability. The person or persons controlling and directing the affairs of an institution, business, etc." Finally, the term "manager" is defined as, "a person who manages. A person charged with the control or direction of an institution, business, or the like. A person who controls and manipulates resources and expenditures..."

Management, then, is primarily about resources and objects. It is about the movement, employment, and manipulation of resources and objects as a means to achieve a predetermined end. This end is the purpose or goal of an organization, institution, or team. It can be the efficient and effective manufacture or production of a product, the building of a structure, providing a service, or some other end. To achieve this end, managers perform the traditional functions of management.

Henri Fayol first identified the traditional functions of management in 1916. These functions are planning, organizing, directing, controlling and coordinating. Though sometimes called by different names these are still the generally agreed functions of a manager or managers.

A wide range of methods and tools are available to assist managers in performing the functions of management. These methods and tools provide insight into the effective and efficient manipulation of resources and objects. The objects manipulated may include capital, raw materials, and equipment. It may also involve managing time and workspace. In terms of time, this means efficiently and effectively utilizing the time available to achieve an end (planning and time management). In terms of space, it means efficiently and effectively utilizing the workspace available to achieve an end (organizing the physical environment).

For instance, Pert Charts, Gantt Charts, and simulation models are tools available to assist in the planning function. Time and motion studies and process or work flow charts assist with the organizing function. The controlling function often includes the use of charts and graphs associated with statistical process control or quality control. Often, managing includes the tools of financial management. These would include ledgers, spreadsheets, and financial statements. The employment of each of these tools and the overall ability of a manager to perform the functions of management is dependent on the person's ability to understand, apply, and interpret the various tools that facilitate the functions of management.

Viewed in this manner, managing or the ability to manage is a competency set. It is the combination of knowledge, skills, and abilities that result in a set of competencies. Much as a person learns and develops competencies in any given field or profession, a person may likewise learn and develop the managerial competency set. The knowledge, skills, and abilities of management are not necessarily specific to a given field or profession. The same or very similar knowledge, skills, and abilities cross many fields and professions. It is this competency set that enables managers to do things right. Managers do things right because they have mastered the necessary managerial competencies, including the proper employment of the methods and tools of management.

However, it is also worth noting that the methods and tools of management are rational. They are based on the ability to reason. This does not infer that they are wrong, incorrect, or inappropriate. They are simply means to ends that are based in reasoning. As means to ends, they are essentially neutral. They are not right or wrong, correct or incorrect, appropriate or inappropriate. How a manager employs the methods and tools can be right or wrong, correct or incorrect, and appropriate or inappropriate.

When properly utilized, the methods and tools of management are the means to an end that maximizes benefit and minimizes harm for Self and the collective Self that is the organization or institution. These methods and tools seek to give order and predictability (benefit) by reducing or eliminating disorder and unpredictability (harm). They improve efficiency and effectiveness (benefit) and reduce inefficiency and ineffectiveness

292 | THE UNEVOLVED AND EVOLVED ETHICS

(harm). They reduce or eliminate chance and randomness (harm). Further, they reduce or eliminate chaos (harm).

Certainly, their use is wrong, incorrect, and inappropriate if their use results in harm for Others and one or more collective wholes not the organization or institution. Likewise, they are wrong, incorrect, and inappropriate if they result in the treatment of Others, human beings, as objects to be manipulated. Unfortunately, human beings are often viewed as objects or resources. This assertion is supported by the use of the terms "human resource" or "human capital" to describe a workforce. Both terms imply a view of human beings as objects. Both terms imply a view of human beings as a means to an end. This view is wrong, incorrect, and inappropriate but is often considered acceptable.

A human being should always be viewed as an end in themselves and not as a means to an end. By this is meant, no human being should be treated solely as a means to achieving an end. To do so is to strip away humanity. It disrespects and denies the value, worth, and dignity of the person or persons treated solely as a means to an end. It disrespects the value, worth, and dignity of the person or persons as a human being. It denies the higher-order self-esteem (dignity) of each human being so treated. However, I must recognize that treating a human being as a means to an end is consistent with the discussion of alliances in the last chapter.

When discussing alliances, I indicated that people enter alliances to facilitate satisfaction of the four lower-level needs of Self. In addition, entering alliances may also facilitate the ability of Self to satisfy the wants, desires, cravings, and obsessions of Self. I included the example of alliances with employers to illustrate this point. Each Self enters these alliances with the intent to utilize the alliance as a means to satisfy the lower-level needs of Self, as well as the means to satisfy the wants, desires, cravings, and obsessions of Self.

As a result, each Self in the alliance, including the employer and all employees, is using the alliance, as well as those Others in the alliance, as a means to an end that serves the interest, welfare, and good of Self. The extent to which the acts and behaviors of Self maximize benefit and minimize harm only for Self does range from wrong to more wrong. The extent to which the acts and behaviors of Self minimalize or ignore harm to Others and the collective Self also ranges from wrong to more wrong.

Therefore, the acts and behaviors of managers range from wrong to more wrong to the extent they treat employees solely as a means to an end. The acts and behaviors of managers range from wrong to more wrong to the extent they treat employees only as "human resources" or "human capital" to be used. In each instance, these acts and behaviors range from wrong to more wrong to the extent or degree that they deny the worth, value, and dignity of human beings.

It is the issue of treatment of human beings that is central to the division between management and leadership. Managers manage resources, objects, but leaders lead people, human beings. Managers manage time and workspace (environment), but leaders lead human beings. Managers employ the methods and tools of management to efficiently and effectively manage resources, but leaders lead people. Unfortunately, learning and employing the methods and tools of management does not necessarily prepare anyone to lead. It only prepares them to manage. Developing management competencies does not result in leadership. It results in managing.

As a verb, the term "lead" means, "to act as a guide; show the way. To afford passage to a place. To go first; be in advance. To result in; tend toward." The term "leader" is defined in part as "a person or thing that leads. A guiding or directing head." Finally, the term "leadership" is defined in part as "the position or function of a leader. Ability to lead. An act or instance of leading." Therefore, leading can generally be defined as taking the lead, showing the way, or setting the course. It is the ability and willingness to guide or influence the way or course for others to follow. It means to set an example for others to follow. However, there is a tie to managing contained in the definition of "leader."

The tie is that part of the definition that indicates a leader is "a guiding or directing head." The functions of management do require that managers plan, organize, *direct*, control, and coordinate. However, leading does not require either the knowledge or ability to employ the functions of management. Therefore, leading does not require the management competency set. Rather, leading requires the willingness and ability to take the lead, to go first and to show the way. It requires the willingness and ability to set an example or model the way for Others to follow. Further, it requires the willingness and ability to influence the acts and behaviors of Others through the example set.

It is this willingness and ability to set the example and model the way that sets leadership apart from management. However, to accommodate the notion of managers as leaders, it is common to discuss leadership in organizations or institutions using the terms formal leader and informal leader.

Formal leaders occupy a formal position or formal status within an organization or institution (alliance). Formal leaders occupy established, formal positions charged with guiding and directing the activities of the organization or institution. As such, formal leaders are managers. They are "The person or persons controlling and directing the affairs of an institution, business, etc." Formal leaders are responsible for understanding, implementing, and interpreting the methods and tools of management. In this sense, formal leaders are managers, including the most senior managers, afforded the title "leader" by virtue of their formal position within the organization or institution.

Informal leaders are different. Informal leaders may have no formal position or formal status within an organization or institution (alliance). As a result, informal leaders cannot direct. They can only influence or guide by the example set. They can only influence the acts and behaviors of Others through the example they model. They can only show the way or set the course through their acts and behaviors. Therefore, informal leaders more closely reflect the definition of a leader. However, leadership is not just about setting the course, setting the example, or modeling the way. Leadership is also about the example or course set. It is about the model set. It is the example, the course, or the model set that directly ties leadership to ethic.

If the underlying ethic of a leader is the Evolved Ethic, the example set is consistent with this ethic. The example manifests concern for the interest, welfare, and good of Others and the collective whole. If the guiding and motivating ethic is the Evolved Ethic, the example set maximizes benefit and minimizes harm for Others and the collective whole. Finally, if the guiding and motivating ethic is the Evolved Ethic, the example set minimalizes or ignores harm for Self when acting and behaving for the best interest, welfare, and good of Others and the collective whole.

If, on the other hand, the underlying ethic of a leader is the Unevolved Ethic, the example set manifests that ethic. The example set manifests concern for the best interest, welfare, and good of Self. The example set will maximize benefit and minimize harm for Self and minimalize or ignore harm for Others and the collective whole. It may well ignore harm for multiple levels of the collective whole in the interest of Self.

From this discussion, it is clear that, in the context of this theory of ethics, there are two types of leadership. One type is Evolved leadership. The other is Unevolved leadership. Evolved leadership is very consistent with the notion that leaders can consistently know the right thing to do and consistently do it. This is Evolved leadership. Unevolved leadership, cannot consistently know or consistently do the right thing. Rather, this leadership will consistently do what is right for Self and the best interest, welfare, and good of Self. This is Unevolved leadership. The difference between the two types of leadership becomes increasingly obvious through an examination of the characteristics of each type.

Throughout this discussion of ethics, I have consistently associated a variety of characteristics with both the Evolved and Unevolved Ethics.

These same characteristics are very useful for distinguishing Evolved Leaders from Unevolved Leaders. For example, I associate integrity and the willingness and ability to consistently manifest integrity with the Evolved Ethic. Further, I associate nurturing and the willingness and ability to consistently demonstrate nurturing acts and behaviors with the Evolved Ethic. By contrast, I do not associate the willingness and ability to consistently manifest either integrity or nurturing with the Unevolved Ethic. Yet both integrity and nurturing are considered important characteristics of leaders.

As a second example, I associate values such as fairness, faithfulness, truthfulness, and the many other values derived from the lesser virtues with the Evolved Ethic. These are values often associated with good character and good leadership. But I associate values such as unfairness, unfaithfulness, and untruthfulness, and the many other values derived from the vices with the Unevolved Ethic. These are values often associated with poor character and poor leadership. It is characteristic of the Evolved Leader to manifest the values associated with good character and leadership consistently, but it is not characteristic of the Unevolved Leader to manifest these values consistently or evenly.

Going a step further, I also associate principles such as truth, justice, equity, equality, and other related principles with the Evolved Ethic. Each of these principles is generally agreed to be important to both good character and good leadership. The objective implementation of these principles recognizes the worth, value, and dignity of Others. In addition, the objective implementation of these principles reduces or eliminates harms such as favoritism, preferential treatment, bias, and discrimination within the collective whole.

By contrast, I associate principles such as untruth, injustice, inequity, inequality, partiality, and other related principles with the Unevolved Ethic. Each of these principles is generally agreed to be contrary to both good character and good leadership. The subjective implementation of these principles results in harm such as favoritism, bias, and discrimination within the collective whole. They also fail to recognize the worth, value, and dignity of Others. But then, both objectivity and subjectivity are very important when considering the characteristics of leaders and leadership.

I associate objectivity, the absence of regard or concern for Self and the best interest, welfare, and good of Self, with the Evolved Ethic. Objectivity maximizes benefit and minimizes harm for Others and the collective whole at all levels of the collective whole. On the other hand, I associate subjectivity, the presence of regard or concern for Self and the best interest, welfare, and good of Self, with the Unevolved Ethic. Subjectivity maximizes benefit and minimizes harm for Self.

This difference between objectivity and subjectivity has a significant impact on the discussion of leaders and leadership. This difference suggests that the Evolved Leader will objectively act and behave for the best interest, welfare, and good of Others and the collective whole at all levels. In contrast, the Unevolved Leader will subjectively act and behave, to some extent or degree, for the best interest, welfare, and good of Self. The Evolved Leader will set aside or ignore the best interest, welfare, and good of Self, while the Unevolved Leader will set aside or ignore the best interest, welfare, and good of Others and the collective whole in favor of Self. For instance, objectivity or subjectivity reflects in the willingness and ability to either include or exclude Others.

I associate the willingness and ability to include Others, regardless of differences, as characteristic of the Evolved Ethic. Further, I associate the willingness and ability to accept the beliefs, attitudes, opinions, ideologies, and philosophies of Others with the Evolved Ethic. This does not infer the willingness to adopt the beliefs, attitudes, opinions, ideologies, and philosophies of Others but to objectively accept that Others hold these beliefs, attitudes, opinions, ideologies, and philosophies.

To include and accept is consistent with the Evolved Ethic. To include and accept gives respect, value, and worth. It gives dignity. However, including and accepting regardless of difference is also consistent with Maslow's use of the term "democratic character structure" when describing characteristics of the Self-actualized. Indeed, Maslow's list of characteristics of the Self-actualized presents a remarkable and appropriate list of characteristics that can be associated with Evolved leaders. As first presented in Chapter 6, the list includes:

> Clearer, more efficient perception of reality.
>
> More openness to experience.
>
> Increased integration, wholeness, and unity of the person.
>
> Increased spontaneity, expressiveness; full functioning; aliveness
>
> A real self; a firm identity; autonomy; uniqueness.
>
> Increased objectivity, detachment, transcendence of self.
>
> Recovery of creativeness.
>
> Ability to fuse concreteness and abstractness, primary and secondary process cognition, etc.
>
> Democratic character structure.
>
> Ability to love, etc.[13]

I would not associate this list of characteristics with the Unevolved Leader or Unevolved Leadership. On the contrary, I associate the willingness and ability to subjectively exclude Others as characteristic of the Unevolved Ethic. Further, I associate the unwillingness and inability to accept the beliefs, attitudes, opinions, ideologies, and philosophies of Others as consistent with the discussion of tolerance and intolerance, both of which I associate with the Unevolved Ethic. Tolerating the beliefs, attitudes, opinions, ideologies, and philosophies of Others is not the same as accepting. Tolerating the beliefs, attitudes, opinions, ideologies, and philosophies of Others still implies loss or sacrifice for Self.

The willingness and ability to subjectively exclude denies respect, worth, and value. It denies dignity. It denigrates Others as well as the beliefs, attitudes, opinions, ideologies, and philosophies of Others. This inevitably leads to contention and conflict within the collective whole.

Therefore, I would certainly not associate democratic character structure or the ability to Love with the Unevolved leader and Unevolved Leadership. However, neither would I associate increased objectivity, detachment, or transcendence of Self with the Unevolved Leader. Indeed, I would anticipate increased subjectivity, increased attachment to Self, and the inability to transcend Self with the Unevolved Leader.

But objectivity and subjectivity also play a role in the willingness and ability or unwillingness and inability to accept responsibility and accountability for the acts and behaviors of Self. It plays a role in the willingness and ability or unwillingness and inability to accept responsibility and accountability when the acts and behaviors of Self result in harm for Others and the collective whole.

In other locations throughout this discussion of ethics, I noted that the Evolved Ethic guides and motivates acts and behaviors that manifest the willingness and ability to accept responsibility and accountability for the acts and behaviors of Self. Consistent with this characteristic, the Evolved Leader will manifest the willingness and ability to accept responsibility and accountability for the acts and behaviors of Self. The Evolved Leader will not attempt to minimalize or avoid harm for Self through the use of rationalizations, justifications, explanations, and excuses. Further, the Evolved Leader will not employ self-deception strategies to shift responsibility and accountability away from Self.

On the other hand, the Unevolved Leader is more likely to attempt to avoid responsibility and accountability for the acts and behaviors of Self. The Unevolved Leader is more likely to attempt to shift responsibility and accountability away from Self. This is consistent with the willingness and ability to employ rationalizations, justifications, explanations, and excuses to minimalize or avoid harm for Self. Likewise, it is consistent with the willingness and ability to employ self-deception strategies to shift responsibility and accountability away from Self. It is consistent with the willingness and ability to maximize benefit and minimize harm for Self.

However, the willingness and ability to maximize benefit and minimize harm for Self even manifests itself in the relationships Unevolved Leaders enter and leave, as well as the focus of acts and behaviors of Self within these relationships. Both the Evolved and Unevolved Leader will seek and attempt to build relationships. However, consistent with the characteristics of the two ethics, the acts and behaviors of the Unevolved Leader within relationships will be significantly different from the acts and behaviors of the Evolved Leader.

For instance, within relationships, the characteristic focus of the Unevolved Leader is the best interest, welfare, and good of Self. The Unevolved Leader will likely only enter relationships that serve the best interest, welfare, and good of Self in some manner. Further, the Unevolved Leader will only stay in relationships that serve the best interest, welfare, and good of Self in some manner. This leader will, generally speaking, only stay in relationships that maximize benefit or minimize harm for Self. They will abandon relationships that do not preserve, protect, or promote the best interest, welfare, and good of Self.

Similarly, this leader will not hesitate to exercise "free agency" if a different relationship will better enable Self to maximize benefit and minimize harm for Self. The relationship could be a friendship, a marriage, a relationship that involves employment, or any other form of alliance. The Unevolved leader will then utilize rationalizations, justifications, explanations, and excuses to minimalize the harm that results for Others or the collective whole. In other instances, the Unevolved Leader will simply ignore these harms. However, these acts and behaviors are not consistent with the characteristics associated with the Evolved Ethic or Evolved Leadership.

The focus of the Evolved Leader is the best interest, welfare, and good of Others and the collective whole. The Evolved Leader places the best interest, welfare, and good of Others and the collective whole above Self. The Evolved Leader acts and behaves to maximize benefit and minimize harm for Others and the collective whole. This leader is much less likely to exercise "free agency" to maximize benefit and minimize harm for Self. This leader is much less inclined to abandon a relationship and will minimalize or ignore harm to Self that results, which is more consistent with the characteristics of the Evolved Ethic.

Within relationships, the focus of the Unevolved Leader is the four lower-level needs as well as the wants, desires, cravings, and obsessions of Self. Even excess is often a hallmark of the Unevolved Leader. This excess may manifest in wants, desires, cravings, and obsessions tied to each or all of the four lower-level needs. However, it may be especially apparent in wants, desires, cravings, and obsessions tied to the lower-level esteem need. These are wants, desires, cravings, and obsessions tied to power, wealth, status, position, prestige, eminence, and recognition for Self. These are wants, desires, cravings, and obsessions that manifest great regard and concern for Self.

Indeed, the Unevolved Leader will place value, perhaps even great value, on the trappings and trinkets of success: the perks, honors, and tributes that outwardly signify the success of Self. In addition, the Unevolved Leader is likely to place great value on the deference and admiration of Others. Trappings, trinkets, deference, and admiration of Others all manifest self-importance, self-promotion, self-glorification, and self-aggrandizement. Any harm that results for Others and the collective whole is simply minimalized or ignored in the interest of Self. At best, this harm is rationalized, justified, explained, and excused in favor of Self. The Evolved Leader does not act in this fashion.

The Evolved Leader does not focus on wants, desires, cravings, and obsessions tied to the four lower-level needs of Self. The Evolved Leader is not concerned with excess for Self. The Evolved Leader is not concerned with power, wealth, status, position, prestige, eminence, honors, tributes, and recognition for Self. Further, the Evolved Leader will not focus on the trappings and trinkets of success. The Evolved Leader will not engage in self-promotion, self-glorification, and self-aggrandizement. Finally, the Evolved Leader is unlikely to expect or place value on the deference and admiration of Others. Each of these is simply out of character with the Evolved Ethic. Therefore, each would be out of character with the Evolved Leader.

The Evolved Leader will enter alliances and, to some extent, will satisfy the four lower-level needs of Self through these alliances. However, the Evolved Leader satisfies needs and not wants, desires, cravings, and obsessions through these alliances. The focus of the Evolved Leader remains the best interest, welfare, and good of Others and the collective whole. In addition, the characteristic inclination of the Evolved Ethic toward cooperation and collaboration, harmony and community, within relationships becomes still another characteristic difference between Evolved Leaders and Unevolved Leaders.

Throughout this discussion of ethics, I associated cooperation and collaboration, community, with the Evolved Ethic. Further, I contrasted community with the competition associated with the Unevolved Ethic. The characteristic inclination toward either community or competition will manifest in the acts and behaviors of the Evolved and Unevolved Leaders.

The leadership of Unevolved Leaders will manifest an inclination toward competition. The acts and behaviors of the Unevolved leader will manifest concern for "I," "Me" wins or "I," "Me" loses. The result will often be higher levels of contention and conflict within the collective whole. The greater the distance the ethic of the Unevolved Leader lies from the PoT, the higher the levels of contention and conflict. Correspondingly, the less the Unevolved Leader is willing to engage in mutual benefit, reciprocity, and compromise, the greater the contention and conflict.

By contrast, the leadership of the Evolved Leader will manifest an inclination toward community. It will manifest an inclination toward cooperation and collaboration. The acts and behaviors of this leader will manifest concern for the best interest, welfare, and good of "We," "Us" at multiple levels of "We," "Us." The acts and behaviors of the Evolved Leader will manifest regard and concern for the impact (harm) of competition at multiple levels of "We," "Us" and will seek to minimize these harms through cooperation and collaboration. As a result, the level of contention and conflict within relationships (alliances) will, to some extent or degree, be lower.

Even the approach to influencing or guiding will differ between the Evolved and Unevolved Leaders. The difference in approach will also impact the level of contention and conflict within relationships. For instance, it is more characteristic of Unevolved leaders, including those in formal leadership positions, to employ power and/or wealth to influence or guide which includes the use of position power in formal leadership settings. The use of power may include the overt or covert use of force, threats, or other forms of coercion. It may include the use of money or other inducements. In addition, it is characteristic of Unevolved Leaders to influence or guide through the use of emotion or emotional appeal or the use of reasoning or reasoned appeal. Further, Unevolved Leaders may employ the use of clever tricks or contrivances to influence and guide. Finally, they may employ cunning, guile, duplicity, deception, and craftiness to influence or guide.

In each case, these approaches characteristically treat people as objects. These approaches characteristically treat people as a means to an end that serve to benefit the Unevolved Leader. In each case, these approaches demonstrate the willingness to deny the value, respect, worth, and dignity of Others in the interest of Self. Finally, in each case, these approaches serve the best interest, welfare, and good of the Unevolved Leader.

However, these approaches all harm the collective whole. This harm includes the harms previously mentioned in this discussion of ethics, including the building of contention and conflict within the collective whole. This harm to the collective whole is minimalized or ignored by the Unevolved Leader in the interest, welfare, and good of Self. The example set or modeled by the Unevolved Leader will suggest that it is right, correct, and appropriate to act and behave to maximize benefit and minimize harm for Self. The example set will suggest that it is right, correct, and appropriate to minimalize harms that result for Others and the collective whole so long as Self benefits. The example set will suggest that it is right, correct, and appropriate to use people as means to an end or ends for Self.

On the contrary, it is not characteristic of the Evolved Leader to employ the use of power or wealth to influence or guide. It is not characteristic of the Evolved Leader to employ emotional appeal or reasoned appeal to influence or guide. Likewise, it is not characteristic of the Evolved Leader to employ clever tricks or contrivances to influence or guide. Finally, it is not characteristic of the Evolved Leader to employ cunning, guile, duplicity, deception, or craftiness to influence or guide.

Rather, the Evolved Leader will characteristically influence and guide by example. They will guide and influence through acts and behaviors that suggest it is right, correct, and appropriate to maximize benefit and minimize harm for Others and the collective whole. They will guide and influence through acts and behaviors that model integrity and nurturing. They will guide and influence through acts and behaviors that give value, worth, respect, and dignity to Others. They will treat Others as ends in themselves and not as means to ends.

There is another important characteristic of Evolved leaders that also concerns the self-esteem (dignity) need. This is the willingness and ability to give and share the knowledge, skills, talents, and abilities of Self to help Others grow and develop.

In Chapter 6, I associated both the self-esteem (dignity) and self-actualization needs with the willingness and ability to give and share the knowledge, skills, talents, and abilities of Self with Others. I indicated this willingness and ability to give and share the knowledge, skills, talents, and abilities of Self often takes the form of teaching, mentoring, and coaching. Further, especially concerning the self-actualization need, teaching, mentoring, and coaching often take the form of modeling or setting an example for Others to follow. Through teaching, coaching, mentoring, and the example set or modeled, Self helps Others satisfy these two highest-level needs.

However, it is only characteristic of the Evolved Ethic and, therefore, Evolved Leaders to freely give and share the knowledge, skills, talents, and abilities of Self to maximize benefit and minimize harm for Others. This willingness and ability to give and share the resources of Self maximizes benefit and minimizes harm for the collective whole at multiple levels of the collective whole. However, it is uncharacteristic of the Unevolved Ethic or Unevolved Leaders to give or share freely.

The Unevolved leader is not ethically inclined to give or share freely for the benefit of Others. The Unevolved Leader is inclined to give or share only when Self benefits from the giving or sharing. The Unevolved Leader is inclined to give or share only when there is sufficient reward for Self and will give or share only to the extent or degree the reward equals the loss to Self or the interest, welfare, or good of Self. As discussed earlier, this is giving or sharing to receive. In effect, it is buying or purchasing some benefit for Self. As an example, the Unevolved Leader may help Others grow and develop if doing so results in saving more time for Self. Likewise, the Unevolved Leader may help Others grow and develop if doing so results in less work or effort on the part of Self. Similarly, the Unevolved Leader may help Others grow and develop if doing so enables Self to more efficiently or effectively achieve some other end that benefits Self. In each of these instances, the teaching, coaching, or mentoring maximizes benefit for Self first and foremost.

In other instances, the Unevolved Leader may demonstrate concern for the growth and development of Others if there is some external pressure to do so. This external pressure may be a policy or law. It may be a condition of employment. In these instances, the Unevolved Leader will meet the policy, law, or condition of employment to minimize harm for Self. However, even under these circumstances, the Unevolved Leader will feel the loss (harm) to Self required by the policy, law, or condition of employment and may comply only grudgingly or to the extent Self receives reward or minimizes harm to Self. But in none of these instances, is the Unevolved Leader acting or behaving primarily to maximize benefit and minimize harm to Others or the collective whole. In none of these instances is the Unevolved Leader placing the best interest, welfare, and good of Others above the interest, welfare, and good of Self. In each case, the focus of the Unevolved Leader is still Self.

This focus on Self and the best interest, welfare, and good of Self leads to the conclusion that the Unevolved Leader cannot and will not consistently help Others satisfy the self-esteem (dignity) or self-actualization needs. Indeed, the teaching, coaching, and mentoring of the Unevolved Leader will likely only teach Others to focus on the best interest, welfare, and good of Self. It will only teach Others to act and behave in a manner that maximizes benefit and minimizes harm for Self.

To illustrate this characteristic difference between Evolved and Unevolved Leaders, I can examine the use of delegation of responsibility and authority, as well as micro-managing or over-managing in formal leadership situations.

Traditionally, the delegation of responsibility and authority is viewed as a means to encourage the growth and development of Others. Delegation of responsibility and authority builds trust, confidence, self-reliance, and assurance. It increases knowledge, competency, mastery, and proficiency. Therefore, the delegation of responsibility and authority gives value, worth, and dignity to Others. It helps Others satisfy the need for self-esteem (dignity). All of which benefits the collective whole. But delegation of responsibility and authority carry the risk of harm for the Self that delegates. It is this risk of harm to Self that will often separate the acts and behaviors of the Unevolved Leader from the Evolved Leader.

The Unevolved Leader will characteristically act and behave to minimize or eliminate the risk of harm for Self. For example, in many instances, the Unevolved Leader may simply refuse to delegate any responsibility or authority to Others. In other instances, the responsibility delegated may be so trivial as to negate the developmental value of the experience. In still other instances, the Unevolved Leader may delegate responsibility but not the authority to meet the responsibility. Finally, the Unevolved Leader may view delegation of responsibility and authority as decreasing the position or status of Self. They may view delegation of authority and responsibility to Others as a sacrifice or loss to Self. To minimize this harm to Self, the Unevolved leader may also choose not to delegate any responsibility or authority to Others. By refusing to delegate responsibility and authority to Others, the Unevolved Leader preserves and protects the best interest, welfare, and good of Self.

In each of these examples, the acts and behaviors of the Unevolved Leader minimize or eliminate the risk of harm for Self. In each instance, the acts and behaviors of the Unevolved Leader serve the best interest, welfare, and good of Self. The Unevolved Leader will rationalize, justify, explain, and excuse the reluctance to delegate responsibility and authority to Others. Any harm that results for Others and the collective whole is minimalized or ignored within these rationalizations, justifications, explanations, and excuses.

On the other hand, the willingness and ability to practice delegation of authority and responsibility is more consistent with the characteristics of the Evolved Ethic and the Evolved Leader. This leader is more likely to risk harm for Self in the best interest, welfare, and good of Others and the collective whole. This leader is more likely to place the growth and development of Others above the interest, welfare, and good of Self. Therefore, this leader is more likely to demonstrate the willingness and ability to delegate responsibility and authority to assist in the growth and development of Others.

In each instance, the collective whole benefits when Others within the collective whole grow and develop. The collective whole benefits each time the knowledge, competency, mastery, and proficiency of Others increases and enables them to further contribute to the success of the collective whole.

While not inclined to delegate responsibility and authority, Unevolved Leaders in formal leadership situations will often manifest the inclination to micro-manage Others. This inclination to micro-manage or Others is especially consistent with the emphasis on minimizing harm for Self. Micro-managing Others does minimize harm for Self and serve the best interest, welfare, and good of Self. However, it hinders the growth and development of Others. It hinders the growth and development of knowledge, competency, mastery, and proficiency. As such, it does not give worth, value, and dignity to Others. Quite the opposite is true. Micro-managing decreases the worth, value, and dignity of Others.

On the other hand, it would be uncharacteristic of the Evolved Leader to micro-manage. It would be uncharacteristic of the Evolved Leader to act and behave in a manner intended to minimize harm for Self. It would be more characteristic of the Evolved Leader to risk harm to Self to the benefit of Others and the collective whole. It would be more characteristic of the Evolved Leader to act and behave to assist in the growth and development of Others. Finally, it would be more characteristic of the Evolved Leader to act and behave in a manner that gives worth, value, and dignity to Others and the collective whole. In the end, micro-managing Others is simply out of character with the Evolved Ethic.

Similarly, it is inconsistent with the characteristics of the Evolved Ethic to control or hoard information within a formal leadership setting. Rather, the giving and sharing of information is consistent with acts and behaviors that maximize benefit and minimize harm for Others and the collective whole. By contrast, the tight control or hoarding of information is very consistent with acts and behaviors that maximize benefit and minimize harm for Self. Regardless of the reason for hoarding information, acts or behaviors that result in controlling or hoarding information always serve the best interest, welfare, and good of Self. Indeed, the hoarding of information within an organization or institution is often associated with power.

In any organization or institution, information is often viewed as a source of power. The ability to control information is a source of power for those Selves in a position to control or hoard information. The more vital the information, the greater the power derived. Therefore, controlling or hoarding information maximizes benefit and minimizes harm for those Selves in a position to do so. However, the control and hoarding of information does result in harm for Others in the organization or institution. It results in the same harms that always results when a Self or Selves acts and behaves to maximize benefit and minimize harm for Self. It builds distrust and uncertainty. It builds acrimony and resentment. It builds competition. The same result occurs within organizations and institutions when formal leaders engage in "empire building" and other territorial games (turf wars).

I describe "Empire building" as acts and behaviors intended to enlarge the area of control or responsibility and authority of a formal leader. It may include acts and behaviors intended to enlarge the amount of key information, as well as key functions, tasks, or projects controlled by a formal leader. It can include acts and behaviors intended to enlarge the size of the workforce controlled by a formal leader. It can also include acts and behaviors intended to enlarge control of budget or budget authority. With expanded control of information, functions, projects, workforce, budget, and information come increased position power, status, and prestige for Self.

Territorial games can include "Empire building" but can also describe acts and behaviors intended to ward off attempts by other formal leaders to encroach on the area of control or responsibility and authority of a formal leader. This can include acts and behaviors intended to preserve and protect the size, information, functions, projects, or tasks, within the area of control or responsibility and authority of a leader. It can include acts and behaviors intended to preserve and protect the size of the workforce within the area of control or responsibility. It can include acts and behaviors intended to preserve and protect budget or budget authority.

However, territorial games can also extend to acts and behaviors on the part of one or more formal leaders to discredit or disparage another formal leader. These games can extend to acts and behaviors intended to harm the reputation or character of another formal leader within the collective whole. Generally, these acts and behaviors intend to gain some advantage or benefit for Self. In other words, the act or behavior intends to maximize benefit and minimize harm for Self. But these acts and behaviors inevitably result in harm for the collective whole.

It is always the collective whole that bears the harm that results when formal leaders engage in these activities. However, the formal leader or leaders engaged in territorial games will minimalize or ignore this harm in the interest of Self. They will employ rationalizations, justifications, explanations, and excuses to minimalize or ignore the harm to Others and the collective whole.

So, it is perhaps easy to suggest that acts and behaviors associated with all territorial games and turf wars in general, are consistent with the Unevolved Ethic and Unevolved leadership. These acts and behaviors are consistent with maximizing benefit and minimizing harm for Self. They are consistent with the ethic that encourages the view of "I," "Me" wins or "I," "Me" loses. However, both "empire building" and territorial games in general are inconsistent with the Evolved Ethic and Evolved Leadership. The Evolved Leader is unlikely to engage in acts or behaviors intended to increase the power and control of Self.

The Unevolved leader is also more likely to subjectively use and interpret the methods and tools of management in a manner that maximizes benefit and minimizes harm for Self. Likewise, the Unevolved formal leader is more likely to introduce and employ technology in a manner that maximizes benefit and minimizes harm for Self. The harm that results for Others or various levels of the collective whole is then minimalized or ignored in the best interest, welfare, and good of Self. As an example, Unevolved formal leaders are more likely to introduce technology that reduces or eliminates the need for a human workforce.

The reduction or elimination of the human workforce may benefit the best interest, welfare, and good of Self in many ways. It may maximize benefit by reducing direct payroll as well as indirect personnel costs. It may maximize benefit by improving profit, which may result in additional compensation for the unevolved leader. It may even maximize benefit by reducing the need to actually lead.

Reducing a human workforce does reduce the need to be able to lead. The formal leader does not have to lead technology, simply manage its use. However, it may also result in harms for the collective whole at various levels of the collective whole. For instance, it may harm the collective whole that is a local city or community. It may harm the collective whole that is a state or province. It may even harm the collective whole that is a nation-state.

One example of harm for the collective whole would include unemployed workers. It includes the loss of payroll and other employment benefits such as medical insurance. It includes the loss of income taxes generated by payroll. It includes the greater number of former employees seeking government assistance in one form or another. But it also includes the building of distrust, doubt, suspicion, insecurity, cynicism, and pessimism. It includes the building of bitterness and enmity within the collective whole. But the Unevolved Leader will simply rationalize, justify, explain, and excuse these harms. The Unevolved Leader will minimalize or ignore these harms in the best interest, welfare, and good of Self.

This is not to suggest that the Evolved Leader would not employ the methods and tools of management to reduce inefficiency or ineffectiveness. Nor does it suggest the Evolved Leader would not employ technology. It does suggest a more objective employment of these methods, tools, and technology. It does suggest more objective consideration of harm for

Others and the various levels of the collective whole when considering the possible implementation of technology. It does suggest the Evolved Leader will not implement or interpret the methods and tools of management in a manner that gives primary consideration to the best interest, welfare, or good of Self. Rather, the Evolved Leader will implement the methods, tools, and technology in a manner that serves the best interest, welfare, and good of Others and various levels of the collective whole.

In Chapter 3, I indicated that acts and behaviors guided and motivated by the Evolved Ethic range from right to more right as they increasingly maximize benefit and minimize harm for Others and the collective whole. However, I also indicated that the nearer ethic lies to the PoT, the more difficult it becomes to distinguish which ethic is guiding and motivating acts and behaviors. This holds the same for leadership. The close proximity of the ethic to the PoT will make it difficult to distinguish Evolved Leaders and Leadership from Unevolved Leaders and Leadership. However, the ability to distinguish the Evolved Leader from the Unevolved Leader is further complicated by the many years leadership has been taught in classes, courses, seminars, and workshops.

Leadership education and training often attempts to teach the characteristics and qualities of leaders. The characteristics and qualities taught are those most often identified with leaders and good leadership. They are characteristics and qualities often cited as desirable for both formal and informal leaders. However, on close examination, it is clear that much of this training teaches characteristics and qualities associated with the Evolved Ethic and Evolved Leadership. Unfortunately, much of this training teaches only the ability to mimic these characteristics and qualities. It teaches the ability to mimic these characteristics and qualities as a means to maximize benefit and minimize harm for Self.

Unfortunately, the Evolved Ethic cannot be taught and learned in a classroom. It cannot be taught or learned in a seminar or workshop. Characteristics and qualities consistent with or derived from the Evolved

Ethic can be taught and can be learned in a classroom, but not the ethic itself. The ethic must develop over time and through effort. It must develop through the practice of the lesser masculine and feminine virtues. It must develop through acts and behaviors that maximize benefit and minimize harm for Others and the collective whole. It must develop through the growth and strengthening of the Transcendent Morality to enable Self to accept harm for Self in the interest of Others and the collective whole. Finally, it must develop through practice in a wide variety of situations and circumstances. This takes both time and effort. It takes the evolutionary shift of ethic across the Point of Transcendence. This shift is unlikely to occur during a class, course, seminar, or workshop.

Self may experience a significant emotional event while attending a leadership class, course, seminar, or workshop. However, as discussed in Chapter 7, a significant emotional event does not and cannot cause a permanent shift in ethic. It may cause a short-term shift in the pattern of acts and behaviors of Self, but it is unlikely to cause a permanent shift in the pattern of acts and behaviors that indicates a shift in ethic. Only if the significant emotional event triggers a significant ethical event is ethic likely to move along the Unevolved-Evolved Continuum. But even a significant ethical event, by itself, does not result in the Evolved Ethic. A significant ethical event is only the beginning of the journey to develop the Evolved Ethic. If Self is unwilling to give the time and effort to develop the Evolved Ethic, then ethic will simply remain as it was prior to the significant emotional event and acts and behaviors will return to the long-term pattern and leadership will remain Unevolved Leadership. The long-term pattern of acts and behaviors will still focus on maximizing benefit and minimizing harm for Self.

Nevertheless, all of this does not mean we should stop teaching the qualities and characteristics of the Evolved Ethic in our leadership classes, courses, seminars and workshops. Quite the opposite is true. It is important to expose individuals to these qualities and characteristics. However, it is also important that these qualities and characteristics be taught in the context of encouraging the growth of the Evolved Ethic. It is the growth of the Evolved Ethic over time that is likely to have the greatest impact on the long-term well-being of humanity and the planet on which we live. Failure to grow the Evolved Ethic will likely contribute to the eventual decline of humanity.

While this concludes the discussion of Evolved and Unevolved Leadership, there are several other leadership-related topics worthy of mention before wrapping up this chapter and the overall discussion of the two ethics. These topics include followership, change management, and team building. I specifically include these three topics due to the impact of ethic when discussing each. I begin with followership.

Followership and Ethic

Followership is the willingness and ability to be led. It is the willingness and ability to follow the example of a leader. It is the willingness and ability to follow the path or course set by a leader. In formal leadership situations, it is the ability and willingness to be guided and directed by a formal leader. Regardless of whether leadership is Evolved or Unevolved, it is necessary to recognize that each follower has an ethic. That ethic guides and motivates the acts and behaviors of the followers.

In this discussion of followership, we can suggest that serving the best interest and good of Self or serving the best interest and good of the collective whole directly impacts the degree to which each Self will contribute to the success of the collective whole. It is the extent to which Self can and will set aside concern and regard for Self only. It is also the extent or degree to which Self can set aside self-promotion, self-importance, self-admiration, and self-aggrandizement to promote the interest, welfare, and good of the collective whole. This impacts the extent or degree Self will manifest cooperative and collaborative acts and behaviors within the collective whole. It is the extent or degree Self will contribute the knowledge, experience, skills, talents, and abilities of Self for the success of the collective whole or withhold these resources in the interest of Self.

If the ethic of followers is the Unevolved Ethic, acts and behaviors will contribute to the success of the collective whole only to the extent or degree the interest of Self benefits from the contribution. If the ethic of followers is the Unevolved Ethic, their contribution will likely manifest regard for Self over regard for Others and the collective whole. The contribution of these Selves will reflect an assessment of benefit and harm to Self. That assessment will influence the level or degree to which Self contributes to the success of the collective whole. In addition, the ethic of these Selves will likely encourage competition. This will lead to some level of contention and conflict as each follower acts and behaves for the best interest, welfare, and good of Self. How leaders and followers respond to this contention and conflict often determines the effectiveness of the collective whole. This is especially true in formal leadership settings.

If formal leaders and followers engage in mutual benefit and reciprocity, competition may remain relatively minimal, and the collective whole will be more likely to succeed. Similarly, if the formal leaders and followers are willing and able to employ compromise, the level of competition may remain relatively minimal, and the collective whole is more likely to succeed. If, on the other hand, the formal leaders and followers are unwilling or unable to engage in mutual benefit and reciprocity, the level of competition may increase and this will hamper the ability of the collective whole to succeed. Similarly, if the formal leaders or followers are unwilling to employ compromise or consistently violate compromises in the interest of Self, the level of competition may also elevate and hamper the success of the collective whole, that is, the organization or institution.

However, it should be clear that regardless of the ethic of formal leaders, it is still the ethic of followers that determines the degree or extent followers will manifest the willingness and ability to place the best interest, welfare, and good of the collective whole above the best interest, welfare, and good of Self. It is the ethic of followers that determines the degree or extent to which followers will manifest the willingness and ability to act and behave to maximize benefit and minimize harm for the collective whole. It is even the ethic of followers that will determine the example followers will follow and whether they will follow the example of a formal leader or an informal leader.

This is significant since followers will follow the lead or example that most appeals to both the ethic and state of ethical development of Self. This comment suggests that followers will follow the lead or example that most closely resembles the ethic of Self. It suggests that if the ethic of the follower or followers is the Unevolved Ethic, they are more likely to follow the lead of an Unevolved Leader. This is often the example that offers the greatest amount of benefit and the least amount of harm for Self. This is often the easiest and most convenient example or model to follow. It is the example or model that requires the least amount of effort to follow. It is the example that requires the least expenditure of the resources of Self to follow regardless of the resource or resources required.

However, the state of ethical development will also enter into this willingness to follow. If the state of ethical development of a follower is the rational state, this follower may well follow an Unevolved Leader, either formal or informal, whose state of development is also the rational state. This preference will follow the emphasis of the rational state of development on minimizing harm for Self. On the other hand, if the state of ethical development of the follower is the irrational state, this follower will likely follow an Unevolved Leader, formal or informal, whose state of development is the irrational. This preference follows the emphasis on benefit (pleasure) for Self.

Beyond the state of ethical development, followers are more likely to follow the example or model of the leader whose values and principles most closely resemble the values and principles of Self, even if those values and principles result in harm for Others and the collective whole. Similarly, they will follow the example of the leader whose beliefs, attitudes, and opinions most closely resemble the beliefs, attitudes, and opinions of Self, even if those beliefs, attitudes, and opinions result in harm for Others and the collective whole. This willingness to follow the example or model that most closely mirrors the ethic of Self is significant in both formal and informal leadership situations.

It is also the ethic of followers that often requires the use of various forms of external motivation to encourage the willingness of followers to act and behave for the best interest, welfare, and good of the collective whole.

External Motivation and Ethic

External motivation describes the use of external incentives to overcome the characteristic focus on the best interest, welfare, and good of Self guided and motivated by the Unevolved Ethic. External motivation acknowledges the notion that Self should give or share the resources of Self only to the extent there is sufficient reward for the giving or sharing. It concedes the notion, motivated by the Unevolved Ethic, that Self should give or share the resources of Self only to the extent that the reward for Self justifies the loss to Self. This is regardless of whether the resource given or shared is the time, effort, knowledge, experience, skills, talents, or abilities of Self.

However, it is Self who determines whether the external reward justifies the sacrifice to Self. It is Self who makes this subjective assessment. The extent or degree Self values Self, and the resources of Self over Others and the collective whole significantly impacts this assessment. Clearly, the greater Self values Self and the resources of Self, the greater the external incentive required. This is regardless of how rational or irrational the value Self places on Self and the resources of Self.

External incentives can include monetary incentives or prizes, such as a bonus. However, they can also include awards, honors, and other forms of recognition. The appeal of monetary incentives may be tied to the wants, desires, cravings, and obsessions of Self. A monetary incentive can enhance the ability of Self to satisfy wants, desires, cravings, and obsessions of Self. The appeal of non-monetary incentives is often tied to the lower-level esteem need. It is tied to status, prestige, recognition, and reputation for Self. Therefore, both forms of external incentive can be powerful for those followers whose ethic is the Unevolved Ethic.

On the other hand, followers whose ethic is the Evolved Ethic will not generally be attracted to external incentives tied to wants, desires, cravings, and obsessions of Self. They are not generally attracted to external incentives tied to the lower-level esteem need. They will not generally be attracted to incentives tied to status, position, prestige, recognition, or reputation for Self. These followers are internally motivated to give and share the knowledge, experience, skills, talents, and abilities of Self in the best interest, welfare, and good of Others and the collective whole. They are internally motivated to contribute to the success of the collective whole. They are internally motivated to contribute to the success of a purpose or cause greater than Self. Further, they are willing and able to minimalize or ignore harm that results for Self as a result of this contribution. Therefore, external incentives will not hold special appeal to followers whose ethic is the Evolved Ethic.

However, just the need for leaders to employ the use of external motivation to induce the willingness to accept a sacrifice to Self is not the only impact of ethic in formal leadership settings or situations. Indeed, the ethic of followers can and does impact a wide variety of situations and circumstances within the formal leadership setting. Two important situations and circumstances are team building and leading change.

Team Dynamics and Ethic

Consistent with the discussion of relationships in the last chapter, teams are alliances. Teams can form quite naturally in a formal leadership setting. In other instances, formal leaders may establish a team or teams to serve a specific purpose. This purpose might include the performance of a specific function or to complete a project, task, or study. These are often termed functional or work teams.

Regardless of how a team forms, the ethic of followers who comprise the team will guide and motivate the acts and behaviors of Self within the context of the team. This is the case when discussing the acts and behaviors of the team leader or the team members. Ethic will determine the extent or degree to which the acts and behaviors of the team leader and team members serve the best interest, welfare, and good of Self or the best interest, welfare, and good of the collective whole that is the team. Serving the best interest, welfare, and good of Self or the best interest, welfare, and good of the team means the extent to which each Self will contribute to the success of the team. It is the extent or degree Self will manifest cooperative and collaborative acts and behaviors. It is the extent or degree Self will contribute the knowledge, experience, skills, talents, and abilities of Self for the success of the team or withhold these resources in the interest of Self. Finally, it is the degree or extent to which followers believe the success of the team serves the good of Self in some manner.

If the ethic of the team leader and team members is the Unevolved Ethic, each Self will act and behave, to some extent, to maximize benefit and minimize harm for Self. This will lead to some level of competition within the team. It will lead to some level of contention and conflict as each team member acts and behaves for the best interest, welfare, and good of Self. This competition is sometimes referred to as personality conflicts within the team. However, as discussed in Chapter 7, the pattern of acts and behaviors termed personality is a reflection of ethic. How the team leader and members respond to this level of competition will often determine the effectiveness, and, perhaps, even the longevity of the team.

If the team leader and team members engage in mutual benefit and reciprocity, competition may remain relatively minimal and the team is more likely to succeed. Similarly, if the team leader and team members are willing and able to employ compromise within the team, the level of competition may remain relatively minimal and the team is more likely to succeed. If, on the other hand, the team leader or one or more team members is unwilling or unable to engage in mutual benefit and reciprocity, the level of competition may increase, and this will hamper the ability of the team to succeed. Similarly, if the team lead or one or more team members is unwilling to employ compromise or consistently violates compromises in the interest of Self, the level of competition may also elevate and hamper the team's success.

In practical application, teams may establish "rules of operation" or "rules of engagement" concerning respect, courtesy, civility, and decorum expected during team meetings. Teams may also establish penalties for violating these "rules of operation" or "rules of engagement." The obvious intent of the rules is to minimize contention and conflict within the team. They exist to constrain or restrain the ethic of those Selves participating as team lead or team members. They exist to restrain acts and behaviors that manifest concern and regard for Self. But they also exist to restrain acts and behaviors that manifest disregard for Others and the collective whole that is the team. In other words, they exist to encourage right, correct, and appropriate acts and behaviors and to discourage wrong, incorrect, and inappropriate acts and behaviors within the team. They exist to encourage cooperation and collaboration and discourage contention and conflict within the team.

Ultimately, the extent or degree to which the team leader and team members are willing and able to supplant contention and conflict with cooperation and collaboration, even for short periods of time, the team is more likely to succeed. The extent or degree the team leader and team members are unwilling or unable to supplant contention and conflict with cooperation and collaboration, the team will likely be less successful, possibly even unsuccessful.

Change and Ethics

Finally, ethic also impacts the willingness of followers to accept or tolerate change. This stems from consideration or assessment of benefit and harm that lies within the change. If the guiding and motivating ethic is the Evolved Ethic, Self will more likely accept and adapt to change that benefits the collective whole. This willingness and ability to accept and adapt to change is based on the characteristic concern for the best interest, welfare, and good of the collective whole. It is based on the willingness and ability to transcend consideration or regard for Self.

If, on the other hand, the motivating ethic is the Unevolved Ethic, Self is more likely to tolerate and adapt to change that benefits Self, but be intolerant and resistant to change perceived as carrying harm Self. This is regardless of whether or not the change maximizes benefit and minimizes harm for Others and the collective whole. This willingness to tolerate change that benefits Self and resist change perceived as carrying harm for Self is consistent with the Unevolved Ethic. For example, a Self whose ethic is the Unevolved Ethic may welcome or resist a formal change to a process or procedure. Those who perceive benefit for Self will welcome the change. This benefit may take the form of reduced time or effort needed to complete the process or procedure. It may eliminate a step or steps necessary to complete a process or procedure. It may reduce or eliminate workload. In this instance, Self will more willingly tolerate and adopt the change.

On the contrary, a Self who perceives harm for Self will resist the change. This harm may take the form of increased time or effort needed to complete the process or procedure. It may add a step or steps necessary to complete the process or procedure. It may add workload. In this instance, followers will, to some extent, be intolerant and resist the change regardless of whether the change maximizes benefit and minimizes harm for Others and the collective whole. This is also consistent with the Unevolved Ethic.

As in so many other circumstances, the willingness to adopt or resist change within a collective whole often hinges on this assessment of potential benefit or harm for Self. If the potential harm for Self outweighs the potential benefit, Self will often resist change. If the potential benefit for Self outweighs the potential harm, Self will often tolerate and adopt change. When faced with change, each Self in the collective whole, whose ethic is the Unevolved Ethic, will make this benefit/harm assessment. Those who determine the change will benefit Self will more quickly accept and adopt the change. Those who determine the change will result in harm for Self will resist the change. It falls to leaders, especially formal leaders, to understand this impact of ethic on change and efforts to implement change.

Team building and leading change are certainly not the only formal leadership situations in which ethic will guide and motivate the acts and behaviors of followers within the collective whole. Team building and change simply provide two excellent examples to highlight the impact of ethic on the acts and behaviors of followers. Certainly, ethic will impact the productivity of followers. It will impact the attendance or absenteeism of followers. It will impact the quality and excellence demonstrated by followers. Indeed, the willingness and ability to consistently perform at the level of excellence is driven by ethic.

Performance at the level of excellence benefits Others and the collective whole. Excellence maximizes benefit and minimizes harm for Others and the collective whole at all levels. Therefore, excellence requires that Self be both willing and able to consistently give and share the resources of Self to benefit Others and the collective whole. It requires that Self be both willing and able to fully utilize the knowledge, skills, talents, and abilities of Self to benefit Others and the collective whole. It requires that Self be willing and able to give, share, and utilize these resources without regard to harm for Self.

However, here it is necessary to stop for a moment and recognize that many would argue excellence does and should serve the best interest, welfare, and good of Self. They would argue that Self should be the beneficiary of excellence. They might argue that excellence is tied to concepts such as reputation and prestige, status and position. This is a very self-regarding, self-preserving, and self-promoting argument. It is an argument that rationalizes, justifies, explains, and excuses the use of the resources of Self to benefit primarily Self. It is an argument based in the Unevolved Ethic.

If Self is unwilling or unable to give, share, and utilize the resources of Self without regard for Self, then Self will not consistently perform at the level of excellence. If Self is unwilling and unable to act and behave for the preservation, promotion and advancement of Others and the collective whole, the acts and behaviors of Self will not reflect excellence. Instead, Self will give both Others and the collective whole a level of time, effort, and other resources that maximize benefit and minimize harm for Self. Further, Self will likely do so only when there is a clear benefit to Self for doing so. This is not excellence in acts and behaviors. These are simply acts and behaviors guided and motivated by the Unevolved Ethic. It then falls on the formal leader to coax a higher level of performance from followers, often through the use of external motivation discussed earlier in this chapter.

In summary, the guiding and motivating ethic of each Self has significant implications for leaders and leadership. Ultimately, ethic determines whether leadership will be Evolved Leadership or Unevolved Leadership. It determines whether a leader will be an Evolved or Unevolved Leader. It determines whether the example or model set will maximize benefit and minimize harm for Others and the collective whole or maximize benefit and minimize harm for Self.

Many years ago, I was surprised when authors of various articles suggested there was a shortage of leaders in this country and around the world. These many years later, I would suggest those authors were only partially correct. There is a shortage of Evolved Leaders. Perhaps even a critical shortage of Evolved Leaders. On the other hand, there is no shortage of Unevolved Leaders. Unevolved Leaders exist in vast numbers. Unfortunately, there is also no shortage of followers whose ethic is the

Unevolved Ethic. In the end, it is the guiding and motivating ethic that determines whether a leader and followers will consistently act and behave in a manner that is right, correct, and appropriate.

CHAPTER 10:
CONCLUSION

To conclude this discussion of ethics, I begin by saying I sincerely hope you enjoyed this examination and exploration of ethics. I sincerely hope you found something useful within these pages. I further hope you will take some time to reflect on all the various aspects of ethics covered within these pages.

I should also say this discussion intended to provide a mirror of sorts. It intended to provide a means to reflect on the ethic of Self, a means for looking inward to see the ethic of Self and not outward to see the ethic of Others. The intent was never to provide a means to judge Others. It was not to provide a means of criticizing or drawing conclusions about the ethic of Others.

I believe if every person who reads this discussion of ethics will give a little time and effort to reflect on this discussion of ethics, it might just cause a positive shift in the ethic of Self. If each person gives just a little time and effort to contemplating the acts and behaviors of Self, it might cause a positive shift in the ethic of Self. Further, if everyone who reads this is willing and able to give the time and effort necessary to practice the lesser masculine and feminine virtues, to practice maximizing benefit and minimizing harm for Others and the collective whole, it might cause a positive shift in the ethic of Self. Finally, if each person who reads this discussion can learn and practice the willingness and ability to minimalize or ignore harm for Self, to practice the enabling virtues of Love and Courage, the Transcendent Morality, it might cause a shift in ethics on an unprecedented scale.

Appendix 4 may help the reader with this reflective and contemplative activity. This appendix is a list of questions intended to raise awareness of the ethic of Self. It is intended to encourage an objective assessment of the acts and behaviors of Self. Further, it is intended to raise awareness of Others and the collective whole. It is intended to raise the level of consciousness of Self beyond awareness of only Self and the best interest, welfare, and good of Self.

The questions all place emphasis on consideration of the interest, welfare, and good of Others and the collective whole. In addition, the questions emphasize the harm that results for Others and the collective whole when Self acts and behaves to maximize benefit and minimize harm for Self. In effect, this list of questions provides a tool to assist Self in meditating on the acts and behaviors of Self and the impact of these acts and behaviors.

The term "meditate" means "To think contemplatively; muse; reflect." The term "Meditation" means "The act of meditating. Thought; reflection; contemplation. A thinking over." In the context of this theory of ethics, meditation is an active, objective contemplation of the acts and behaviors of Self. It is an active, objective review and analysis of the acts and behaviors of Self. It is also an active, objective review and analysis of harm that results for Others and the collective whole. It is an active, objective review and analysis of both the obvious and the less obvious harm that results from the acts and behaviors of Self.

To be effective, Self should practice this meditative exercise on a daily basis. Daily reflection and contemplation ensure that the acts and behaviors of Self are still fresh in memory. It ensures that acts and behaviors do not slip out of short-term memory. It also helps Self become habituated to assessing the acts and behaviors of Self. It helps Self become habituated to considering the benefit or harm that results for Others and the collective whole from the acts and behaviors of Self.

Delaying the activity for a day or even more, increases the possibility that acts or behaviors of Self will slip from short-term memory. Delay also offers the possibility that Self will build rationalizations, justifications, explanations, and excuses intended to exempt Self from considering self-interested, self-regarding, self-preserving, and self-promoting acts or behaviors. In this sense, delay in assessing the acts and behaviors of Self becomes a self-deception strategy in its own right. Delay becomes a self-deception strategy very similar to the strategy of "sleeping on it" described earlier in Chapter 3.

By delaying this contemplative or reflective activity, Self gains time to create the rationalizations, justifications, explanations, and excuses necessary to overlook or ignore acts and behaviors of Self. Self gains time to create the rationalizations, justifications, explanations, and excuses Self needs to feel good about Self despite failure to manifest right, correct, or appropriate acts or behaviors. Self gains time to feel good about Self despite manifesting wrong, incorrect, or inappropriate acts or behaviors.

The amount of time needed to complete this meditative activity will vary from day to day. The best guideline is to devote the amount of time necessary to complete the activity. Devote the amount of time necessary to review the acts and behaviors of Self objectively; the amount of time necessary to objectively consider the benefit and harm that result from the acts and behaviors of Self. Devote the amount of time necessary to consider even the most routine or mundane acts and behaviors of Self. Ethic motivates even the most routine or mundane acts and behaviors. Through giving the time and effort necessary to assess the acts and behaviors of Self objectively, Self will become more aware of the ethic of Self. With greater awareness of the ethic of Self comes the opportunity to begin the journey to move ethic in a positive direction along the Unevolved-Evolved Continuum.

Horace Mann is quoted as saying, "Be ashamed to die until you have won some victory for humanity." On the surface, this may sound somewhat daunting – a victory for humanity. But it doesn't have to be so daunting. What if that victory for humanity is no more than a victory over the ethic of Self? What if that victory for humanity is no more than a victory over selfish concern and regard for Self at the expense of harm for Others and the collective whole? What if that victory for humanity is recognizing the error that lies within a morality that dictates the best interest, welfare, and good of Self trumps the best interest, welfare, and good of the collective whole? What if that victory is to finally recognize that acts and behaviors that maximize benefit and minimize harm for Others and the collective whole serve the best interest, welfare, and good of all humanity as well as all sentient beings and the very planet on which we and all future generations will live? Would that be a victory for humanity? I believe it would. Further, I believe it is a victory within reach of every individual Self.

Mann is also quoted as saying, "Doing nothing for others is the undoing of ourselves." I believe this comment is truly prophetic. I believe if humanity cannot begin to change the dominant ethic from the Unevolved Ethic to the Evolved Ethic, that humanity will be its own undoing. I believe the current generations of humanity will be the undoing of future generations as well as the undoing of all sentient beings and the planet itself. But to avoid this undoing of ourselves requires time and effort. It requires the time and effort necessary to learn and practice acts and behaviors that manifest the willingness and ability to give, share, care, and love Others and the collective whole. It requires Love and Courage to do so without regard and concern for the best interest, welfare, and good of only Self.

I believe if every Self who reads this examination of ethics is willing and able to care just a little more; to give and to share just a little more; and to love just a little more, without regard for Self, we might see a shift in ethics of epic proportion. If every Self who reads this is willing and able to do for Others without regard for Self, we might see a tremendous shift toward the Evolved Ethic. Instead of the "thousand points of light" envisioned by former President George H. W. Bush in his 1988 speech to the Republican Convention, we might find millions of points of light scattered across this planet we call home. We might find millions of points of light leading the way to a far brighter tomorrow. We might find a world in which, in the words of John Lennon, "We all shine on". I believe this world is possible.

In July of 1969, Neil Armstrong, when stepping on the surface of the moon said, "This is one small step for (a) man, one giant leap for mankind." To land a human being on the moon was a tremendous scientific and technological victory for humankind. I believe victory over the Unevolved Ethic would be a truly evolutionary step for mankind. An evolutionary step that begins with each and every individual Self. As Bono once said, "There is no them, there's only us."

Thank you!

APPENDIX 1:
THE VIRTUES AND VICES

The purpose for providing this list is to demonstrate that for each of the 12 lesser virtues associated with the virtue component of the Evolved Ethic, there is a corresponding vice associated with the egoistic component of the Unevolved Ethic. This list presents only the most obvious antonym or opposite vice for each virtue. It does not attempt to list every possible synonym for each virtue or for each vice

Virtues	Vices
Compassion	Apathy
Generosity	Voracity
Empathy	Indifference
Modesty	Immodesty
Patience	Impatience
Honesty	Dishonesty
Loyalty	Disloyalty
Bravery	Cowardice
Moderation	Immoderation
Perseverance	Ambivalence

APPENDIX 2:
THE VIRTUES AND DERIVED VALUES

Following is the list of the ten lesser virtues and values that derive from each. This list does not attempt to list every possible synonym for the values listed.

Virtues	Derived Values
Honesty	Truthfulness, forthrightness, openness, genuineness, and straight-forwardness
Loyalty	Trustworthiness, faithfulness, steadfastness, staunchness
Bravery	Boldness, directness, candidness, and fearlessness, realness, and frankness
Perseverance	Earnestness, resoluteness, decisiveness, and firmness
Moderation	Reasonableness, sensibleness, temperateness, soundness, and judiciousness
Compassion	Kindheartedness, thoughtfulness, gentleness, and tenderness
Empathy	Responsiveness, receptiveness, pleasantness, friendliness, attentiveness, and openness
Modesty	Unpretentiousness, naturalness, unaffectedness, genuineness, and humbleness
Patience	Calmness, quietness, coolness, unobtrusiveness, even-temperedness, levelheadedness
Generosity	Unselfishness, openhandedness, evenhandedness, fair-mindedness, and kindness

APPENDIX 3:
THE VICES AND DERIVED VALUES

Following is the list of the ten vices and the values that derive from each. Each vice contrasts one of the ten lesser masculine or feminine virtues. This list does not attempt to list every possible synonym for either the vices or the values listed.

Vices	Derived Values
Dishonesty	Untruthfulness, unfairness, disingenuousness, deceptiveness, deviousness, unscrupulousness.
Disloyalty	Unfaithfulness, falseness, faithlessness, craftiness, deceitfulness, ruthlessness.
Cowardice	Fearfulness, faintheartedness, feebleness, weakness, spinelessness.
Ambivalence	Indecisiveness, irresoluteness, tentativeness, apprehensiveness, impulsiveness.
Immodesty	Boastfulness, brashness, cockiness, affectedness, pretentiousness, snobbishness, and pompousness
Immoderation	Intemperateness, excessiveness, insensibleness, unreasonableness, rapaciousness, injudiciousness
Apathy	Heartlessness, mercilessness, coldness, callousness, harshness.
Indifference	Unresponsiveness, inattentiveness, thoughtlessness, carelessness, impassiveness.
Impatience	Tempestuousness, hotheadedness, excitedness, rashness, hastiness, carelessness, recklessness.
Voracity	Selfishness, self-centeredness, miserliness, stinginess, avariciousness, rapaciousness, greediness

APPENDIX 4:
MEDITATION AID

There are a number of questions that can assist with contemplation of the acts and behaviors of Self. These are:

How many times during the day did I manifest acts or behaviors that served only the good or best interest of Self?

How many times during the day did I manifest selfish, self-regarding, self-interested, self-centered, or self-promoting acts and behaviors?

How many manifest acts and behaviors served only Self and self-interest at the expense of Others or the collective whole?

How many manifest acts and behaviors manifest a basis in the vices associated with the Unevolved Ethic?

How many times during the day did I fail to manifest right, correct, or appropriate behaviors?

What motivated that failure to manifest right, correct, or appropriate behaviors?

Was it fear or concern for Self?

Was it to avoid harm (pain or the privation of pleasure) for Self?

How many times over the course of the day did I excuse myself from manifesting a right, correct, or appropriate act or behavior?

How many times did I rationalize or justify not manifesting right, correct, or appropriate behaviors?

How many times did I rationalize or justify manifesting wrong, incorrect, or inappropriate behaviors in the interest of Self?

What impact or harm resulted from these self-interested acts or behaviors?

How many times and in what manner did I place concern for Others and the collective whole over concern for Self?

How many times and in what ways did I unselfishly or selflessly act for the benefit of Others or the collective whole?

How many times and in what manner did I act selflessly for the good of Others and the collective whole?

How many times and in what manner did acts and behaviors manifest the virtues associated with the Evolved Ethic?

How many times and in what ways did I accept harm (pain or the privation of pleasure) for Self in the interest of Others or the collective whole?

How many times did I accept harm (pain or the privation of pleasure) for myself and manifest a right, correct, or appropriate act or behavior?

ENDNOTES

1   Bennis, W.G. & Nanus, B. (1985). *Leaders: The strategies for taking charge.* New York: Harper & Row

2   *The Basic Writings of John Stuart Mill:On Liberty, The Subjection of Women, and Utilitarianism.* (New York:The Modern Library, 2002), p 239.

3   For about Moral Hypocrisy and the need to appear moral, I recommend the article "Moral hypocrisy: appearing moral to oneself without being so," by C.D. Batson in the Journal of Personality and Social Psychology, 77(3), 525-537.)

4   For about Moral Hypocrisy and the need to appear moral, I recommend the article "Moral hypocrisy: appearing moral to oneself without being so," by C.D. Batson in the Journal of Personality and Social Psychology, 77(3), 525-537.)

5   Maslow, A.H. (1943). "A theory of human motivation".*Psychological Review* 50 (4): 370-396

6   Abraham H. Maslow, *Maslow on Management* (New York:John Wiley & Sons, Inc, 1998), 56.

7   Ibid, 56

8   Ibid, 56

9   Abraham H. Maslow, "Psychological Data and Value Theory," *New Knowledge in Human Values,* ed. Abraham H. Maslow (New York:Harper & Row, 1959), 127.

10 Ibid, 128.

11 Ibid, 127.

12 Ibid, 127.

13 Ibid, 127.